THE POLITICS OF
BUDGET CONTROL

THE POLITICS OF BUDGET CONTROL: CONGRESS, THE PRESIDENCY AND THE GROWTH OF THE ADMINISTRATIVE STATE

John Marini, Ph.D.
University of Nevada, Reno

CRANE RUSSAK
A member of the Taylor & Francis Group
Washington, DC • Philadelphia • London

$AAZ6781$

USA	Publishing Office:	Hemisphere Publishing Corporation 1101 Vermont Ave., NW, Suite 200 Washington, DC 20005-3521
	Sales Office:	Taylor & Francis Inc. 1900 Frost Road, Bristol, PA 19007-1598
UK		Taylor & Francis Ltd. 4 John St., London WC1N 2ET

THE POLITICS OF BUDGET CONTROL: Congress, the Presidency and the Growth of the Administrative State

1 2 3 4 5 6 7 8 9 0   E B E B   9 8 7 6 5 4 3 2

This book was set in Times Roman by Hemisphere Publishing Corporation. The editors were Lisa Speckhardt and Radhika Rao Gupta, the production supervisor was Peggy M. Rote, and the typesetter was Laurie Strickland. Cover design by Tammy Marshall. Printing and binding by Edwards Brothers, Inc.

A CIP catalog record for this book is available from the British Library.

∞ The paper in this publication meets the requirements of the ANSI Standard Z39.48-1984 (Permanence of Paper)

Library of Congress Cataloging in Publication Data

Marini, John
    The politics of budget control : Congress, the presidency, and the growth of the administrative state / John Marini.
        p.   cm.
    includes bibliographical references and index.

    1. Budget—United States. 2. Government spending policy—United States. I. Title.
HJ2052.M368 1992
353.0072'221—dc20   91-40591
ISBN 0-8448-1716-3 (case)   CIP
ISBN 0-8448-1717-1 (paper)

To my mother, Margherita Marini, the memory of my father,
Dominic A. Marini (1898-1984), and Nancy and Francesca

Contents

Preface

The federal budget has attained unparalleled significance at the heart of American politics in the last quarter of the twentieth century. The modern budget system has become the mechanism by which a distinctively American administrative state was put in place and made operative. However, the administrative state rests uneasily within the structure of the Constitution of the United States. In terms of legitimacy, the American tradition is one of limited, constitutional government. State theory presupposes the unlimited capacity of government to pursue public purposes. The presence of an American administrative state has produced a disjunction between the theoretical and practical dimension of national politics, between the principles that legitimize action and the practice of the institutions of government. The administrative state rests upon theoretical assumptions that cannot gain constitutional legitimacy. The attempt to consolidate an administrative apparatus within the framework of American government has had the effect of undermining the efficient operation of the constitutional system of separated powers. It has made it more difficult for the institutions of government to function amicably in pursuit of a national interest. It is for this reason that the relations between the political branches of government, Congress, the presidency, and the bureaucracy have become increasingly hostile in the last decades.

In America, the administrative state traces its origins to the Progressive movement. Progressive leaders were hostile to the Constitution because it presupposed a limitation upon the power of government. The executive budget system was among the most important political reforms demanded by Progressives. A presidential budget, along with party reform, would allow activist presidents the ability to pursue the interests of a national majority. Consequently, the United States was the last modern industrial nation to adopt an executive budget system. Congress was reluctant to give presidents the authority to formulate budgets, because it was thought such prerogative would undermine the separation of powers. Fifty years later, the move to increase the legislature's power—and reduce the president's control—over the budget, arose from the realization that the president and the national majority constituted the greatest threat to the continuation of an administrative bureaucracy committed to the achievement of social justice. Throughout much of American history, conflict over control of public finances had been contained because of a consensus concerning the purposes and size of the federal government. Administrative functions at the national level were few, in keeping with a constitutional system which underscored the limited character of all government.

The growth of the administrative state began the process of undermining the consensus in support of limited government. Subsequently, it also eroded support for limited or balanced budgets. Moreover, the president and Congress, the national majority and the organized interests, became rival forces and constituencies committed to purposes that were often adverse to the national interest. The president, responding to a majority, came to oppose the consolidation of the administrative state. Congress and the organized interests developed a stake in the maintenance of administrative centralization. The federal budget, a potential instrument for fueling the growth of the administrative state, subsequently came to be the point of control from which both political branches attempted to maintain, expand, or limit the size of the public sector. The failure of the institutions of government and the political parties to achieve a new consensus, or political realignment, concerning the purposes and level of public spending by the national government made budget control nearly impossible. The Constitution, which separated the powers of government, provided the conditions for budget strife.

By the middle 1970s, the struggle for control of budgets and bureaucracies had become the central battleground in executive-legislative relations. The national budget, with taxing and spending power, had become the focal point of the American administrative state. It was the place where political institutions and public bureaucracies attempted to accommodate the various interests and constituencies seeking a share of the national wealth. The growth of the public sector, which accompanied the increased size of public budgets, began a process that undermined the distinction between the public and private sphere, between government and society. Moreover, it became increasingly difficult for the political institutions to recognize the difference between governing and budgeting. At one time, there was widespread agreement that governments should tightly control expenditures; budgets provided the means of limiting claims based upon available resources. Moreover, there was a consensus concerning the federal government's administrative functions: they were few. This was not merely because state and local governments undertook most administrative tasks, but because of agreement concerning the autonomy of the economic marketplace, and the distinction between the public and private sphere.

In terms of public finance, limited government meant limited and balanced budgets in normal times. Public spending and public debt were viewed in moral terms, as evils to be avoided so as to limit the tax burden upon the working man. The progressive income tax changed the manner in which political leaders looked at taxation, public spending, and public debt. In addition, Franklin Roosevelt's "New Deal" succeeded in destroying the legitimacy of the opinion that private solutions to economic problems were intrinsically preferable to public ones. The budget became a means of aggrandizing the public sector, and a stabilizing device in the economy of the nation. Furthermore, increased government expenditures during the Depression, and the economic theories of John Maynard Keynes, provided the conditions and the rationale for utilizing the budget as a means of implementing federal fiscal policy. The federal budget became an important tool in the presidential attempt to manage the economy. As long as presidents and Congress were agreed upon national priorities, there were few unmanageable conflicts concerning economy policy or budget control. The Nixon presidency revealed fundamental differences between the political branches concerning management of the economy, the budget, and the bureaucracy. A half century after FDR, by the end of the Reagan presidency, the federal budget, which had gained political importance as a device to stabilize economic conditions, had become itself a hostage of the economy it was meant to control. Economic conditions were more important than political decision makers in determining the level of spending, revenue growth, or the size of budget deficits.

The centralization of administration in Washington during the 1960s and early 1970s began the process of eroding the consensus concerning the role of the national government that was forged during the New Deal. The increased size and power of the federal government, and the new regulatory bureaucracy created during the Great Society, polarized society as well as the political institutions and the parties. The divergence between the parties led to heightened conflict among the political branches of government. The Democratic Party, which dominated the legislative branch, was committed to the maintenance of an administrative state. The Republican Party, increasingly able to capture the executive branch, sought to limit the size of government. The 1972 reelection of Richard Nixon produced a crisis in the budget process that led to fundamental reform. In Nixon's view, Congress had become so wedded to the interests of the bureaucratic state, it could no longer control its appetite for increased public expenditures. Nixon sought to limit public spending by impounding expenditures that broke the executive budget. The Democratic majority in Congress was unable to challenge the president's authority in formulating economic policy or establishing national priorities without control of the budget. Furthermore, by the end of the Nixon administration, it had become clear that the presidency was no longer the most progressive institution within the American government. Congress, after Watergate, enjoyed a resurgence of power and prestige. The 1974 Congressional Budget and Impoundment Control Act gave Congress the technical capability and the institutional means of controlling the totals of spending. Congress was at once a dominant force in the formulation of fiscal policy, and a major force in setting the priorities of the nation.

Congress succeeded in challenging presidential control of the budget, but the price of success was an institutional inability to reach agreement on expenditures, except at ever higher levels. The reforms in Congress during the 1970s, which accommodated the growth of the administrative state, weakened the leadership of Congress, and empowered individual members. It also made it possible for members of Congress to disassociate themselves as individuals from the fate of the institution as a whole. The political fortune of individual congressmen was no longer dependent upon the performance of Congress as a body. Power moved from committee chairs to sub-committee chairs. The links between Congress and the permanent bureaucracy undermined presidential attempts to manage the executive branch. The budget process was dominated by those interests in Congress and the bureaucracy that supported the priorities of the administrative state. The growth of the federal government could not be seriously challenged without control of the levers of public spending. Ronald Reagan raised the question of the legitimacy of the administrative state and turned it into a partisan issue. The Reagan presidency was the political response of a national majority to the perceived growth and consolidation of the federal bureaucracy.

The American government was among the last of modern industrialized societies to centralize administration in the national government. The consolidation of the administrative state was not the result of technological necessity: It was an act of political will. The Constitution, and the politics of federalism, had inhibited Washington from attempting such centralization. The Progressive movement and the New Deal had advocated and attempted to legitimize, in theory, the doctrine of an administrative state. But it was not until the Great Society that the task was accomplished. Originally, the president provided the greatest impetus for its creation. Congress, representative of local interests and state power, was opposed. Subsequently, after its implementation, Congress became the greatest benefactor and defender of the administrative state, the president its most ominous and dangerous foe.

The federal budget has come to be the principle instrument of politics in the American administrative state. The inability to control the budget is a symptom of a deeper crisis which arises from the failure of the administrative state to function effectively, or gain legitimacy, within a constitutional regime of separated powers. In a constitutional system, the powers of government are thought to be limited; in the administrative state only resources are limited. In a constitutional regime, the most important political questions are those of principle or public right; in the administrative state they revolve around money and finance. The constitutional system attempted to embody the principles of republican government into a structure of democratic institutions. Although the institutions were separated, and constituencies and perspectives differed, each branch participated in defining and pursuing the common good. The administrative state has undermined the capacity of the institutions to pursue a public interest. It reflects a concern with administrative detail rather than principle, rule making rather than lawmaking, and the attempt to placate every private interest, rather than the obligation to pursue a common good.

Any work of this sort incurs numerous debts. The many footnotes provide some acknowledgment of my obligation to scholars living and dead. In addition, I would like to thank my wife, Nancy Jane Simkin, for her tireless efforts in editing the manuscript at every stage of its development. She has spared the reader a lot of unnecessary fatigue. This book is dedicated to my mother, the memory of my father, and my wife and daughter.

John Marini
Reno, Nevada

INTRODUCTION

The growth of the administrative state has transformed politics in America, but many Americans are unaware of its existence. In their view, the institutions of government appear to operate as they always have, as part of a constitutional system. Nonetheless, a "sense of the state" pervades contemporary American politics. It is "the sense of an organization of coercive power operating beyond our immediate control and intruding into all aspects of our lives." We have called this organization an "*administrative state*, a *bureaucratic state*, a *capitalist state*, a *corporate state*, a *postindustrial state*, a *welfare state*." No matter what it is called, one thing is clear: the administrative state in America is a relatively new, but alien, phenomenon. After all, "it is the absence of a sense of the state that has been the great hallmark of American political culture."[1]

The presence of the administrative state can be measured by the pervasiveness of the regulatory apparatus, and the increase in resources devoted to the public sector. The most revealing account of the struggle over resources and

[1]Stephen Skowronek, *Building a New American State: The Expansion of National Administrative Capacities, 1877-1920* (Cambridge: Cambridge University Press, 1982), p. 3.

political authority is to be found in the politics surrounding the budgetary process. Public budgeting is much concerned with power and finances, and hence involves important questions of economics, as well as politics. But the budget process is not primarily a matter of economics, so it is not merely a technical process, but a political one. Budgeting in the national government is complicated by a constitutional separation of powers between the executive and legislative branches of government. Both institutions, Congress and the presidency, have important roles in every phase of allocating, appropriating, and expending money. In addition, the administrative apparatus, put in place by the growth of the public sector, has become a source of power in its own right. The struggle for control of budgets and personnel often involves the two branches of government in a struggle for control of the bureaucracy and the priorities of spending. Increasingly, the political branches have come to rely on the judiciary to adjudicate political disputes arising out of the administrative process.

The advent of the administrative state and the growth of state budgets has accelerated competition for resources. It has created new constituencies nurtured by public subsidies. It has also tended to blur distinctions once thought fundamental to liberal regimes: those between the public and private spheres, and those between the state and society. It was inevitable, therefore, that fundamental questions would be raised concerning the legitimacy of the idea of the state itself. Although politics in the American administrative state revolves around money and budgets, and affects nearly every economic and political interest, it is dependent upon a consensus within the political branches concerning the legitimacy of the size and power of the public sector. No such consensus exists. In the final analysis, economic interests and political opinions rest upon ideas concerning the justice and legitimacy of the use of power.

The theory upon which the administrative state is based is alien to the tradition of American political thought. It developed as a practical outgrowth of German idealist philosophy that dominated thinking in the last years of the eighteenth and the early part of the nineteenth century. It was meant to provide a solution to those defects of modern liberal governments that Jean Jacques Rousseau had exposed with such great force.[2] The American Constitution was adopted before modern theories of the state attained any currency. As a result, the Constitution of the United States did not create a state in the modern sense of the term. It created a national government, of limited power, with few administrative purposes to fulfill. The concept of the state as it was to evolve "focused around the idea of centralization of power, normally in an absolute monarch (later an elected parliament and chief executive), whose authority was rationalized and extended over a nation through a developed, impersonalized

---

[2]See particularly, Roger D. Masters, ed., *Rousseau's The First and Second Discourses* (New York: St. Martin's Press, 1964), and Roger D. Masters, ed., *On the Social Contract* (New York: St. Martins Press, 1978).

public administration."[3] The central idea of the state stands in sharp contrast to the government created by a limited Constitution.

The American constitutional system created a regime of limited and separated powers. The administrative state is in principle unlimited in power.[4] The budget is the most important political mechanism of the administrative state. As a formal plan of government in a fiscal year, it is a centralizing device that presupposes a conception of the state as an active mechanism pursuing positive administrative purposes. In its origins, the national budget was viewed as a threat both to a federal system and the separation of powers among the branches of government. It is not accidental that the United States was the last modern industrial nation to adopt a national budget system. The budget process, with taxing and spending power, has become the focal point of the administrative state.

The American government is the classic example of a regime founded on what was essentially a theoretical notion, the doctrine of the separation of powers.[5] The national budgetary process provides a unique vantage point from which to view the separation of powers as it works in practice. In America, the budget process is the point at which the president and Congress must necessarily interact. The questions of taxing and spending go to the heart of the administrative state. In parliamentary regimes it is considered an unacceptable loss of confidence in the leadership for the majority party to fail to carry its budget.[6] But in the American system, the differentiation of the executive and legislative function has predominated over majority and minority party roles within the legislature. In addition, the American federal system enables the legislature and the executive to represent different interests by providing different constituencies; the two majorities thus created are a congressional, locally derived national majority, and a presidential, nationally derived majority.

As a consequence of the separation of powers and the federal system, the budgetary system has attempted to minimize expression of partisanship by preventing consideration of a unified (or party) budget. Hence party leadership committees have no systematic role in budgetary considerations. The committee system reflects the necessity of allowing legislators the ability to satisfy local constituencies. At the same time, the committee system requires the majority

[3]Richard J. Stillman, II, *Preface to Public Administration: A Search for Themes and Direction* (New York: St. Martin's Press, 1991), p 15.

[4]In practice, the administrative bureaucracy poses severe problems for the proper working of the separation of powers. Consequently, the institutions of government, Congress, the presidency, and increasingly the Courts, have operated in a manner that undermines the specific virtue of each of the respective branches.

[5]See especially, Charles Sherman, ed., *John Locke's Second Treatise of Civil Government* (Appleton-Century-Crofts, 1965), Chaps. 11 and 12; and Franz Newman, ed., Montesquieu's *Spirit of the Laws*, Nugent translation, (New York: Hafner Publishing Company, 1949), Book 11.

[6]See Kenneth Bradshaw and David Pring, *Parliament and Congress* (Austin: University of Texas Press, 1972), pp. 306-350.

party to compromise—with the minority as well as with the executive who may
or may not be of the majority party—in exchange for cooperation that would
enable the majority party to pursue a party policy in national affairs. If the
institutional arrangements have tended to minimize partisan division within the
Congress over control of the budget, they have the potential to maximize the
tension between the executive and the legislature concerning their respective
roles in the budgetary process. As Richard Rose has noted:

> When a parliamentary system faces a budget crisis, the problem is basically money.
> The political system has the authority to make a decision, and everybody knows
> where the metaphorical buck stops. In Washington, the problem of the budget is
> political, for nobody wants to admit where the buck stops. The President denies
> responsibility for the faults of a budget enacted by Congress, and Congress blames
> the President for presiding over a government that cannot keep its accounts in
> order.[7]

As the federal budget increased in economic significance, not to mention size,
and became the instrument of fiscal policy, it also came to be regarded as the
primary mechanism of executive aggrandizement. The unity of the executive—
as well as his national constituency and perspective—was once considered sufficient reason for concluding that the president was best suited to the pursuance
of a responsible and efficient fiscal policy. As the use of federal expenditures in
the public interest became public policy, it was widely believed that the executive was best suited to the implementation of a policy of federal spending.
When the consensus concerning the ends of government was shattered during
the Nixon presidency, the budget became the focal point of contention between
the executive and legislative branches. It came subsequently to be argued that
the initiating role of the executive in the formulation and submission of the
budget had resulted in a diminution of the congressional role in policy formation.

The creation of the executive budget system was initially accomplished by
a willing Congress in order to remedy what was thought to be an institutional
weakness in budgetary matters. Prior to 1921 the United States government did
not have anything that could properly be called a federal budget. Federal agencies negotiated directly with Congressional committees to obtain funding, and
the president had no significant ongoing involvement in the process. This was
not an unsatisfactory arrangement in a time when balanced budgets were the
rule, and revenues were usually sufficient (except in wartime) to cover the costs
of government. The increase in the size and scope of public spending, as well as
a new conception of the social responsibilities of government, led to the realization that legislatures were unsuited to the management of public expenditures in
the public interest. Through the use of such devices as deficiency appropria-

---

[7]Richard Rose, *The Postmodern President: George Bush Meets the World* (Chatham, NJ: Chatham House Publishers, 1991), p. 207.

tions, agencies often expended funds at rates that forced Congress to provide additional money during the fiscal year. As a result, Congress not only failed to manage resources in an effective manner, it was impelled to yield more and more discretionary power to the agencies of the executive branch.

Finally in 1921 with the passage of the Budget and Accounting Act, Congress sought to remedy its own managerial deficiencies by placing responsibility for the coordination of the entire budget in the hands of the president. By forcing all agency requests to go through the budget procedures in the executive branch, Congress would be relieved of direct pressure from them. The president was made responsible for preparing an annual budget and submitting it to Congress; executive agencies were barred from presenting estimates directly to Congress unless specifically requested by either House to do so. The Bureau of the Budget was created to assist the president in the discharge of these new responsibilities. Budget reform was just one reform that emerged from the Progressive period; it was part of the attempt to strengthen executive authority. As Allen Schick, then of the Congressional Research Service, noted:

> The shift in Budget control is part of a much larger twentieth century story of governmental reform biased in favor of centralized executive power. Perhaps nowhere was this bias more pronounced or pervasive than in the executive budget movement that swept all levels of American government in the first decades of this century. A generation of reformers came of age with the belief that Congress—any legislative body—is a defective organization for making budgetary decisions. In the words of a leading reformer, "to be a budget it must be prepared and submitted by a responsible executive."[8]

In the past half century, the executive budget system operated with few legislative changes. There were, nonetheless, significant modifications achieved through executive orders, reorganization plans, and other administrative actions. These changes reflected the shifting relationship of the executive and the legislature on the one hand, and the rise and demise of a majority consensus on the other.

Since the New Deal, a fundamental consensus has been achieved concerning the importance of fiscal policy to economic stability. If there were often quarrels over the kind and amount of public spending, there was little partisan disagreement as to the positive role the federal government should play in the economy. Consequently, Washington was thought to bear the major responsibility for economic growth and cyclical stability. The once-orthodox concept of the balanced budget—the raising of sufficient revenue to meet the money costs of government—became of secondary importance to the conscious use of public

[8]Allen Schick, "Budget Reform Legislation: Reorganizing Congressional Centers of Fiscal Power," *Harvard Journal on Legislation*, 1 (February 1974), 308.

expenditures as a "balancing factor" in the attempt to influence the economy as a whole.[9]

Just a few generations ago, prior to the New Deal, it was still a widely held view that public spending itself was a burden on the economy and the working man and should be kept to a minimum. Since then, total government spending has increased from 10 percent of the GNP in 1929 to nearly 35 percent of the GNP by 1990.[10] More interestingly, since the mid-1960s roughly one fifth of the national income of the United States flows through the federal budget.[11] This mammoth rise in spending and the growth of a centralized administrative apparatus through which public money is channeled has precipitated, to an unprecedented degree, an executive–legislative struggle for control of both the spending power and the administrative bureaucracy.

The contemporary problem is complicated by the fact that the presidential–Congressional partnership in public spending, which reached full bloom in the Great Society, was an outgrowth of the consensus established by the Democratic coalition, which had dominated both branches of government for more than a generation. It remains the animating force in Congress. The apparent splintering of the old coalition has not resulted in a new consensus concerning the method in which public spending ought to be pursued. The majority in Congress has favored the use of the national bureaucracy to administer the standards for spending. It wished to centralize economic planning in the attempt to strengthen the public sector. This has resulted in the transformation of the federal system. By the mid-1970s, the federal government had come to rely "increasingly on state and local jurisdictions to deliver national programs." In order to obtain much needed national funding, "state and local jurisdictions have had to meet federal requirements and standards and so have become agents of national policies in such critical areas as social services and education, economic growth and employment, environmental protection, and urban renewal."[12] Nonetheless, during the Reagan years when intergovernmental transfers were cut, local governments were asked to shoulder federal and state mandated programs without being given the resources to do so. The intergov-

---

[9]Accordingly, fiscal policy has been defined as a "policy under which the government uses its expenditures and revenue programs to produce desirable and avoid undesirable effects on the national income, production, and employment." Arthur Smithies, "Federal Budgeting and Fiscal Policy," H. Ellis, ed., in *Survey of Contemporary Economics* (Philadelphia: Blakiston Co., 1948), p. 174.

[10]*Economic Report of the President, 1990* (Washington, D.C.: Government Printing Office, 1989), pp. 294, 388.

[11]See the Brookings Institution annual series, *Setting National Priorities*, beginning in 1970, especially, Barry M. Blechman, Edward M. Gramlich, and Robert W. Hartman, *Setting National Priorities: The 1976 Budget,* and Joseph A. Pechman, ed., *Setting National Priorities: The 1983 Budget* (Washington, D.C.: The Brookings Institution, 1975, 1982).

[12]Gerald Caiden, "Reform and Revitalization in American Bureaucracy," in Robert Miewald and Michael Steinman, eds., *Problems in Administrative Reform* (Chicago: Nelson Hall, 1984), p. 254.

ernmental system had been transformed in the 1970s to become a complex policy arena. Federal policy had resulted in "a decisive shift from income security programs to human services, from general revenue sharing to economic stimulus programs and aid to distressed regions, from local discretionary use to national entitlement formulas, and from relatively simple bureaucratic arrangements to complicated bargaining arenas."[13] The disagreements between Congress and presidents concerning the levels of social spending reached a peak in the Reagan administration. It was Reagan's view that high levels of social spending resulted in limiting the individual's freedom to choose (by allowing less disposable income) the spending goals that should be pursued. As control of more income has been put into the hands of governments (and bureaucracies) at all levels, it was social rather than individual goals that had become paramount. Reagan attempted to alter the priorities of the public sector, slowing the growth of government and reducing taxes to allow greater individual choice. In attempting to reorder spending priorities, the struggle for budget control dominated politics in the Reagan years. The reluctance of recent presidents—not only Republicans—to sustain a national spending partnership has resulted in a deep division that may not be a temporary phenomenon. It is possible that, with the advantages of incumbency and the continued support of groups who are beneficiaries of federal spending, a Congressional majority with an interest in increased public spending can continue to dominate the legislative branch. On the other hand, it seems likely that presidents who obtain a national majority (regardless of party) will oppose that view.[14]

The critical period for the consolidation of the administrative state occurred during the Nixon administration. This was the period of greatest turbulence in legislative–executive relations. It was also the time of the most far-reaching reforms in the budget process. It was fashionable in the aftermath of Watergate to applaud the ascendancy of the legislature as a necessary corrective of the presidential abuse of power. Consequently, legislative attempts to assert Congressional power in areas long considered to be the domain of the executive were widely praised as vital to the preservation of a constitutional balance. Perhaps the most important effort in this regard was the passage of the Congressional Budget and Impoundment Control Act of 1974. This act resulted in the creation of a legislative budgetary system. The executive budget system, created by the Budgeting and Accounting Act of 1921 (and made the focal point of the managerial presidency in Roosevelt's creation of the Executive Office of the President), had come to be regarded as the means whereby presidents had attained important control over the purse strings and thereby the priorities of the

---

[13]Ibid.

[14]If the current situation persists, it may be increasingly difficult for the executive to retain sufficient power to resist the encroachments of the legislature. This is particularly so as Congress becomes more closely allied with the executive bureaucracy as a consequence of their similar interest in sustaining a centralized administration.

national government. The impetus for budget reform grew out of the desire of the Congressional majority to enable the legislature to establish priorities for public spending. They also intended to inhibit the president's ability to refuse to spend funds appropriated by Congress. In a peculiar reversal of roles, the president had increasingly come to be viewed as the guardian of the public treasury against a spendthrift Congress.

The Budget Act marked the first time in this century that Congress success-fully changed its own practices rather than those of the executive in regard to the budget.[15] By the institution of a legislative budget process complete with new budget committees in the House and Senate and a new Congressional Budget Office,[16] Congress attempted to ensure that the spending priorities of the old majority would not go unheeded. Whether Congress had finally overcome what were once thought to be institutional limitations to the formulation of a unified budget policy remained to be seen. As one budget authority observed at the time, "If Congress were to have a centralized and cohesive budget machine, it would be an executive in legislative disguise."[17]

The Congressional Budget and Impoundment Control Act was widely con-sidered among the most important pieces of legislation in the last generation,[18] yet it passed both Houses by nearly unanimous vote.[19] It was not treated as a partisan measure. Similarly, the Budgeting and Accounting Act of 1921 (now widely considered as a key to the aggrandizement of the executive) had passed with little controversy. Why did two such important reform measures become law without partisan controversy and with virtually no public awareness? The answer appears to lie in the prevailing climate of respectable opinion that re-flects a legitimizing opinion. In this case, the opinion that legitimized the cre-ation of a national–executive budget was derivative of the progressive notion that a government ought to be organized to achieve positive purposes. The move to establish a legislative budget 50 years later arose from the realization that the president and the national majority may have become the greatest obsta-cles to progress and the perpetuation of a neutral administration committed to the achievement of social justice.

By distributing power among competing branches, the separation of powers

---

[15]Although there were provisions for a legislative budget procedure in the Legislative Reorgani-zation Act of 1946, these were never successfully implemented because of Congressional inability to reform its own committee structure and its internal operations.

[16]This was to be the legislative counterpart of the Office of Management and Budget located in the executive branch.

[17]Allen Schick, *Congress Versus the Budget, Hearings before a House Select Committee on Committees.* 93rd Cong., 1st sess., 1973, vol. 2, pt. 3, p. 630.

[18]Nixon, in signing the bill less than a month before his resignation, noted "this bill is the most significant reform of budgetary procedures since the Congress and this country began." Presum-ably, he thought it more important than the Budget Act of 1921. *Weekly Complication of the Presidential Documents* 10 (July 12, 1974), p. 800.

[19]The vote was 401 to 6 in the House; 80 to 0 in the Senate. *Congressional Roll Call, 1974* (Washington, D.C.: Congressional Quarterly, Inc., 1975), pp. 12, 14.

prevents any one branch from speaking authoritatively for the whole. Consequently, opinion and its political legitimization become crucial in justifying the actions of each of the respective branches. In the formative years of the republic, the separation of powers was viewed primarily as a means of imposing limitations upon the power of government in order to reconcile executive energy with the requirement of democratic representation. It was precisely this difference that animated the dispute between Alexander Hamilton and Thomas Jefferson. It was Hamilton's fiscal "monarchism," Jefferson believed, that constituted the gravest threat to the underlying principle of democracy, thereby threatening liberty. The separation of powers between the political branches necessitated a continuous struggle over control of the administration—or the government itself. The unifying element which sought to bridge the gap between the respective branches was the party. It was the party, based on principle, that provided a consensus upon which a majority could rule.

A new interpretation of the separation of powers emerged out of a new concern with social and economic justice. It took the form of an attack on the Constitution itself. The Constitution traditionally viewed—indeed, required—a rigid interpretation of the powers of the respective branches in order to maintain liberty. The concern to protect liberty had led to the protection of the "privileged" few; it inhibited the positive use of governmental power in the interests of the many. In the hands of the Progressives a new interpretation of the separation of powers achieved legitimacy. This view held that the political branches of government should be distinguished from the administration of government.[20] In creating an executive budget with the Budget and Accounting Act, Congress implicitly recognized that the president was solely responsible for the conduct of nonpartisan administration.

The distinction between the political branches and the bureaucracy posed novel problems for the continued viability of the separation of powers. The administration, it could be said, rested outside the traditional checks and balances imposed by the separation of powers.[21] The impact of bureaucracy on the concept of separation of powers is troublesome. Its implications for constitutional government are profound:

---

[20]The rise of the modern theory of budgeting goes hand in hand with the rise of an administrative state. The budget, like the administration, is a neutral mechanism. It was clear, however, that it served to strengthen centralized executive control.

[21]Consequently, the Progressive attitude toward power was far different from that of the Founding Fathers. Because the bureaucracy was intended to achieve humane purposes—its neutrality was assured—the dependence upon motives and ambition to sustain independence and resist encroachments by other branches was unnecessary. But its motives in relation to the other branches (and vice versa) become extremely important. In this regard, Peter Woll has suggested, "The system of motivated conflicts tends to break down in the interaction of the bureaucracy and Congress. Many agencies of Congress are relatively independent of both presidential and judicial control; in these cases Congress and its particular committees involved feel no compelling need to oppose bureaucratic interests." *American Bureaucracy,* 2d ed., (New York: W.W. Norton & Co., 1977), p. 25.

Although technical constitutional norms prevail, the constitutional system to limit government power through the separation of powers no longer functions in the manner or to the degree thought to be necessary by the Framers of the Constitution. . . . The premises of the constitutional system are no longer valid today. This is a further reason to support the view that present bureaucratic power does not fit neatly into the pattern of limited government established by the Constitution of 1789.[22]

Nonetheless, the 1974 Budget and Impoundment Control Act originated in a renewed concern to reinvigorate the separation of powers. This time it was alleged that the executive branch had usurped the preponderance of power.[23] But did the new act attempt to restore a new political balance between the branches? Or did it simply seek to achieve a new equilibrium wherein both branches would have equal access to the bureaucracy? The struggle over control of the bureaucracy and budgets reached its peak in the administration of Richard Nixon. He was the first president to clearly question the legitimacy of the administrative state. In doing so, he confronted a Congress dominated by interests committed to its perpetuation. He also challenged the idea of the neutrality, or nonpartisan character of the bureaucracy. He concluded that the permanent government, created by Democrats, was sympathetic to its interests and the continued growth of the public sphere. The hostility to the Nixon administration, which erupted into open warfare in his second term, resulted from Nixon's failure to recognize the legitimacy and the neutrality of the federal bureaucracy. This was important because it constituted an implicit repudiation of the progressive view made operative in the New Deal and Great Society that government could be an "engine of compassion."[24] Nixon failed to regard "enlightened administration" as being beyond partisanship. It appeared to be his view that the presence of a nonpartisan bureaucracy had resulted in a distortion of the principle of representation: It had prevented the majority from ruling. The purpose of decentralization (the heart of the New American Revolution) and executive reorganization was to bring the bureaucracy under political control, thereby restoring a representative government. The problem of bureau-

---

[22]Ibid., p. 24.

[23]David Frohnmayer suggested that "The extent of the shift to executive power is now so great as to throw into question the continuing viability of the separation of powers." "The Parchment Barriers; An Essay on the Vitality of a Constitutional Idea," in *Impoundment of Appropriated Funds by the President, Joint Hearings Sub-committee on Separation of Powers,* 93rd Cong., 1st sess, S. 373. p. 722.

[24]Robert Eden has suggested that "FDR offered a comprehensive interpretation of partisanship. The New Deal reassessment justified a new partisan division within American society, not merely in public life and electoral politics, but in every major sector of the economy. It made enlightened administration, as a higher kind of partisanship, newly respectable in American public life. But it also sought to precipitate or sharpen a moral division in the internal governance of the private sector, fostering a new definition of social responsibility that was inseparable from partisan struggles in the public arena." "The New Deal Reevaluation of Partisanship," in Peter W. Schramm, ed., *The Future of American Political Parties,* forthcoming.

cratic centralization may present the greatest difficulty to representative government. Long ago, Tocqueville, in pointing to the difficulty of maintaining representative institutions in a bureaucratic society, asked the question: "How is it possible to reconcile extreme centralization with representative democracy? This is the grand problem of the times."[25]

The centralization of administration in Washington during the 1960s and early 1970s began a process that led to the erosion of the consensus forged during the New Deal. At the same time, the institutions of government at all levels were transformed. Revenue flowed to the center and Washington became the focal point of administrative politics in America. The consequences for the political system were profound. The Democratic Party, which controlled the political branches of the national government after the election of 1964, initiated an American version of the administrative state. Special interests and constituencies were mobilized in support of certain categories of expenditure. Naturally, the legislative branch became the focus of such attention. It was almost inevitable that budgeting would become the most important part of modern bureaucratic government.

The new regulatory bureaucracy created during and after the Great Society attempted much more detailed control of the political, economic, and even social problems that affected nearly every interest in the nation. These problems were to be solved, no longer primarily within the political institutions, but through the administrative process and subsequently the courts. The increased administrative power of the national government quickly became a political and partisan issue, and tended to polarize society as well as political institutions. The Democratic Party, which created the administrative state, was able to dominate the legislative branch and was committed to the maintenance of administrative centralization. The Republican Party, increasingly able to capture the executive branch, sought to limit the size of the public sector and attempted to decentralize administrative authority. The two institutions of government fought to establish dominance in controlling national priorities, as well as the bureaucracy itself. It was clear by 1973 that Congress could not be a player in either realm without having greater control over the budget. The Democratic majority was unable to challenge effectively the President's authority in formulating economic policy or establishing national priorities because it did not have the organizational means and technical capability to do so. With the Budget Act of 1974, Congress became a dominant force in the formulation of fiscal policy, and a major player in setting national priorities. Congress succeeded in challenging executive control of the budget and the bureaucracy, but the price of success was an institutional inability to reach agreement within the legislature

---

[25]Alexis de Tocqueville, *Etudes Economiques, Politiques, et Litteraires*, p. 74. Quoted in Louis Smith, "Alexis de Tocqueville and Public Administration," *Public Administration Review*, Vol. 12, No. 3, 1942, p. 237.

concerning expenditures, except at ever-higher levels of spending. Moreover, the reforms in Congress during the 1970s, which accompanied the growth of the administrative state, had weakened the leadership of Congress and empowered individual members. Power moved from committee chairs to subcommittee chairs. The links between Congress and the permanent bureaucracy undermined presidential attempts to manage the executive branch. The budget process was dominated by those interests in Congress and the bureaucracy that supported the priorities of the administrative state. The growth of the federal government could not be challenged seriously without control of the levers of public spending.

The election of Ronald Reagan indicated that the administrative state had not ceased to be a troublesome problem in American politics. He posed another serious threat to those committed to the maintenance or growth of the public sector. Reagan used the budget process to establish his own priorities, which included a reduction in the size of government. He took advantage of the reconciliation procedure of the Budget Act to force reductions in expenditures, while at the same time reducing tax rates. However, the 1982 recession, coupled with the rapid collapse of inflation, prevented a reduction of expenditures. Instead, the growth of the defense budget and the maintenance of social spending led to an explosion of deficit financing and increased the national debt. Furthermore, the budget process could no longer limit expenditures without fundamental changes in the laws. Nearly half of all federal expenditures now take the form of direct transfer payments, which are called entitlements, to individuals. The political difficulty of raising new sources of revenue, coupled with a mistrust of presidential power, led Congress to attempt to reduce the deficit by procedural devices, such as the Gramm–Rudman–Hollings Deficit Reduction Act. Congress lacked the will to act but refused to trust Republican presidents, including Reagan's successor, George Bush, with the power to reorder spending priorities or to cut the remaining controllable portions of the budget. The result has been a stalemate, budget gimmickry, and ever-increasing budget deficits.

The American government was among the last modern industrialized societies to centralize administration or consolidate an administrative state. The Constitution and the politics of federalism had inhibited Washington from attempting such centralization. The progressive era and the New Deal had legitimized, in theory, the development of an administrative state. But it was not until the Great Society that the task was accomplished. Originally the presidency provided the greatest impetus for its creation. Congress, representative of local interests and state power, was opposed. Subsequently, after its implementation, Congress became the greatest benefactor and defender of the administrative state, with the presidency its most ominous and dangerous foe.

Since 1968, much of American politics and budgetary strife has revolved around the executive–legislative struggles to control the resources and the power associated with the administrative state. When a political consensus existed concerning the priorities of spending, conflict over the budget was contained. At one time governments controlled expenditures; the budget process provided the means of limiting claims based upon available resources. The budget, which had gained political importance in the New Deal as a device to stabilize economic conditions, had become a hostage of the economy it was meant to control. Indeed, some would say that in the most important respect, politicians have substituted budgeting for governing. They have done so precisely because they have abdicated their responsibility to make choices based upon available resources. They have failed to do so because of a lack of consensus concerning fundamentals, not the least of which is agreement concerning the size and composition of the public sector. As Aaron Wildavsky has noted, "the budgetary process is an arena in which the struggle for power over public policy is worked out. Budgeting is a forum for the exercise of political power, not a substitute for that power."[26] Now it appears that budgets control governments rather than governments controlling budgets.

With the growth of the administrative state, the consensus in support of limited government was fragmented, and support for limited (or balanced) budgets also began to wane. The problem of budget control is further complicated by a failure of the parties and institutions of government to achieve a new consensus or political realignment concerning the purposes of public spending. The Constitution, which separated the powers of government, has provided the conditions for budget strife. Nonetheless, the administrative state rests somewhat uneasily within the confines of a constitutional order; it is a presence waiting to be legitimized. It is for this reason that the legitimacy of the administrative state can and will be challenged by those whose power derives from the Constitution.

---

[26]Aaron Wildavsky, *The New Politics of the Budgetary Process* (Glenview, Illinois: Scott, Foresman & Co., 1988), p. 439.

Chapter 1

Congress, the Presidency, and Administrative Organization

Though men be much governed by interest, yet even interest itself, and all human affairs, are entirely governed by opinion.

David Hume, Essays

The creation of the American presidency had presented numerous difficulties for those who framed the Constitution.[1] It was at once a representative office and a constitutional one. The Framers attempted to create an executive who was dependent upon the majority of the people, but sufficiently independent to act unrestrained in his own sphere when necessity and the public interest demanded.[2] They also separated the powers of government to ensure that government would not become tyrannical, thereby protecting the liberties of the people. With this separation, the constitutional system obscured responsibility concerning the administration of government. The struggle between Congress

[1]Joseph Story has suggested, "What is the best constitution for the executive department, and what are the powers with which it should be entrusted, are problems among the most important, and probably the most difficult to be satisfactorily solved, of all which are involved in the theory of free governments." *Commentaries on the Constitution of the United States,* 1833 ed. (New York: Da-Capo Press Reprint, 1970), p. 277.

[2]Cf. Alexis de Tocqueville, *Democracy in America* (New York: Vintage books, 1945), vol. 1, p. 125.

and the president for control of administration has been an ongoing problem in American history. The growth of the administrative state has only aggravated the problem.

A significant cause of the inability of the executive and the legislature to function amicably in recent years arises from the splintering of the old Democratic coalition and the failure of the leadership of the parties to create a new consensus upon which the majority can rule. In addition, the growth of an administrative apparatus that is not accountable simply to the president or the Congress has complicated the relationship between the political branches. Even more important than the formal powers accorded the branches of government is the legitimacy of opinions that sanction the use of power. That legitimacy derives from conceptions concerning justice and the public good. Changes in social and political conditions often result in a questioning of the legitimacy of power and institutions. The differences in ideas concerning justice and power serve as the catalyst that transforms parties and, subsequently, the actions of those who occupy the offices of government. The separation of powers provides the practical means by which minorities and majorities can stake their claim to power and legitimacy by control of one or both of the political branches of government.

Nearly twenty years ago, the historian Arthur M. Schlesinger, Jr. noted in his celebrated book, *The Imperial Presidency,* that "the American Constitution was established, for better or worse, on an idea new to the world in the eighteenth century and still uncommon in the twentieth century—the idea of separation of powers."[3] The Founding Fathers saw conflict as the guarantee of freedom; thus, "instead of concentrating authority in a single institution, they chose to disperse authority among three independent branches of government."[4] It was precisely the danger of authority becoming too concentrated in a single institution that brought forth Schlesinger's attack on the "imperial presidency".

The tension created by the two great functions of government when contained in separate institutions has spawned numerous controversies concerning the proper role of the executive and the legislature. From the beginning, various crises have resulted in a reexamination of the legitimacy of institutions, which reflects the legitimacy of ideas and the dominant opinions holding sway over those who govern. Although the structure of government appears the same, the opinions that animate those who guide its institutions have not been so immune and the institutions themselves have thereby undergone subtle change. If not, why would Schlesinger, long a friend of presidential power, have been forced to make such a reappraisal thereof? Had the presidency changed or had the legitimacy of the opinion that had sanctioned the use of that power changed? If so, why?

[3](Boston: Houghton Mifflin Co. 1973), p. 1.
[4]Ibid.

For much of the twentieth century, the presidency has been perceived to be the more progressive instrument of reform in American politics, and Congress a source of deadlock, at best. In short, it seemed perfectly clear that the fundamental conflict in American politics revolved around the tension that existed between liberal presidents and conservative Congresses. Willmoore Kendall attempted to explain what he called the "unexplained mystery" of American politics, the heart of which was the fact that "one and the same electorate maintains in Washington, year after year, a president devoted to high principle and enlightenment, and a Congress that gives short shrift to both."[5] The patrons of presidential power had a simple answer: the Congress was undemocratic. It maintained internal procedures—such as the filibuster and the seniority system—that were hostile to majority rule. Moreover, the Constitution itself— through the devices of separation of powers and a bicameral legislature, staggered elections, and a federal system that encouraged rural overrepresentation—tended to obstruct the transformation of majority sentiment into governmental action. The presidency was the democratic element in a regime characterized by undemocratic roadblocks to the unencumbered rule of the majority.

Those who favored presidential leadership as being most representative of the progressive elements of the American regime insisted that the president was the embodiment of the moral sentiment of the community. Kendall did not disagree; his preference for the congressional majority and local constituencies against the centralizing effects of presidential leadership rested at bottom on his disagreements with what that moral vision was. He noted:

> The congressional election, provide[s] a highly necessary corrective against the bias toward quixotism inherent in our presidential elections . . . . And it is well they do; the alternative would be national policies based upon a wholly false picture of the sacrifices the electorate are prepared to make for the lofty objectives held up to them by presidential aspirants. And executive–legislative tension is the means by which the corrective works itself out.[6]

Kendall's praise of the tension created by the separation of powers would be echoed within a decade by those who had once regarded it as undemocratic and antimajoritarian. It was the separation of powers and a resurgent legislative branch that would save the republic from the "imperial" presidency. Kendall and his critics viewed the problem as a structural or institutional one. That this was not the case became apparent in the intervening years. The presidency had been thought to "embody high principle and enlightenment" because the president spoke for a national majority. However, the legislature, with its representation of interests, provided a diversity and a provincialism that was comforting

---

[5]Willmoore Kendall, "The Two Majorities," *Midwest Journal of Political Science*, 4 (November 1960):328.

[6]Ibid., p. 344.

to those who distrusted the moral purpose embodied in the presidency and the power that derives from the majority. But the institutional differences, derivative of the nature of the two branches, could not be as important as the legitimacy of the opinion that gave a moral authority to the majority and thereby the presidency.

It was precisely this moral authority of the majority that became suspect in the waning years of the 1960s. It had become apparent to some that it was neither the president nor the majority that was the exclusive source of morality in the American regime. Many who had previously seen majority rule as being the key to democratic government had come to view the majority suspiciously, as itself undemocratic or even racist. It was the difference in opinion concerning the meaning of equality that prompted the new mistrust of the majority. Therefore it is not surprising that the authoritative opinion, in transferring its allegiance from the president to the Congress, sought a restraint upon the power of the majority.[7]

The separation of powers does not prevent majorities from ruling: it makes it difficult for majorities that appear to be illegitimate from ruling simply. It is therefore a practical means of ensuring that the structural or institutional framework serves as a support for the animating principles of the regime. It is the principle of equality itself that is the cornerstone upon which any legitimate government must be based. The only legitimate organizing principle compatible with equality and the rights of individuals derived therefrom is majority rule, which rests equality on the consent of the governed. But a majority must be reasonable or mindful of the rights of minorities to be considered legitimate.[8] The separation of powers through democratic representation in the legislature offers a practical organizational means to protect minorities. The practical struggle for control of the administration in the early years of the nation was animated by the necessity to reconcile executive energy with democratic representation.

ORGANIZATIONAL LEGITIMACY AND MAJORITY CONTROL: THE IMPORTANCE OF OPINION

The importance of tension as the creative force in the practical relations between the legislature and the executive in the institutional framework of government cannot be overestimated. The struggle for control of the purse and the

---

[7]See William G. Andrews, "The Presidency, Congress, and Constitutional History," in Aaron Wildavsky, ed., *Perspectives on the Presidency,* (Boston: Little Brown & Co., 1975), pp. 24-40.

[8]As Thomas Jefferson noted in his first Inaugural Address: "All, too, will bear in mind this sacred principle, that though the will of the majority is in all cases to prevail, that will, to be rightful, must be reasonable; that the minority possess their equal rights, which equal laws must protect, and to violate . . . would be oppression." In Henry Steele Commanger, ed., *Documents of American History,* (New York: Appleton-Century Crofts, 1963), vol. 1, p. 187.

details of administration often lie at the bottom of legislative–executive tensions.[9] Consequently the majority is the natural point of control to be occupied by a statesman who aims at organization or reform. However, the creation of a majority is one of the great difficulties in American politics. As Madison noted, in the extended republic of the United States,

> and among the great variety of interests, parties, and sects which it embraces, a coalition of a majority of the whole society could seldom take place on any other principles than those of justice and the general good: whilst there being thus less danger to a minor from the will of a major party, there must be less pretext, also to provide for the security of the former, by introducing into the government a will not dependent on the latter, or, in other words, a will independent of the society itself.[10]

If a will independent of society cannot exist, it is not clear that the majority can rule simply.[11] The separation of powers provides for a competition between the legislature and the executive for the right to establish or determine the legitimacy of the opinion that it indeed represents the majority. It does so by channeling political divisions into a struggle over control of the administration of the government itself. The mobilization of that opinion, which is the key to the successful organization of government, has resulted in the development of political parties based on the division of what Tocqueville has called the "two opinions which are as old as the world and are perpetually to be met with, in all free countries, the one tending to limit, the other to extend indefinitely the power of the people."

Political parties in the United States arose from a difference concerning the founding principles of the regime.[12] The first party struggle grew out of a dispute concerning the meaning and means of giving organizational authority to those principles. Tocqueville has noted that "the political parties that I style great are those which cling to principles rather than to their consequences; to general and not to special cases; to ideas and not to men."[13] In America the ideas that animated the regime were derived from the "laws of nature" and were articulated in the principle of equality em-

---

[9]Henry Adams noted in his *The Life of Albert Gallatin:* "In governments, as in households, he who holds the purse holds the power. The Treasury is the natural point of control to be occupied by any statesman who aims at organization or reform, and conversely no organization or reform is likely to succeed that does not begin with and is not guided by the Treasury. The highest type of practical statesmanship must always take this direction." (Philadelphia: J.B. Lippincott & Co., 1879), p. 267.

[10]Alexander Hamilton, James Madison, and John Jay, *The Federalist*, No. 51, Clinton Rossiter, ed. (New York: Mentor Books, 1961), p. 325.

[11]This is merely the practical difficulty that derives from the necessity of reconciling majority rule with minority rights, or consent and "enlightened consent."

[12]See Harry V. Jaffa, "Nature and Origin of the American Party System" in his *Equality and Liberty* (New York: Oxford University Press, 1965), pp. 3–41.

[13]Tocqueville, *Democracy in America*, vol. 1, p. 182.

bodied in the Declaration of Independence. As a result, the clash of great parties over the formal powers of government and the organization of government itself occurred on the basis of whether that power was conducive to the perpetuation of those principles, or had itself served as a stumbling block to their attainment.

Great parties, as Tocqueville noted, are not those concerned merely with private interests. Rather, great party struggles concern "moral principles of a high order, such as the love of equality and independence . . . they suffice to kindle violent passions."[14] The first great party struggle in the United States, which culminated in the election of 1800, had revolved around the attempt to "recreate" the principles of the Declaration of Independence that had been subverted by Hamilton's monocratic fiscal arrangements and a centralized administration. "The party that desired to limit the power of the people," Tocqueville observed, "endeavored to apply its doctrines more especially to the Constitution of the Union, whence it derived its name of Federal. The other party, which affected to be exclusively attached to the cause of liberty, took that of Republican."[15] Jefferson and the Republicans were fearful that an aristocratic passion lay at the bottom of the Federalist attempts at organizing the federal government.[16]

The separation of powers necessitates, as a practical matter, legitimizing the power to rule by showing that its authority derives from the animating principles. The separation of powers ensures that a majority and minorities will have the organizational means through which they can seek their claims to legitimacy. During the times of an articulated moral purpose that creates a broad consensus, the president, as national spokesman, is usually regarded as the unquestioned leader of the nation through his leadership of the party and thereby of the majority.

The minor interests may stake their claim to dissent from the moral authority of the majority by retreating to the protection of the institutional forms themselves; the emphasis is on representation and protection of minority rights, sustained often in the legislature or the courts. In times of no moral authority or broad consensus owing to the devitalization of principle in the parties, there is often a period of minor party strife. Unlike great parties Tocqueville noted that minor parties

> . . . are not sustained or dignified by lofty purposes, they ostensibly display the selfishness of their character in their actions. . . . They glow with a factious zeal. Whereas society is convulsed by great parties, it is only agitated by minor ones.[17]

---

[14]Ibid., p. 183.
[15]Ibid.
[16]Tocqueville suggests "that aristocratic or democratic passions may easily be detected at the bottom of all parties." Ibid., p. 186.
[17]Ibid., p. 182.

In the times when minor parties contend, the fragmented interests of localities and organized groups come to the fore and Congress assumes a dominant role.[18]

The history of American democracy has often been a history of extending the power of the people. But this has not meant simply that unfettered executive power could accomplish that purpose. Hamilton and the Federalists had attempted to combine executive energy with a vigorous administration, not to increase the authority of the people but to increase the power and stabilize the economy of the nation. Jefferson, on the other hand, sought to extend the power of the people by appealing to those principles that legitimized that power; in so doing he had created the spirit of party. He attempted, in consequence, to mitigate the effect of executive aggrandizement.[19]

The Federalist purposes at Philadelphia had involved the attempt to wed Republicanism to administrative energy.[20] Jefferson, in turning to his party in the representative branch, had eschewed a vigorous executive administration that was incompatible with liberty. An important practical aspect of the separation of powers is revealed in the attempt to provide executive energy while maintaining the requirements of representative government.

PRESIDENT, CONGRESS, AND ADMINISTRATIVE ORGANIZATION

An important practical question raised as a result of the institutional tension created by the separation of powers is the relationship of the executive and the legislature to the administration apparatus. To put the matter simply, is the president the leader of the executive branch, or a clerk responsible to the legislature.[21] The Constitution did not finally settle the question of how power was to be exercised. Yet as Charles Thach noted, "Nothing is more vital than the relations of the executive head to the chief officers of the administrative departments, and the relations of the latter to the legislature." The Constitution, he suggested, failed to "decide the fundamental question of whether the legislature or the chief executive was the master of the organs of administration."[22]

---

[18]At the time of Tocqueville's visit, he suggested that great political parties did not exist; rather "the parties by which the union is menaced do not rest upon principles, but upon material interests." Ibid., p. 184.

[19]John Zvesper has observed that Jefferson believed that "such systems as the plan of Government, which the late Secretary of Treasury (Mr. Hamilton) had proposed in the (Philadelphia) Convention had justly raised Republican apprehension of a 'Monarchic, Aristocratic Faction', who would wish to impose upon us the substance of the British Government." In Zvesper, *Political Philosophy and Rhetoric* (London: Cambridge University Press, 1977), p. 162.

[20]See Edward S. Corwin, "The Progress of Constitutional Theory Between the Declaration of Independence and the Meeting of the Philadelphia Convention," *American Historical Review*, 30 (April 1925): 511-36

[21]Herbert Storing has suggested that there are "two great themes that always have run through any substantial consideration of the Presidency—the themes . . . of 'clerkship' and 'leadership' . . ." In the introduction to Charles Thach, *The Creation of the Presidency* (Baltimore: Johns Hopkins University Press, 1969).

[22]Ibid., p. 140.

James Hart similarly noted that although the Constitution created the presidency, it had "by clear implication left the creation of the great departments to Congress."[23] Consequently, the creation of the executive branch had remained an incomplete task at the conclusion of the Convention. It was left to the first Congress and administration of George Washington to determine the practical details of the operation of the administration and its relation to the political branches of government.[24]

Hart insists that

> . . . the legislative decisions of 1789, in its bearing upon the crucial relations of the President to department heads . . . had helped . . . to save that great office from the dangerous disintegration which every administrative position taken in 1789 other than that of the House majority would have invited.[25]

If the presidency had indeed been placed upon a firm foundation at the conclusion of the first Congress, an important consequence of the separation of powers was the extent to which substantive political issues were likely to escalate into debate over the formal powers of the branches of government.[26]

The primary organizational problem that resulted was the necessity to secure the maintenance of the distinction between the proper spheres of legislative supremacy (which is embodied in the principle of representation) and executive independence (to ensure the possibility of a vigorous administration).[27] A competent government must have the capacity for both deliberation and decision-making. A difficulty to be overcome from the beginning was the widespread belief, predominant at the Convention, that a nonmonarchial executive was inherently weak.[28]

On the other hand, it was necessary to reconcile an energetic executive with the liberties of the people.[29] Hamilton himself delivered a speech in Phila-

---

[23]*The American Presidency in Action* (New York: The Macmillan Co., 1948), p. 152.

[24]One critic notes, "The broad outlines of the presidency . . . were drawn during Washington's administration. It was 'the result of Congress's decisions to allow or to require the executive to plan policy and to exercise broad policy-making discretion in implementing legislatively unarticulated but shared objectives." Abraham P. Sofaer, *War, Foreign Affairs, and Constitutional Power, The Origins* (Cambridge: Ballinger Publishing Co., 1976), pp. 128-129.

[25]Hart, *The American Presidency*, p. 248.

[26]See Peri E. Arnold and L. John Roos, "Toward a Theory of Congressional-Executive Relations" *Review of Politics*, 36 (July 1974): 410.

[27]Hamilton noted in *Federalist*, No. 70: "Those politicians and statesmen, who have been the most celebrated for the soundness of their principles . . . have declared in favor of a single executive and numerous legislature. They have . . . considered energy as the most necessary qualification of the former, and have regarded this as most applicable to power in a single hand; . . . they have . . . considered the latter as best adapted to deliberation and wisdom, the best calculated to conciliate the confidence of the people and to secure their privileges and interests." p. 424.

[28]Montesquieu had contributed to this opinion. In *The Spirit of the Laws* he had noted the superior executive strength in monarchies. See Book 11, Chapter 6, p. 156; Book 5, Chapter 10, p. 54. (New York: Hafner Publishing Co., 1966).

[29]Joseph Story suggests "that organization is best which will at once secure energy in the executive and safety to the people." *Commentary on the Constitution*, p. 280.

delphia in which he declared the difficulty of securing a vigorous republican executive.[30] And yet, as Thomas Pangle has noted, "the need to limit government does not imply the need to weaken government . . . . The executive is the key to the achievement of both limited and forceful government."[31]

A primary requirement to counter the objection of monarchy (and yet provide energy) was to ensure the possibility of securing unity in the executive and at the same time provide an adequate means to ensure independence in a manner not inconsistent with a republican form of government. When James Wilson proposed a single executive on the opening day of the Convention's debate on the presidency, he maintained that this would allow the "most energy, dispatch, and responsibility to the office."[32] As to independence, the most powerful support for independence in such a regime, said Wilson, would be his connection with the people and a capacity to secure (through a majority) the legitimizing opinion that the president represented the people, and could ensure a continuing national interest:

> The tenure of his office, it is true is not hereditary, nor is it for life; but it is a tenure of the noblest kind. By being the man of the people, he is invested; by continuing to be the man of the people, his investiture will be voluntarily, and cheerfully, and honorably renewed.[33]

Even though the president was to be indirectly elected, as Thach noted, "it is somewhat remarkable that the electoral procedure set up by the Constitution should so soon have been regarded as the equivalent of popular election, that the position of the President as the one, great national representative should have been readily accepted."[34]

The separation of powers, insofar as it ensured a unitary executive and a diversified legislature, could be taken to have shown the extent to which a monarchy could be moderated or liberalized[35] and a republic, primarily through the principle of representation, could be made extensive.[36] Together, the powers provided the possibility of a federal republic capable of energetic administration, in which the interests and the requirements of the use of executive power would not be adverse to the rights of the people.

At the Convention, when Wilson wrote into the report of the committee of

[30]See Max Farrand, *The Records of the Federal Convention* (New Haven: Yale University Press, 1966), vol. 1, p. 289.

[31]*Montesquieu's Philosophy of Liberalism* (Chicago: University of Chicago Press, 1973), p. 134.

[32]See Thach, *Creation of the Presidency,* p. 167.

[33]Yales and Seaton, *Annals of the Congress of the United States* (Washington, D.C., 1834), vol. 1, p. 400.

[34]Thach, *Creation of the Presidency,* p. 167

[35]Edward S. Corwin suggests that "the Presidency was designed in measure to reproduce the monarchy of George III with the corruption left out, and also of course the hereditary feature." *The President: Office and Powers* (New York: New York University Press, 1940), p. 15.

[36]*The Federalist,* No. 9, p. 72.

detail the sentence "The executive power of the United States shall be vested in a single person," it marked the final abandonment of the concept of the omnipotence of the legislature, and the substitution therefore of the characteristically American doctrine of coordinate departments. The unrestrained legislature and subordinate executive had its day, and, so far as the United States was concerned, had ceased to be.[37]

If the President need not be a clerk, it was not unambiguously clear that he could always be a leader. One thing was clear, however: as a practical matter this arrangement would ensure that a tension between the requirements of effective administration and adequate representation of interests would exist.[38]

CREATION OF THE TREASURY DEPARTMENT: A PRACTICAL PROBLEM

The problem created by the establishment of the Treasury Department was indicative of the extent to which control over the purse strings constituted a special problem for the conduct of executive–legislative relations. This difficulty concerned the manner in which the department should be organized: simply as an executive department, like the Departments of War and Foreign Affairs, or as an arm of the legislative branch.[39] The creation and organization of the Treasury department, which culminated in the Treasury Act of 1789, was the "center of the first great Congressional debate on administrative responsibility."[40] Was the department primarily responsible to the president or the Congress?

This debate was an instructive one, for it presented in microcosm many of the very problems that the creation of an energetic executive had incurred. It

---

[37]Thach, *Creation of the Presidency,* p. 167.

[38]Murray Dry has observed: "As representative government starts from a consent to government in order to secure natural rights, and as the free development of different faculties produces division between rich and poor, few and many; the difference between the Federalists and Anti-Federalists, and then the Jeffersonians, turns on how such a government should be organized and what was the most needful for it to succeed, popular participation or effective administration. The separation of powers supports representative government by channeling and limiting political divisions into debates on the scope of the different branches' powers." "The Separation of Powers and Representative Government," *The Political Science Reviewer,* (Fall 1973), 73-74.

[39]For the view that Foreign Affairs and the War departments were recognized explicitly as executive departments as opposed to the Treasury Department, see *Annals of Congress,* vol. 2, pp. 2132, 2158, 2174-2176. Also, the statutes creating both the departments of War and Foreign Affairs read: "that there shall be an executive department to be denominated—War, Foreign Affairs." Concerning the Treasury Department, on the other hand, there was no agreement as to whether it constituted an executive department in the same sense as the other two; as a result, the originating language read simply: "that there shall be a department of Treasury." Similarly, the Secretary of War and the Secretary of Foreign Affairs were thought to be executive agents of the president; as such, they were under no obligation to appear before Congress routinely to present reports of the activities of their respective departments. But Treasury was another matter.

[40]Vincent J. Browne, *The Control of the Public Budget* (Washington, D.C.: Public Affairs Press, 1949), p. 29.

was clear that unified control of the expenditures of government presented difficulties for maintenance of the separation of powers. Elbridge Gerry argued against a single officer on the grounds that he could set his will against both Congress and the president.

> We find such an officer unprecedented in the several States; and I believe it would not be agreeable to have a single officer, and his assistants, collecting the money, or controlling the revenue arising in these states; yet you make it one of his powers that money shall not be drawn without a warrant from the financier. It appears to me, that by so doing, we shall establish an office giving one person a greater influence than the President has, and more than is proper for any person to have in a republican Government.[41]

Gerry's argument to the assembly was not as persuasive as that of Jeremiah Wadsworth, who argued that "it seems to be a prevailing sentiment among all conditions of men, that we ought to have the highest degree of responsibility in every department of Government."[42] The necessity to ensure responsibility led the majority to choose a unitary head for the Treasury Department.

Having agreed upon a single department head, it was necessary to determine the powers such an official should have and what his relationship with Congress should be. Should he be authorized to appear on the floor of Congress when making his reports? Should the reports be submitted in writing? There was concern that an able minister, armed with an expertise in the subject matter, might present his report in person, thereby creating

> an undue influence within these walls, because members might be led, by the deference commonly paid to men of abilities who give an opinion in a case they have thoroughly studied, to report the minister's plan, even against their own judgment.[43]

Even among those House members who generally favored the technical information that could be obtained from the Treasury Department, there was a fear that an energetic Secretary might seek to initiate legislation by means of his reports. Madison attempted to allay these fears by pointing to the danger of a bad administration:

> There is a small probability . . . that an officer may derive a weight from this circumstance, and have some degree of influence . . . but compare the danger likely to result from this cause, with the danger and inconvenience of not having well-formed and digested plans, and we shall find infinitely more to apprehend. Inconsistent, unproductive, and expensive schemes, will be more injurious to our constituents than the undue influence which the well-digested plans of a well-formed officer can have. From a bad administration of the Government, more

[41]*Annals of Congress*, vol. 1, p. 402.
[42]Ibid., p. 406.
[43]Ibid., p. 615.

detriment will arise than from any other source. The want of information has occasioned much inconvenience and unnecessary burdens under some of the State governments. Let it be our care to avoid these rocks and shoals in our political voyage, which have injured, and nearly proved fatal to, many of our contemporary navigators.[44]

In the end, it was decided that a single department head should "prepare and report estimates of the public revenue and the public expenditure." He is to "make reports and give information to either branch of the Legislature, in person or in writing (as he may be required), respecting all matters referred to him by the Senate or House of Representatives, or which shall appertain to his office."[45]

The importance of the Secretary of the Treasury was apparent to George Washington, for he appointed Alexander Hamilton as the first Secretary, and also the first cabinet officer to be appointed under the government of the United States.[46] Upon assuming his duties in late September 1789, Hamilton was quick to establish himself as a force to be reckoned with in the legislature as well as in the executive administration because he "did not share the restrictive views of certain House members concerning the scope and nature of his responsibilities."[47] His enemies' worst fears were confirmed concerning an able minister's efforts in exerting influence. In several measures of great importance—the assumption of the national debt, the excise bill, and the establishment of a national bank—Hamilton's influence was decisive despite considerable opposition. Senator Maclay confided in his diary,"Were Eloquence personified and reason flowed from her tongue, her talents would be in vain in our assembly; . . . Congress may go home. Mr. Hamilton is all powerful, and fails in nothing he attempts."[48]

The dominance of Hamilton and the Treasury Department in Congress was a source of growing alarm.[49] As Congressman William Findlay noted in his *Review of the Revenue System Adopted by the First Congress:*

> The first proof of a systematic plan for subverting the principles of the government by the instrumentality of fiscal arrangements, was given by law for establishing the

[44]Ibid., p. 628.

[45]The act was approved on September 2, 1789, and provided for a Secretary of the Treasury, to be deemed the head of the Department. *Statutes at Large,* vol. 1, p. 65–66.

[46]Browne, *Control of the Budget,* pp. 32-33.

[47]Lynton Caldwell, *The Administrative Theories of Hamilton and Jefferson* (Chicago: University of Chicago Press, 1944), p. 219.

[48]Cited in Georgia Galloway, *History of the House of Representatives,* 2nd ed., (New York: Thomas Crowell, 1976), p. 18.

[49]In a letter to Mason in 1791, Jefferson asked: "What is said in our country of the fiscal arrangements now going on? I really fear their effect when I consider the present temper of the Southern states. However, all will pass; the excise will pass, the bank will pass. The only corrective of what is amiss in our present government will be augmentation of numbers in the lower house, so as to get a more agricultural representation, which may put that interest above that of the stock-jobbers." Cited in Zvesper, *Political Philosophy,* pp. 106-107.

treasury department, by which a transfer is made of the exclusive right to originate money bills, to the Secretary of the Treasury, and this proof is rendered indubitable by the use that has been uniformly made of it. . . . Hamilton's system had greatly increased the spirit and enterprise of speculators, and occasioned in this way the most detestable and enormous frauds, and promoted a depravity of morals and a great decline of republican virtue.[50]

In December 1791, Hamilton presented to Congress his Capital Report of Manufactures "which made clear the kind of society his funding, assumption and bank had been designed to promote."[51] Hamilton's success in convincing George Washington and the Congress had prompted Jefferson to threaten to retire from the government. At the end of February 1792, Washington met with Jefferson to listen to his grievances and urge him to stay in the administration. Jefferson made it clear that

> there was only a single source of [discontent]—namely, the Treasury system, which was encouraging immoral speculation and had introduced "its poison into the government itself" by making "particular members of the legislature into instruments of the Treasury." By this means, and by extravagant Constitutional constructions, permitting "congress to take everything under their management which they should deem for the public welfare" the system had been fixed.[52]

Jefferson was fearful that Hamilton's financial schemes would undermine the authority of the representatives of the people and eventually the people themselves by encouraging speculation and the creation of a public debt. The "chicken of the treasury," he feared, might succeed in establishing the doctrine "that a public debt is a blessing . . . a perpetual one is a perpetual blessing."[53] Madison, too, joined in the cautioning against the increase of a public debt."[54] The true supporters of the union, Madison maintained, were not those who tried to pervert its government into "one of unlimited discretion" nor those who espoused monarchy and aristocracy or a "system of measures more accommodated to the depraved examples of those hereditary forms than to the true genius of our own." Thus it was "not Adams' political monarchism, but Hamilton's economic monarchism" that had produced "the beginnings of American party politics." The abiding issue that embodied these disputes was "executive [monarchical] corruption of the legislature, and a subsequent corruption of the people by government promotion of speculation."[55]

[50]Cited in ibid., p. 146.
[51]Ibid., p. 76.
[52]Jefferson cited in ibid.
[53]Cited in ibid.
[54]"The real friends of the union," Madison noted, are those who consider "a public debt as injurious to the interests of the people, and baneful to the virtue of government, are enemies to every contrivance for unnecessarily increasing its amount, or protecting its duration or extending its influence. Ibid., p. 116.
[55]Ibid., p. 81.

ADMINISTRATIVE CENTRALIZATION AND FISCAL CONTROL

It was clear from Hamilton's point of view that effective administration was of prime importance to the success of the national government. He had emphasized in the *Federalist* that "the true test of a good Government . . . is its aptitude and tendency to produce a good administration."[56] Indeed, he suggests:

> The administration of government, in its largest sense, comprehends all the operations of the body politic, whether legislative, executive or judiciary, but in its most usual and perhaps in its most precise signification, it is limited to executive details, and falls peculiarly within the province of the executive department.[57]

If Hamilton was acutely aware of the "share which the Executive in every Government must necessarily have in its good or ill administration,"[58] Madison would subsequently argue that "the term Administration" applies equally to "both the Executive and the Legislative branches."[59]

Hamilton and the Federalist party desired a national administration "which left substantial freedom of action to high officials and kept Congress out of most administrative details."[60] The device that Hamilton chose, as Secretary of the Treasury, to ensure that executive discretion in financial matters would be a practical reality was the method of the general appropriation.[61] This general appropriation of lump sums allowing broad construction of their use by the Secretary would ensure that administrative details would remain in executive hands.

In the first administration of George Washington, with Federalist control of both Houses and both branches of government, Hamilton successfully forged a close working relationship with Congress. He was so successful in this regard that in September 1789, a new House Committee of Ways and Means (set up in July of that year to advise Congress on fiscal matters) was discharged from further consideration of financial affairs and its duties were referred to the Secretary of the Treasury.[62]

---

[56]*The Federalist*, No. 68, p. 414.

[57]*The Federalist*, No. 72. Hamilton, in elaborating execution, notes that "the actual conduct of foreign negotiations, the preparatory plans of finance, the application and disbursement of the public monies, in conformity to the general appropriations of the legislature, the arrangement of the army and navy, the directions of the operations of war; these and other matters of a like nature constitute what seems to be most properly understood by the administration of government," p. 435. Murray Dry has suggested, "If Hamilton was right in connecting good government to good administration; then good government in America would have to be presidential government." "Congress," in George and Scarlett Graham, eds., *Founding Principles of American Government*, (Bloomington: Indiana University Press, 1977), p. 237.

[58]*The Federalist*, No. 68, p. 414.

[59]Gaillard Hunt, ed., *The Writings of James Madison* (New York: G. Putnam's & Sons, 1900-1910), vol. 5, p. 423.

[60]Leonard D. White, *The Federalist* (New York: The Macmillan Co., 1948), p. 552.

[61]This was in opposition to a line item device, which would allow Congress greater discretion in specifying the purposes of public spending.

[62]*Annals of Congress*, vol. 1, pp. 894-895; 904-905. See also White, *The Federalist*, p. 324.

As Arthur Smithies has suggested, Hamilton "performed for the Congress all functions now performed by its financial committees."[63] During the first Congress, Hamilton succeeded in maintaining himself as "agent and advisor to Congress," as George Galloway noted,[64] in matters relating to public finance and the national economy. Shortly, however, Hamilton's attitude toward the budget and finance became "a central point of attack for his adversaries,"[65] particularly his insistence upon discretionary use of funds, which resulted from the device of lump sum appropriation. From 1791 to 1794, Smithies notes, "there was one appropriation for the Civil list, one for the Department of War, one to cover Treasury warrants outstanding, and one to cover other listed expenditures."[66] This discretion in fiscal administration was criticized as resembling "monarchism."

The early pattern of centralized executive administration was challenged when Republicans increased their numbers in the House. In early 1792, John Mercer of Maryland attacked a bill submitted by Hamilton tying revenue-producing measures to a military personnel pay increase. He stated on the floor of Congress:

> I have long remarked in this House that the Executive, or rather the Treasury Department, was really the efficient Legislature of the country, so far as relates to revenue, which is the vital principle of Government. The clause of the Constitution confining to the immediate Representatives of the people . . . the origination of money bills, is converted into a Committee of Sanction, that never withholds its assent; a convenient cloak to divert the blame of odious measures from the real authors.[67]

Hamilton's fiscal arrangements had mobilized political opposition concerning the question of what the proper tasks of the national government should be.[68] They also resulted in an institutional struggle between the executive and the legislature to determine the limits of the Secretary of the Treasury's role in financial affairs. In January 1794, the House appointed the Baldwin Committee to examine the operations of the Treasury Department; the Committee presented a report detailing the methods of collecting and disbursing public money.[69] Its intention was to discredit Hamilton's performance as Secretary.

The Jeffersonians were in the vanguard of the attack on Hamilton, and their power was reflected in their increased strength in the popularly elected House of Representatives. Led by Albert Gallatin, they devised a strategy to limit

[63]*The Budgetary Process in the United States* (New York: McGraw-Hill, 1955), p. 50.
[64]Galloway, *The House of Representatives*, p. 18.
[65]Smithies, *The Budgetary Process*, p. 50.
[66]Ibid.
[67]*Annals of Congress*, vol. 3, p. 349.
[68]See Wilfred Binkley, *American Political Parties: Their Natural History* (New York: Alfred A. Knopf, 1943), pp. 62-71.
[69]*Annals of Congress*, vol. 4, p. 248.

executive discretion through the imposition of specific (line item) appropriations of public money detailing its use, thereby curtailing the use of lump sum grants.[70] This, however, required the development of an independent congressional role in financial affairs.[71] Consequently, Congress moved toward the creation of standing committees and a temporary House Committee on Ways and Means was reappointed under a resolution proposed by Gallatin.[72] This committee, of which Gallatin was a member, considered both revenue and appropriations measures and attempted by amendment to ensure that specific appropriations were to be "solely applied to the objects for which they are respectively appropriated."[73] Gallatin, unlike Hamilton, "believed that the doctrine of energy was the doctrine of tyranny."[74] "Whenever the Executive have acquired an uncontrolled command over the purse of the people, prodigality ensued."[75] His attack on Hamilton, consequently, was both principled and expedient. It was necessary to destroy Hamilton's influence and weaken his control over congressional finances in order to enable a separate congressional capability in this regard.

When Hamilton requested the opportunity to appear on the floor of Congress to answer questions concerning the public debt, he was refused on the grounds that it would contribute to the practice of mixing the two branches of government. "Members objected to having the heads of departments originate legislation or even voice an opinion that might influence Congress."[76] From 1793 on, Hamilton was subject to increasing attack by members of the Congress. As Binkley notes:

> They attacked his "premiership" and his "unconstitutional" promotion of money bills. They attacked him by offering a series of resolutions charging him with violation of law, neglect of duty, transgression of proper limits of his authority, and indecorum in his attitude toward the House. . . . Although the resolutions failed to carry, the new Congress was to render Hamilton's position as secretary scarcely tenable.[77]

Hamilton resigned office in January 1795; his post was filled by Oliver Wolcott, Jr., a man of similar opinions, but without the brilliance of Hamilton.

The assault on Hamilton was but one part of a general revolt against the use

[70]See Lucius Wilmerding, Jr., *The Spending Power: A History of the Efforts of Congress to Control Expenditures* (New Haven: Yale University Press, 1943), pp. 61-63.

[71]See John S. Saloma, *The Responsible Use of Power: A Critical Analysis of the Congressional Budget Process* (Washington, D.C.: American Enterprise Institute, 1965), pp. 107-120.

[72]The House Ways and Means Committee was not made a permanent or standing committee until 1802. See Browne, *Control of the Budget*, p. 38.

[73]Saloma, *The Congressional Budget Process*, p. 110; cf. Adams, *Life of Gallatin*, p. 157.

[74]Leonard D. White, *The Jacksonians: A Study in Administrative History* (New York: Free Press, 1954), p. 562.

[75]Gallatin, cited in Zvesper, *Political Philosophy*, p. 162.

[76]Louis Fisher, *Presidential Spending Power* (Princeton: Princeton University Press, 1975), p. 13.

[77]Wilfred Binkley, *American Political Parties*, p. 38.

of executive authority to further nationalization and administrative centralization, which was thought to be incompatible with representation and liberty. His opponents found particularly distasteful his recommendation of a national bank, with the implication that financial policy was to be used to create a national economic interest.

In relation to the budget, it is commonly observed that Hamilton's conception of the role of the Secretary of the Treasury was a forerunner of the executive budget system.[78] Yet his success was limited to a few short years when his esteem in the Congress was high. The Hamiltonian view was compatible with government that had high purpose and sought to achieve great results. As Henry Jones Ford noted:

> Hamilton almost at a stroke lifted the nation out of bankruptcy, established its credit and secured its revenues. His plans were marked by boldness of conception and unity of design. . . . They surpassed popular comprehension and affronted popular prejudice to an extent that would have made them impracticable in an assembly without another means of action than its own varied impulses. It was because he was in a position to formulate his measures in their entirety and to press them directly upon Congress, unhindered by any committee system with its parcelling of influence that he was able to carry his measures.[79]

With the success of the Jeffersonian Republicans in the waning years of the century, the Hamiltonian dream of the creation for a strong national economy was not deemed an appropriate task of the government of free farmers. Thus the basis of executive–legislative relations in financial affairs for the next century was defined by the defeat of the Federalists by the Jeffersonians in the election of 1800. That defeat resulted in the repudiation of the Hamiltonian conception of financial management as Congress assumed a dominant role in the budgetary process.[80]

Hamilton, as Secretary of the Treasury, had exercised a "mastery of government detail" advocating measures that the Jeffersonians believed would have "rendered them tributary to the financial interests."[81] Jefferson had attacked the "monocrats" as having sold out the principles of the revolution in nationalizing the government in the interest of the commercial and financial classes. Jefferson, in appealing to the party, sought to establish executive leadership of the party in the legislative branch as the means of maintaining popular

---

[78]Cf. Smithies, *The Budgetary Process*, p. 53.

[79]"Budget Making and the Work of Government," *The Annals of the American Academy of Political and Social Science*, 62 (November 1915), pp. 4-5.

[80]With the establishment of the permanent Ways and Means Committee, direct Treasury influence in budget preparation was eliminated. Government agencies presented their requests directly to the House. Until 1921, the Treasury Department could only forward the estimates to Congress as a sort of middle man. Cf. Browne, *Control of the Budget*, p. 62.

[81]Binkley, *American Political Parties*, p. 287.

representation without resorting to an executive discretion that he believed was incompatible with liberty.

ADMINISTRATIVE DECENTRALIZATION: THE EFFECT OF THE REVOLUTION

If Hamiltonian finance emphasized executive discretion, Jefferson, upon assuming the presidency, followed the advice of his Secretary of Treasury, Albert Gallatin, when he indicated his view of spending discretion in his message to Congress:

> In our care, too, of the public contributions intrusted to our direction it would be prudent to multiply barriers against their dissipation by appropriating specific sums to every specific purpose susceptible of definition; by disallowing all applications of money varying from the appropriation in object or transcending it in amount; by reducing undefined field of contingencies and thereby circumscribing discretionary powers over money.[82]

In the years following the Jeffersonian revolution of 1800, Congress engaged in a long battle to acquire full control over federal expenditures.

The specificity of appropriations was one of the great issues over which Congress and the Executive branch fought during the early years of nationhood, and it was the triumph of itemized appropriations that ensured legislative supremacy during the nineteenth century.[83] With control of itemized appropriations, Congress had attained control of the details of administration.[84]

> The theory of our government is, that a specific sum shall be appropriated by a law originating in this House, for a specific purpose, and within a given fiscal year. It is the duty of the executive to use that sum and no more, specially for that purpose, and no other, and within the item fixed.[85]

A rigid adherence to such a formula would make executive leadership impossible; the president would be no more than a clerk. Moreover, it would make effective administration difficult, for it would deny the executive any discretion necessary to adapt general laws to specific purposes. Thus, in practice, it could not and did not work. "The executive branch . . . found means where necessary or useful, to avoid or to evade many of the fiscal limitations that Congress

[82]J. D. Richardson, *Messages and Papers of Presidents, 1789-1897* (New York: Bureau of National Literature, 1897), vol. 1, p. 329.

[83]Allen Schick, "Congress and the 'Details' of Administration," *Public Administration Review*, 36 (September/October 1976), p. 517. As a consequence, as Arthur Smithies noted, "centralized Executive authority in budgetary matters was to remain in abeyance for over a century." *The Budgetary Process*, p. 53.

[84]As Schick has noted, "there are substantially fewer 'lines' in the $375 billion budget for 1976 than there were in the $265 million of expenditures of 1876." "Congress and the 'Details' of Administration," p. 517.

[85]Rep. John Sherman, cited in White, *The Jacksonians*, p. 141.

deemed it proper to impose. . . ." And Congress readily acquiesced in such breaches of authority, for as Leonard White noted, the purposes of individual Congressmen, "who wanted some particular payment made or task undertaken," were often "different from and contrary to the interests of Congress."[86]

What enabled the branches to function amicably in fiscal affairs during this period despite the seeming rigidity of the positions taken was the underlying opinion that the tasks of government were few. (Of course the revenues from custom duties and the sale of public land were sufficient for the ordinary expenditures of government.) More importantly, perhaps, the legitimacy of that opinion was derivative of the partisan consensus created in the appeal to the principles that underlay the election of 1800, which Jefferson, himself, called the "revolution of 1800."[87]

EXECUTIVE ENERGY AND THE SPIRIT OF PARTY: THE IMPORTANCE OF CONSENSUS

Forrest MacDonald has noted:

> the Presidency is dual in nature, entailing two functions so different from one another that the ability to perform them both is rarely to be found in a single person. One function is administrative and executive and is involved in the formulation and implementation of policy. The other is ritualistic and ceremonial.[87a]

He suggests:

> whereas Washington had been honored as a symbol of the nation, Jefferson sought to become a symbol of the people. As to the executive function, the revolution of 1800 . . . required that the government [be] purged of irreconcilable monarchists [and that] Hamilton's fiscal machinery be disbanded.[87b]

Jefferson completely abhorred a commercial aristocracy: a Hamiltonian executive in the service of a national economic class was greatly to be feared. Even if MacDonald is not incorrect in his assertion that Jefferson sought to become a symbol of the people, it may be appropriate to suggest that he wanted to be a leader of his party, the party of liberty. As John Marshall wrote of Jefferson:

> He will embody himself with the House of Representatives. By weakening the office of President, he will increase his personal power. He will diminish his re-

---

[86] Leonard White, *The Jacksonians*, p. 141.

[87] Letter to Spencer Roane, 16 September 1819, in Paul Ford, ed., *Writings of Thomas Jefferson, 1892-99* (New York: G. P. Putnam's Sons, 1904-1905), vol. 12, p. 140. Abraham Sofaer has noted that "the triumph of Republicans over Federalists was called a revolution because of what it was supposed to mean for the allocation of power between the federal and state governments, and among the branches of the federal government." *War, Foreign Affairs and Constitutional Power: The Origins*, p. 168.

[87a] "A Mirror for Presidents," *Commentary* 62 (December 1976): 34.

[87b] Ibid., p. 37.

sponsibility, sap the fundamental principles of government, and become the leader of that party which is about to constitute the majority of the legislature.[88]

Within the framework of parties, the limitations of the separation of powers could be minimized in times of consensus. But depending upon the legitimacy of the purposes of the national government, it was no longer necessary to connect good government with an energetic executive. Jefferson was unconvinced after Hamilton's tenure in the Treasury Department that an energetic executive, even under the Constitution, could not become a despotic one.[89] The Republicans, to whom Jefferson gave his support, in theory if not always in practice, accepted "the idea of unity of executive power, but they had no intention of allowing it to escape a narrow responsibility to Congress . . . they disliked executive discretion . . . and sought to limit rather than extend administrative authority. They could do this the more readily since they had no large programs for the general government to carry forward."[90]

If Jeffersonian principles supplied energy to the party in his administration, the party itself soon became the energizer. As the historian Ralph Volney Harlow has observed, Jefferson had made the Republican party, and as maker he ruled it. The party in its turn made Madison president, and what need was there to bow before the idol it had created?[91] The weakened position of the president in regard to the party resulted in a diminution of executive influence in the legislature. During the presidency of James Monroe, Justice Story observed, "The Executive has no longer a commanding influence. The House of Representatives has absorbed all the popular feeling and all the effective power of the country. Even the Senate cowers under its lofty pretensions to be the guardians of the people and its rights."[92]

In financial matters, the struggle between Andrew Jackson and Congress over the Second United States Bank was indicative of the ambiguity that existed concerning control of the executive administration. During this period, Congress frequently treated the Secretary of the Treasury as its own agent. For example, Congress delegated to him, not the president, the responsibility for

---

[88]Letter to Alexander Hamilton in A. J. Beveridge, *Life of John Marshall* (Boston: Houghton-Mifflin Co.) vol. 2, p. 537.

[89]Jefferson's attitude toward executive power was not unambiguous. He was willing to use that power when necessary—with or without legislative or Constitutional warrant—if that power was used in the preservation or perpetuation of the principles of the revolution. As he suggested, "a strict observance of the written laws is doubtless one of the high duties of a good citizen, but it is not the highest. The laws of necessity, of self-preservation, of saving our country when in danger, are of higher obligation. To lose our country by a scrupulous adherence to written law, would be to lose the law itself, with life, liberty, property and all those who are enjoying them with us; thus absurdly sacrificing the end to the means." *Writings of Thomas Jefferson*, vol. 9, p. 279.

[90]White, *The Jacksonians*, p. 562.

[91]*The History of Legislative Methods in the Period before 1825*, (New Haven: Yale University Press, 1917).

[92]W. W. Story, ed., *Joseph Story; Life and Letters of Joseph Story*, (Boston: Charles C. Little and James Brown, 1851), vol. 1, p. 311.

depositing government money in state banks or the national bank. Jackson's insistence upon depositing the funds in state banks resulted in the removal of two Treasury secretaries before he could find one willing to comply with his demands.[93] In reaction to Jackson's removal of the deposits from the United States Bank, the Whigs demanded "the separation of the purse from the sword."[94] Henry Clay offered a Resolution of Censure in which it was resolved "that the President in the late Executive proceedings in relation to the public revenue, has assumed upon himself authority and power not conferred by the constitution and the laws but in derogation of both."[95]

Jackson's willingness to use the executive power, often in opposition to Congress, in matters concerning a vital public interest, probably made him

> the first president in our history to appeal to the people over the heads of their legislative representatives. On the basis of the strength of that appeal [the Presidency] was thrust forward as one of three equal departments of government, and to each and every of its powers was imparted new scope, new vitality.[96]

The novel theory that Jackson claimed of direct representation of the people grew out of his struggle with Congress over the control of the executive administration. He attempted to differentiate the office of the president from that of the heads of the departments. "The President," he declared, "is the direct representative of the American people, but the Secretaries are not."[97]

If the potential for the use of presidential power attained new dimensions under Jackson, the "new vitality" lasted only as long as party principles provided a consensus upon which a majority could rule. Within a dozen years of Jackson's tenure in office, there occurred "the greatest weakness in the Presidency in American history . . . the period from 1848 to 1860—twelve years in which four men occupied the office, and none of them was reelected."[98]

The power of the president could not be divorced from the uses to which such power could be employed, and the organizational and institutional strength that derived from the legitimacy of party principles could at times overcome the effects of the separation of powers. If Jackson achieved a democratization of the party through the extension and control of a mass-based party organization and leadership of the national presidential nominating convention (particularly by

[93]Cf. Louis Fisher, *President and Congress: Power and Policy* (New York: Free Press, 1972), p. 90.

[94]In his inaugural address, President Tyler proposed "to save the liberty of the people by protecting the public funds from the executive branch." Cited in White, *The Jacksonians*, p. 43.

[95]Ibid., p. 44.

[96]Corwin, *The President*, vol. 3, p. 90.

[97]Jackson, in defending his removal of Secretary of the Treasury Duane, made this claim in his famous "Protest" to the Senate on April 15, 1984. Richardson, *Messages and Papers*, vol. 3, p. 90.

[98]Samuel Huntington, "The Democratic Distemper," *The Public Interest*, 41, (Fall 1975), p. 25.

the time of his reelection in 1832),[99] his strength in opposing Congress derived from the legitimation of the opinion that the president had an independent duty to ensure the rights and interests of the majority. That legitimacy derived from his reanimation of Jeffersonian principles. According to Jackson:

> It is certain, that which ever party makes the Presidency, must give direction to his administration. . . . I have long believed, that it was only by preserving the identity of the Republican party as embodied and characterized by the principles introduced by Mr. Jefferson that the original rights of the states and the people could be maintained as contemplated by the Constitution. I have labored to reconstruct this great Party and bring the popular power to bear with full influence upon the Government, by securing its permanent ascendancy.[100]

Like Jefferson, Jackson did not intend to use the executive power to accomplish great national goals in the manner of Hamilton.[101] Rather, as he showed in his action concerning the great political controversy of the time—the veto of the Second Bank of the United States—he was acting in the interests of the people. In justifying his decision to remove federal deposits from the National Bank, he maintained:

> The case was argued to the people; and . . . the people have sustained the President. . . . Whatever may be the opinions of others, the President considers his reelection a decision of the people against the bank. He was sustained by a just people, and he desires to evince his gratitude by carrying into effect their decision so far as it depends upon him.[102]

Perhaps the one president in the nineteenth century who combined the two disparate elements of executive leadership of which Forrest MacDonald has written was Abraham Lincoln.[103] His success in unifying the "executive" or "administrative" function and the "ritualistic" or "ceremonial" aspect created a vigorous executive compatible with a positive purpose. Amidst the greatest breakdown of consensus in American history, Lincoln was able to articulate a common national goal (the preservation of the union), which required the most vigorous use of executive power. At the same time, he embodied that goal with a purpose laid down in a principle (the rededication to the principle of equality). The recreation of the spirit embodied in the principles of the Revolution

---

[99]White suggests "the most important influence upon the administrative system from Jackson to Lincoln was the wide enfranchisement of adult male citizens and their organization into a national party system." *The Jacksonians*, p. 11.

[100]Jackson noted in the same letter that "it is as true in politics as morals, that those who are not for us are against us." Cited in White, *The Jacksonians*, p. 14.

[101]Arthur Schlesinger, Jr., in *The Age of Jackson* (Boston: Little Brown & Co., 1945), argues that Jackson was forced to adopt Hamiltonian means to attain Jeffersonian ends. Government power was used to check the growing power of business. Cf. pp. 505-23.

[102]Richardson, *Messages and Papers*, vol. 3, p. 7.

[103]See a "Mirror for Presidents," footnote 87a.

gave his party the capacity to create a new consensus upon which the majority could rule.[104]

If Lincoln had articulated a national purpose and recreated consensus, his successor, Andrew Johnson, was challenged by the legislature of the same party for the right to determine the contours of that policy. As Thaddeus Stevens proclaimed, "Congress is the sovereign power, because the people speak through them; and Andrew Johnson must learn that he is your servant and that as Congress shall order he must obey."[105]

Once again, the field of battle was control over details of administration, with Congress attempting to contravene the president's authority over his cabinet and the army. In the end, Johnson learned that the formal powers of the president were not so great in a struggle with Congress. He barely escaped forced removal from his office.

Throughout the rest of the century the familiar pattern of congressional dominance, for the most part, was restored. This was not surprising, for the tasks of government were few and an energetic executive was hardly necessary. It was, from Tocqueville's view of parties, a period of minor parties animated more by interests than by principles.

Perhaps the greatest respectability and the most creative energy resided in the area of enterprise and business. This fact was not lost on Woodrow Wilson. In his attempt to reenergize executive authority, he conceived of the necessity to separate the administrative function of the president from the political function. In an era when the rise of the positive sciences began to exert an influence among the educated classes, Wilson sought to establish the weight of an independent authority on behalf of the president's administrative tasks. But as a result of his utmost regard for public opinion, Wilson sought to justify the attempt not on the theoretical grounds of positive science, but on the practical example of business management.

[104]See Harry V. Jaffa, *Crisis of the House Divided* (Seattle: University of Washington Press, 1973), p. 224.
[105]Wilfred Binkley, *President and Congress*, 3rd ed., (New York: Vintage Books, 1962), p. 166.

Chapter 2

Budgeting and Reform: Executive Budgeting and the Legacy of Progressivism

As a rule, there is far more danger that the President of the United States will render the office less efficient than was intended, than that he will exercise an authority dangerous to the liberties of the country.

James Fenimore Cooper, *The American Democrat*

PROGRESSIVISM AND THE NEW SEPARATION: POLITICS AND ADMINISTRATION

In 1885, Woodrow Wilson voiced an old complaint when he wrote of Congress, "It has entered more and more into the details of administration until it has virtually taken into its own all the substantial powers of government."[1] The institutionalized struggle for control of the details of administration is not a governmental problem that is likely to wither away as long as the separation of powers is operational. It is part of an ambivalence persisting throughout the history of the American republic. Moreover, the disparities in the legislative

---

[1]Woodrow Wilson, *Congressional Government* (New York: Meridian Books, 1956), p. 49. Hamilton had expressed a similar complaint prior to the Constitution itself. He noted, "Another defect in our system is want of method and energy in the administrative. . . . Congress have kept the power too much in their own hands and have meddled too much with details of every sort." Thach, *Creation of the Presidency*, p. 64. Jefferson, too, suggested: "I have viewed the executive details as the greatest cause of evil to us, because they in fact place us as if we had no federal head, by diverting the attention of that head from great to small objects." Quoted in Joseph E. Kallenback. *The American Chief Executive* (New York: Harper and Row, 1960), pp. 30-31.

and executive views concerning control of the administration have nowhere been more evident than in financial matters. But the struggle for the control of the purse strings often mirrors a deeper concern, usually with what the priorities or the purposes of the government itself should be. A comprehensive reconsideration of those purposes was a task Wilson sought to undertake. He and the leaders of the Progressive movement attempted to adapt the separation of powers and the rigid constitutional system to the demands of a new age.

Herbert Croly captured the essence of the Progressive movement when he wrote, "Constitutions are intrusted frankly to the people instead of people to the constitutions."[2] From Croly's (and the Progressives') viewpoint, the Federalists had insisted on checks and balances to limit the power of the people by creation of "some elaborate masterpiece of artificial constructive genius, such as a Gothic cathedral"[3] that increased the power of the national government, but not of the people. In extending the power of the people, the Jeffersonians had sought to limit the power of the government, thus reducing it "to a bed of liquid clay . . . an indiscriminate mass of sticky matter, which merely clogged the movements of every living body entangled in its midst."[4] The goal of the Progressives was to reformulate the separation of powers to enable the national government to act positively in the interest of the people. They believed that

> the *Federalist*'s science of political mechanics was rigid, superficial, self-interested, and outdated. . . . It was a time for debunking and innovation. . . . One science of politics was in ruins, a new one was needed, mechanics yielded to the science of management and administration.[5]

The authors of the *Federalist* had insisted that the doctrine of the separation of powers was intended to ensure liberty. They were "clearly committed to a view of political liberty—an essential part of which is the restraint of governmental power" and the prevention of "a concentration of such power in the hands of a single group of men."[6] But the growth of the corporations and the concentration of economic power in the period following the Civil War resulted in the necessity of governmental action to deal with the pressing national economic and social problems. The leaders of the Progressive movement, in attacking the Constitution, which they believed protected the rights of the few in the name of liberty, launched an attack "upon privilege, and upon those constitutional checks and balances, which, by denying majority rule, protected privilege."[7] The social and

---

[2]Croly, *Progressive Democracy*, (New York: Macmillan Company, 1915), p. 225.
[3]Ibid., p. 248.
[4]Ibid.
[5]Wilson Carey McWilliams, "American Pluralism: The Old Order Passeth," in Irving Kristol and Paul Weaver, eds., *The Americans*, (Lexington, Mass.: Lexington Books, 1976), p. 306. They insisted, McWilliams notes, that "institutions could not be exempted from the laws of evolution." They were "convinced that insitutitions had a creative role and that 'social science' could help shape a more humane political order", p. 305.
[6]M.J.C. Vile, *Constitutionalism and the Separation of Powers* (Oxford: Claredon Press, 1967), p. 14.
[7]Ibid., p. 265.

economic problems of modern society, M. J. C. Vile suggests, "required concerted action by responsible government authorities, whereas the separation of
powers made concerted action impossible."[8]

Vile has indicated that the new separation of powers, which rested on the
distinction between the political branches of government and the bureaucracy, led
to a fundamental shift in the manner in which this doctrine came to be viewed.[9]
The older view was compatible with three dominant considerations or "values"
that animated the necessity to ensure the maintenance of the separation of powers:
they were efficiency, democracy, and justice. But, he notes, "over the past hundred years, a new value emerged—social justice. It is the concern with social
justice which above all has disrupted the earlier triad of government functions."[10]
The desire for the achievement of social justice meant "control of the economy to
insure full employment, the attempt to secure the incomes of farmers and wage-
earners, the control of monopolies, the maintenance of a certain level of public
expenditure, the control of the balance of payments, and so forth."[11] The strength
of the demand for "social justice" and "the structures which ensure its realization must mean that any facile view of the separation of powers is dead."[12]
Progressivism had come into the world carrying the banner of social justice. The
separation of powers came to be seen as an obstacle to the progress of government in the interests of the majority. The president could become the means of
overcoming the institutional barriers presented by the Constitution. In 1879, at
the zenith of congressional authority in the national government, Woodrow
Wilson expressed his growing pessimism concerning the state of American institutions.[13] The problem, he thought, was the separation of powers, and the inability to provide for executive leadership of the majority.[14] This state of affairs had
resulted in a government that was fragmented and purposeless, captive to the
special interests represented in the committees of Congress, which had attained

[8]Ibid., p. 266.

[9]The decline in popularity of the doctrine in the late nineteenth and early twentieth century, Vile
observed, "is closely related to the recognition of the need for collectivist activities on the part of
the government, which requires a co-ordinate program of action by all parts of the government
machine." As a result, Vile noted, the demand for the establishment of harmony between the
legislature and government, which characterized the theory of parliamentary government in Britain
and France and the Progressive movement in the United States, was accomplished by a new separation of powers—that between the political branches of government and the bureaucracy. Vile, p. 6,
14.

[10]Vile, p. 347.

[11]Ibid., p. 348.

[12]Ibid., p. 349. Thus, Vile concludes that "the distinction . . . between politics and administration was . . . to open a new chapter in the establishment of semi-autonomous branches of government in an age which stressed unit and cohesion." p. 6.

[13]"A Political Essay," "Cabinet Government in the United States," "Congressional Government," in Arthur S. Link, ed., The Papers of Woodrow Wilson (Princeton: Princeton University
Press, 1966), vol. 1, pp. 493-513, 548-574.

[14]"In short," Wilson wrote, "the framers of the Constitution, in endeavoring to act in accordance with the principle of Montesquieu's celebrated . . . maxim . . . made their separation so
complete as to amount to isolation." Ibid., p. 497.

"imperial" control over the operations of the administration. They acted almost wholly in "secret" and were responsible to no one.[15]

According to Wilson, the separation of powers had stagnated government, prevented accountability to the majority, and destroyed the possibility of the emergence of a public interest. As he noted, the "paper constitution" had given all of the formal power of government (especially the power of the purse) to the Congress. Thus,

> Congress is the supreme ruling power in the government of the United States. Notwithstanding the paper safeguards set up by the Constitution . . ., notwithstanding the precise limitations of its prerogatives contained in its original written organization; Congress had the hand of power—the power of the purse and of law given to it, and it has stretched forth that hand to brush away all obstructions to the free exercise of its will, and has assumed imperial control of all matters within the scope of the general government.[16]

Wilson decried the system of committee government as "utterly at variance with the true principles of representative government."[17] On the one hand, it did not represent the opinions of the majority of the people, but only the special interests of a minority:

> There is no one in Congress to speak for the nation. Congress is a conglomeration of inharmonious elements; a collection of men representing each his neighborhood, each his local interest; an alarmingly large proportion of its legislation is special, all of it is at best only a limping compromise between the conflicting interests of the innumerable localities represented.[18]

On the other hand, it prevented accountability to the people by conducting the affairs of government in the dark. As Wilson suggests, "its worst feature, its damning fault, is secrecy."[19] Such a government had abdicated its right to rule; a private government does not appeal to public principles.[20] This failure to rest government on principle had prevented the emergence of leaders who were able to articulate principles and mobilize majorities. It had contributed to the demise of political parties.

At bottom, the crisis of his time, Wilson believed, was a moral crisis, the solution to which would determine the viability of free institutions. A major factor contributing to the moral weakness of such a government was its failure to derive any legitimacy from the consent (or opinion) of the governed. The problem, as Wilson saw it, could be reduced to the following:

[15]Cf. ibid., pp. 555-560.
[16]Ibid., pp. 555-560.
[17]Ibid., p. 501.
[18]Ibid., p. 502.
[19]Wilson later noted in his campaign for president that "the government, which was designed for the people, has got into the hands of bosses and their employers, the special interests. An invisible empire has been set up above the forms of democracy." *The New Freedom* (Englewood Cliffs, N.J.: Prentice-Hall, 1961), p. 36.
[20]Ibid.

The two great national parties—and upon the existence of two great national parties, with clashings and mutual jealousies and watching, depends the health of free political institutions—are dying for want of unifying and vitalizing principles. Without leaders, they are also without policies, without aim. . . . Eight words contain the sum of the present degradation of our political parties: *No leaders, no principles; no principles, no parties.*[21]

Wilson, perhaps better than most, understood the importance of opinion, parties, and consent to the legitimacy of democratic government. Indeed the principles of the Declaration of Independence, he thought, could be reduced to one necessity— the necessity of ensuring consent. The underlying consensus of a people must be adapted to the changes in the conditions and attitudes of the people. As a consequence, he regarded majority rule and responsive institutions, as indispensable to the maintenance of freedom.[22]

Although cognizant of the importance of opinion and the necessity of legitimizing majority rule, Wilson failed to understand the extent to which majority rule was derivative of the "enlightened opinion" that "all men are created equal" and from which the rights of individuals themselves are derived. This principle is what makes majority rule a practical necessity. The self-evident truth, not the organizing principle, is what gives a moral authority to public opinion. In his failure to see the necessity to tie majority rule to the animating principle, Wilson did not foresee the possibility that majority rule itself could not ensure the success of free institutions. Nevertheless, free institutions (or a Constitutional majority) are indispensable to the preservation of the rights of individuals, which give rise to rightful majorities. The maintenance of free institutions would depend upon the extent to which "enlightened opinion" would adhere in the opinion of the majority.[23]

Wilson's attempt to ensure that public opinion and majority rule could be established on a firm foundation led to his advocacy of the institutionalization of

[21]"Cabinet Government," in *The Papers of Woodrow Wilson*, p. 507 [emphasis added]. In Wilson's view, the absence of leaders meant no opposition as well. "And if the opposition are then silent, they cannot reasonably expect the country to entrust the government to them. . . . Not daring to propose any policy—having indeed, because of the disintegration of the party, no policy to propose—their numerical weakness became a moral weakness." Ibid.

[22]The Declaration, Wilson observed, "expressly leaves to each generation of men the determination of what they will do with their lives, what they will prefer as the form and object of their ability, in what they will seek their happiness." *Constitutional Government in the United States,* (New York: Columbia University Press, 1908), p. 4. "Liberty fixed in an unalterable law," Wilson noted in this work, "would be no liberty at all." See also Edward J. Erler, *The American Polity: Essays on the Theory and Practice of Constitutional Government,* (New York: Crane Russak, 1991), pp. 60-64.

[23]Wilson apparently did not understand the extent to which, in America, principles and leadership (like equality and consent) are opposite sides of the same coin. Likewise, parties and organization (the procedures for ensuring the practical possibility of attaining democratic ends) may be necessary to the continuation of relating means and ends—but the procedure could never be an end in itself. His observation that without leaders there can be no principles, therefore no parties, may be true—but perhaps it is even truer that without principles there can be no leaders, and American parties would likely wither away.

the executive leadership of the legislature in the form of a Cabinet government. In this way, he thought, leaders would arise who could articulate principles around which a majority could organize and an opposition form. As a result, a government could both guide policy, through the cultivation and molding of the public mind, and be responsive to the opinions of the people by defending its principles against claims of the opposition. Government would then be both responsive and responsible. At the same time, a Cabinet government would serve to undermine the principle of the separation of powers.

WOODROW WILSON AND THE SEARCH
FOR NEUTRAL PRINCIPLES

Alexander Hamilton had viewed administration "in its most usual and perhaps in its most precise signification" as "limited to executive details," and therefore as falling "peculiarly within the province of the executive department."[24] The history of the nineteenth century was largely a period of legislative intrusion into the executive domain. Woodrow Wilson considered his task to be one of reestablishing executive control of the details of administration. Wilson maintained that the security of executive power rested in distinguishing the sphere of politics from the domain of administration. He was not without his political purposes. His ultimate motive was an energetic executive capable of leading public opinion (as well as Congress) so as to secure majority rule and responsible government.

Wilson was convinced that public opinion was of primary importance in a democracy.[25] But opinion, like parties, was dependent upon leadership and principles. Leadership, however, had nearly vanished in this period of "congressional government." The problem was not a lack of understanding of the principles of politics, but the necessity of ensuring that these principles were accepted by "enlightened" statesmen who could provide leadership. "Even if we had clear insights into all the political past, and could form out of perfectly instructed heads a few placidly wise maxims of government . . . would the country act on them?"[26] To that question, Wilson answered in the affirmative, but only with the proper preparation and the proper leadership in the formation of public opinion.[27] The problem, Wilson suggests, is that "the bulk of mankind is rigidly unphilosophical, and nowadays the bulk of mankind votes. A Truth must be-

[24]Hamilton, *The Federalist*, No. 72.

[25]"Wherever regard for public opinion is a first principle of government, practical reform must be slow and all reform must be full of compromises, For wherever public opinion exists it must rule. . . . Whoever would effect a change in a modern constitutional government must first educate his fellow-citizen to want some change. That done, he must persuade them to want the particular change he wants." Wilson, "The Study of Administration," *Political Science Quarterly*, 2 (June 1887), p. 208.

[26]Ibid., p. 209.

[27]See Woodrow Wilson, *The State: Elements of Historical and Practical Politics* (Boston: D.C. Heath, 1980), p. 667.

come not only plain but also commonplace before it will be seen by the people."[28]

Wilson had noted that one good thing had emerged in the practical conduct of government in the period of Congressional domination. The separation of powers had been rendered practically ineffective. "The predominate and controlling force . . . is Congress." As a result,

> All niceties of constitutional restriction and even many broad principles of constitutional limitations have been overridden, and a thoroughly organized system of congressional control was set up which gives a very rude negative to some theories of balance and some schemes for distributed power, but which suits well with convenience and does violence to none of the principles of self-government contained in the Constitution.[29]

Wilson recognized that the organizational forms inherent in the constitutional system had a substantial impact upon political practice. In exposing those forms for what they were, as part of a mere "literary theory" of the Constitution, he would be able to go beyond the limitations imposed by the structure of the Constitution itself. The literal application of the Constitution to the practice of government had resulted in an unworkable and irresponsible government.[30] Wilson hoped to replace the "Newtonian" view of the Framers with his own "Darwinian view."[31]

The true test of the government and its constitution is its capacity to adapt to the "prevailing thought and need of the time."[32] Wilson had observed three stages of political development in the chief nations of the modern world: first, there had been a period of absolute rule, followed by a period of constitution-making and constitutional development, and, finally, a period of administrative development.[33]

It was Wilson's view that the period of constitution-making had ended and a new era was emerging; the people had won their struggle against tyrannical forms; now they "have to develop administration in accordance with the constitution they won for themselves in a previous period of struggle with absolute power."[34] In the final historical stage of development, the leaders of the people, those who articulate and lead public opinion, would become the government. In

---

[28]"Study of Administration," p. 209.

[29]*Congressional Government*, p. 31.

[30]Wilson suggests that "if it were possible to call together again the members of that Convention (of 1787) to view the work of their hand in the light of the century that has tested it, they would be the first to admit that the only fruit of dividing power has been to make it irresponsible." Ibid., p. 187.

[31]*Constitutional Government in the United States* (New York: Columbia University Press, 1908), cf. pp. 54-57.

[32]Wilson, *Papers*, Arthur S. Link, ed., 61 vols., (Princeton: Princeton University Press, 1966), vol. 10, pp. 37-42.

[33]Wilson, "The Study of Administration," p. 204.

[34]Ibid., p. 206.

this way, the changing opinions of the people could be accommodated to the changing times. Also, majority rule would be made compatible with responsible government.

Consequently, Wilson saw nothing wrong with the concentration or centralization of power; the focus of that power had come to reside in a place where it could not be properly utilized—the Congress. Concentration of power in Congress (with its numerous committees) violated a central maxim of Wilsonian theory: "The more power is divided, the more irresponsible it becomes."[35] Wilson's task, therefore, was to reinstitute responsibility in the executive by a cultivation of the opinion that administration is not properly within the sphere of politics. Administration, and its study, are properly within the domain of those universal things commonly associated with science.[36] As Wilson suggested, "Efficiency is the only just foundation for confidence in a public officer, under republican institutions no less than under monarchs."[37] It was his view that "there is but one rule of good administration for all governments alike,"[38] and the perfection of modern government requires the establishment of a "good" system of administration.[39]

The time had come to reestablish the constitutional order along lines that were consonant with the new realities. Through the establishment of administration as the domain of the executive, he could accomplish two crucial purposes; beginning a process of legitimizing (by making commonplace) that opinion in the public mind and attempting to lay the foundations for the constitutional reinterpretation of the proper distribution of power (toward executive predominance) by grounding that opinion in the "permanent truths of political progress."[40] In both cases, it was necessary to establish apparently neutral ground, on the one hand theoretical and scientific, and on the other merely practical and commonplace.

In attempting to justify administration as a function separate from politics, Wilson turned, by analogy, to an activity most commonplace in the life of his time—business.

> The field of administration is a field of business. It is removed from the hurry and strife of politics; it at most points stands apart even from the debatable ground of

[35]*Congressional Government,* p. 77.

[36]It was for this reason, Vincent Ostrom has noted, that "Wilson could conceive of a theory of democratic government but *not* a theory of *democratic administration. The Intellectual Crisis in American Public Administration* (University, Ala.: University of Alabama Press, 1974), p. 27 [emphasis is in the original].

[37]Wilson, *Congressional Government,* p. 255.

[38]Wilson, "Study of Administration," p. 202.

[39]Wilson suggests that "it is the object of administrative study to discover, first, what government can properly and successfully do, and secondly, how it can do these proper things with the utmost possible efficiency and the least possible cost either of money or of energy. The reason administration had been neglected in the prior period of constitution making was the necessity to subject absolute power to democratic control." "Study of Administration," p. 206.

[40]Ibid.

constitutional study. It is a part of political life only as the methods of the counting-house are a part of the life of society.[41]

In distinguishing politics from administration, Wilson defines politics as the enactment of public law, or the formulation of public policy;[42] as such, it is a task most suited to the legislature. Public administration, however, "involves the detailed and systematic execution of the law; as such it is the proper task of the executive."[43] Although the political principles underlying the constitutions of governments may vary with differing regimes, the principles of good administration are the same in every system of government.[44]

If Wilson appears to have rested the legitimacy of his claim upon a scientific authority derived from the study of administration (which subsequently occurred in the discipline of Public Administration), his political and philosophical objective was to rest that opinion upon a stable principle. "The object of administrative study," Wilson claimed, "is to rescue executive methods from the confusion and costliness of empirical experiment and set them upon foundations laid deep in stable principle."[45] Ultimately, that required a change in the way of viewing the distribution of power in the Constitution that was compatible with his purposes.

> The study of administration, philosophically viewed, is closely connected with the study of the proper distribution of constitutional authority. To be efficient it must discover the simplest arrangements by which responsibility can be unmistakably fixed upon officials; the best way of dividing authority without hampering it, and responsibility without obscuring it. And this question of the distribution of authority, when taken into the sphere of the higher, the originating function of government, is obviously a central constitutional question. If administrative study can discover the best principles upon which to base such a distribution, it will have done constitutional study an invaluable service. Montesquieu did not, I am convinced, say the last word on this head.[46]

Montesquieu had failed to discover the best principles for the proper distribution of power because he, like the framers of the Constitution, was concerned with limiting the power of government to ensure the protection of individual liberty. By uniting power in a responsible executive, Wilson hoped to adapt the institutions of government to the requirements of a progressive theory. Ultimately, therefore, administration itself is "raised very far above the dull level of mere technical detail by the fact that through its greater principles it is directly con-

---

[41]Ibid., p. 210.
[42]Cf. ibid., pp. 198 and 212.
[43]Ibid., p. 212.
[44]As Wilson noted, "when we study the administrative systems of France and Germany . . . we need not care a peppercorn for the constitutional and political reasons which [they] give for their practices. . . . If I see a monarchist died [sic] in the wool, I can learn his business methods without changing one of my republican spots." Ibid.
[45]Ibid., p. 210.
[46]Ibid., p. 213.

nected with the lasting maxims of political wisdom, the permanent truths of political progress."[47]

The practical success of the Wilsonian theory entailed the acceptance of the legitimacy of a simple reversal: Congress should concern itself with general policies and lawmaking and the executive should control the details of administration. Wilson was not aware of the fact that it was precisely by means of the control of those details that Congress had "attained all the substantial powers of government."[48] Thus, from his point of view administration is the source of power in modern government. Through control of the details of administration (given Wilson's insistence that the administration is nonpolitical) the president is potentially less dependent upon the formal powers of the office in the political realm, but more dependent upon the shaping and leading of public opinion.[49] In the administrative realm, executive success is dependent upon the implementation of the opinion that politics and administration can indeed be separate. To the extent that the goals of progressivism have been embodied in a popular majority, the legitimacy of a managerial presidency would be unquestioned.[50]

THE THEORY OF BUDGET REFORM: A RATIONAL PROCESS OR MUDDLING THROUGH?

The legacy of Progressivism was a legacy of practical reform that tended to elevate the rhetoric of reform into a moral imperative. Nearly every change in the operation of government or its institutions was advocated and justified as a reform, necessary or otherwise. Consequently, reform became an end in itself. The list is endless: constitutional reform; party reform; civil service reform; electoral reform; reform of the Congress, courts, or the presidency; and budget reform. Nearly every major reform grew out of a breakdown in the legitimacy of the constellation of ideas and principles that had established a consensus in an earlier period. Many important issues, perhaps the most important ones, could only be solved by partisan appeal and resolution in the electoral arena. But increasingly reform had come to be viewed as a technical matter, outside the scope of partisan appeal. Reforms growing out of the Progressive Era thus had a peculiar adaptability to the methods of the positive sciences. And the likelihood of the successful implementation of a reform was enhanced by the extent to which it could appear to be nonpartisan. As a result, economics came

[47]Ibid., p. 210.

[48]Wilson, *Congressional Government*, p. 49.

[49]Thus Wilson suggests that the chief weapon of the president in the political realm in "compelling the Congress" to follow his leadership "is public opinion." *Constitutional Government*, pp. 70-71.

[50]For a broad treatment of the managerial presidency, see Peri E. Arnold, *Making the Managerial Presidency* (Princeton, NJ: Princeton University Press, 1986), especially Chaps. 1 and 2.

to assume an important role in the conduct of administration.[51] Peter Drucker suggests that a basic maxim of American politics might be: "If at all possible, express a political issue and design a political alignment as an economic issue and an economic alignment."[52] But he also notes, "despite its appearance of centrality, economics in the American experience is actually subordinate means to predominantly noneconomic ends."[53] Likewise, the distinction between the political branches and the administration, which characterized the new view of the separation of powers, tended to obscure the fact that budgetary principles of the old liberal state were being gradually discarded.

> One change was the substitution of direct for indirect taxation; another was the surrender of the principle of balanced budgets; a third was the acceptance of an inconvertible paper monetary standard and a new role for loan finance. But most important, there was a steady expansion of state expenditures, and an increase in the number and variety of state economic functions. The evolution of the state budget as a crucial factor in economic life has gone hand in hand with the development of a permanent state bureaucracy.[54]

The growth of the administrative sphere was attained under the guise of its neutrality; similarly, modern budgetary "theory" was legitimized under the banner of "economic rationality." The distinction between politics and administration had its counterpart in the development of the theory of budgeting.

The manner in which the budget is now customarily viewed is largely colored by the successful implementation of the methods of the positive sciences into the practice of modern government. Those theories that gave legitimacy to a positive role for the government in economic affairs were themselves legitimized by the incorporation of scientific methodology as a means to ensure the successful operation of policies designed to achieve social justice. This interrelationship has tended to create a distinction between the theory and practice of budgeting. As a result, it becomes difficult to understand budgeting as a practical procedure once it has become embodied as a principal

---

[51]It was not accidental that economics came to be viewed as the most successful of the social sciences. It was, as Alfred Marshall noted, due to the "measuring-rod" of money. "Money is the one convenient means of measuring human motivation." As R. W. Staveley noted, "The motivation is measured indirectly through its effect, the amount of money an individual is willing to pay for an extra amount of satisfaction; or the extra amount of fatigue he is willing to endure for a given sum of money. Money measures utilities and disutilities. The process of rational choice and therefore human rationality itself is subordinate to the desires . . . being the agency of the economic laws of supply and demand." "Keynes and the Postulates of Classical Economics" (unpublished manuscript).

[52]*Men, Ideas and Politics* (New York: Harper & Row, 1971). p. 255.

[53]Ibid.

[54]James O'Connor, *The Fiscal Crisis of the State* (New York: St. Martins's Press, 1973), p. 72. Marcus G. Raskin has suggested that "the federal budget is an invention of twentieth-century progressive movements which sought to organize the American national state in a 'rational' way." He notes that it "has been an important nail in the coffin of localism." *The Federal Budget and Social Reconstruction: The People and the State,* Institute for Policy Studies, (New Brunswick, N.J.: Transaction Books, 1978), p. xiv.

planning device to ensure the successful participation of government in the economic realm.

The budget itself is a theoretical plan bringing together into one place the money costs of government without regard to considerations other than economy and efficiency. This is not to deny that such considerations will not occur elsewhere, but the budget itself is a neutral mechanism. Modern budgeting, therefore, is no older than the distinction between facts and values, the foundation of the positive sciences.[55] It presupposes the fact that government has positive purposes to perform. By virtue of the organization or the plan itself, the budget becomes a powerful centralizing device. It is not accidental that in the literature concerning budgeting, the budget is associated with the executive.[56]

If the practice of budgeting is as old as the necessity to choose among competing claims upon the public treasury, the use of the budget as a centralizing device was greatly facilitated by the authority conferred upon it by the independent study of public finance and public administration. The study of budgeting as a distinct activity was dependent upon the success of the positive sciences as well as the ascendancy of a positive theory of the state.[57] It required the implicit recognition of the fact that governments must be organized to achieve positive purposes.

In the United States, the structure of the government itself, with its constitutional division of government functions, had served to prevent centralized administrative control. Jesse Burkhead has noted that for this reason

> development of budgeting in the United States ran head-on into the doctrine of the separation of powers. The division between executive and legislative authority in the constitution and the practices of governments had to be greatly altered before budget systems could be established. In this respect the establishment of budget systems in the United States was "revolutionary," it was both a product of and a contribution to a fundamental change in the structure of government.[58]

It was necessary, in the first instance, to alter the common perceptions concerning the desirability of limiting centralized (executive) authority. In a manner not unlike Woodrow Wilson's attempt to distinguish administration from politics, a

---

[55]Rene Stourm, in what is often considered the first systematic work on the budget, noted that a budget is a document containing a preliminary approval plan of public revenues and expenditures. *The Budget.* Translated by Thaddeus Plazinski. (New York: D. Appleton & Company, 1917, original edition, 1889), cf. pp. 144-168.

[56]Eli B. Silverman has suggested that public budgeting, like public administration, "has historically excluded the legislature from its . . . province. Legislatures were linked with policymaking process, a phenomenon . . . distinctly different from the administration process associated with the Executive." "Public Budgeting and Public Administration: Enter the Legislature," *Public Finance Quarterly,* 2 (October 1974), p. 472.

[57]See W. F. Willoughby, "Budget," in *Encyclopedia of the Social Sciences* (New York: Macmillan Company, 1930), vol. 3, p. 40.

[58]*Government Budgeting* (New York: John Wiley, 1956), p. 29.

similar distinction was made in terms of policy and finance.[59] Of course, like administration, finance is clearly within the sphere of executive activity.

In any case, the importance of social science theory in legitimizing that distinction should not be minimized. The budget revolution

> was brought about by a peculiar combination of reformer—the professional political scientists and public servants who wished to transform government into a positive instrument for social welfare, and the conservatives of the business community, who wished to reduce government expenditures and lower tax burdens. Both of these divergent groups subscribe to budget reform under the heading of "economy and efficiency" [that phrase which seems to have such powerful appeal in American politics].[60]

To regard the budget within the framework of modern social science is to become aware of budgeting as an organizational means for ensuring the technical rationality inherent in modern liberal administration. In an influential work on administrative organization, Herbert Simon has suggested that though the final goals of organizational activity, "policy questions," involve value judgments, the means for attaining these final objectives ("administrative questions") involve factual, and hence rational, judgments. Simon contends that "behavior is purposive insofar as it is guided by general goals or objectives; it is rational insofar as it selects alternatives which are conducive to the achievement of the previously selected goals."[61]

Budget-making, as a practical matter, does not involve the necessity to distinguish questions of "finance" from those of "policy." When subordinate to organizational theory, however, budgeting is denied any rationality apart from the theory from which it is derived. "The organization," Herbert Simon insisted, took "from the individual some of his decisional autonomy, and substituted for it an organizational decision making process."[62] It would appear that scientific rationality is different from, although the source of, human rationality. Simon maintains, therefore, that "behavior patterns which we call organizations are fundamental, then, to the achievement of human rationality in any broad sense. The rational individual is, and must be, an organized and institutionalized individual."[63]

The systematic study of budgeting, like the study of administration, is removed from politics and political theory.[64] It is unconcerned with practical, political, or common-sense judgments. It is animated by a technical rationality

[59]As Arthur Smithies has observed, "in practice, governments have attempted to make a basic distinction between 'policy-making' and 'finance'." "Government Budgeting," in Encyclopedia of the Social Sciences (New York: Macmillan, 1968), vol. 2, p. 185.

[60]Burkhead, Government Budgeting, p. 29.

[61]Herbert Simon, Administrative Behavior (New York: Free Press, 1957), p. 5.

[62]Ibid., p. 8.

[63]Ibid., p. 102.

[64]For a general discussion of this problem, see Bernard Crick, The American Science of Politics (Berkeley: University of California Press, 1959).

that can be apprehended in the "factual dimension" of the distinction between the "empirical" and the "normative" realm. Rationality is at best only instrumental. Consequently, Simon can maintain that efficiency "in its broadest sense . . . is often used as a virtual synonym for 'rationality'."[65]

Contemporary scholarship has focused on the budget in one of two ways. In the one instance, it is viewed as a means to ensure the ends of pluralist society; as such it is a part of the political process and thus can only be viewed incrementally. Conversely, it is seen as an end in itself (comprehensive or rational budgeting), in which case the primary concern is to ensure efficiency.[66]

Budgeting can be viewed in an almost wholly theoretical manner, and as such, it is concerned with the budget as a rational or universal document. The characteristic of good budgeting then is its ability to be comprehensive or rational. It should be capable of universality;[67] it should be "intelligible and accurate";[68] and it "should be detailed and should include all of the estimated revenues and expenditures of a government . . . and should present all the information necessary for intelligent interpretation and action."[69] Arthur Smithies contends that a rational budgeting procedure demands that "expenditures should be considered in relation to revenues and all final expenditure commitments should in general result from consideration of the budget as a whole."[70] The separation of "policy" questions from those of "finance" involves the necessity to distinguish theory from practice.

The core of comprehensive budgeting is its insistence that its subject matter is neutral ground and therefore a degree of rationality can be infused into its method.[71] Let the political decision-makers agree upon the goals;

[65]Herbert Simon, Donald W. Smithburg, and Victor A. Thompson, *Public Administration* (New York: Alfred Knopf, 1950), p. 490.

[66]Academic budget theory, building upon concepts of economic thought, has tended to reflect the politics of budgeting at the national level. In the 1960s and 1970s "microbudgeting" or incrementalism was ascendant. Since the middle 1970s (in the wake of the Congressional Budget Act) "macrobudgeting," which has attempted to be comprehensive in its analysis, attained greater currency. It attempted to take into account the new role of Congress in budgeting and also the growth in entitlements. See Lance T. LeLoup, *The Fiscal Congress* (Westport, Conn.: Greenwood Press, 1980), and his "The Myth of Incrementalism: Analytic Choices in Budgetary Theory," *Polity*, 10, No. 4 (Summer, 1978); and "From Microbudgeting to Macrobudgeting: Evolution in Theory and Practice," in Irene S. Rubin, ed., *New Directions in Budget Theory* (Albany: State University of New York Press, 1988); also, Allen Schick, *Congress and Money* (Washington, D.C.: Urban Institute Press, 1980); and his "Macro-Budgetary Adaptations to Fiscal Stress in Industrialized Democracies," *Public Administration Review*, 46, no. 2 (March-April, 1986); and Dennis Ippolito, *Congressional Spending*, (Ithaca, N.Y.: Cornell University Press, 1981).

[67]Rene Stourm, *The Budget*, pp. 150-165.

[68]G. Findlay Shirras, *The Science of Public Finance* (London: Macmillan & Co., 1924), p. 564.

[69]Alfred G. Buehler, *Public Finance* (New York: McGraw-Hill, 1936), p. 165.

[70]Arthur Smithies, *The Budgetary Process in the United States* (New York: McGraw-Hill, 1955), p. 168.

[71]Cf. V. O. Key, "The Lack of a Budgetary Theory," *American Political Science Review*, 34 (December 1940): 1137-1144. As Arthur Smithies suggests, "in one sense the entire budgetary process can be said to have as a single objective the attainment of economy and efficiency." Smithies, *Budgetary Process*, p. 13.

budgetary experts will discover the various ways to reach such goals.[72] They will provide the alternatives in such a way as to elicit the least costs or the greatest benefits and will institute the best procedure (cost–benefit analysis) to achieve those goals of economy and efficiency. These characteristics of comprehensive budgeting have been incorporated into many of the budgetary reforms of the 1960s and 1970s—including those innovative programs intended to rationalize the budgetary procedures of the Great Society (known as the Planning Programming Budgeting System, PPBS)—or even Jimmy Carter's attempt at comprehensive annual budget review, the zero–base budgeting system.

On the other hand, the dominant study of budgeting throughout the 1960s and 1970s has focused on the "politics of the budgetary process."[73] In this view, the budget is so intricately intertwined with the political system as to defy any rational understanding of the whole. Rather, budgeting is a process of incrementalism, a procedure for "muddling through."[74] In the complex environment of the modern state "one cannot be confident that such principles of rationality as comprehensiveness of overview, explicitness of choice, means-end calculations, and clarity of definitions of objectives are appropriate."[75] What is clear to the adherents of the incremental school of budgeting is that any attempt to tamper with the parts of the system will have an undesirable effect upon the whole.[76]

Aaron Wildavsky has clearly enumerated the procedures by which budgetary decisions were once made within the national government:

> Decisions depend upon calculation of which alternatives to consider and to choose. . . . By far the most important aid to calculation is the incremental method. Budgets are almost never actively reviewed as a whole in the sense of considering

[72]These experts usually regard economics as a more exact science than the other social sciences. Thus, it serves as a model for the construction of the proper means to attain ends that have been agreed upon.

[73]See the first edition of Aaron Wildavsky, *The Politics of the Budgetary Process* (Boston: Little Brown & Co., 1964), and several subsequent editions through the early 1980s. By the middle of the 1980s, the politics of budgeting had changed so dramatically that Wildavsky had to write *The New Politics of the Budgetary Process,* (Glenview, Ill.: Scott, Foresman & Co., 1988).

[74]See Charles Lindblom, "The Science of Muddling Through," *Public Administration Review,* 19 (Spring 1959), p. 77-88.

[75]Charles Lindblom, "Decision-making in Taxation and Expenditure," in National Bureau of Economic Research, ed., *Public Finances: Needs, Sources, and Utilization,* (Princeton: Princeton University Press, 1961), p. 299.

[76]When Arthur Smithies suggested (in *The Budgetary Process in the United States,* pp. 192-193) that a Joint Congressional Budget Committee be formed and charged with the task of considering all proposals for revenue and expenditure in a single package and that their decisions be made binding by concurrent resolutions as a modest attempt to improve "the rationality of the budget process," Aaron Wildavsky insisted that "Smithies' budgetary reform presupposes a completely different political system from the one which exists in the United States. . . . In the guise of a procedural change in the preparation of the budget by Congress, Smithies is actually proposing a revolutionary move which would mean the virtual introduction of the British Parliamentary system if it were a success." Wildavsky, *The Revolt of the Masses* (New York: Basic Books, 1971), p. 180.

at once the value of all existing programs as compared with all possible alternatives. Instead, this year's budget, with special attention given to a narrow range of increases or decreases . . . is a product of previous decision.[77]

It was precisely those devices (incremental process, fragmented decision-making) that Wildavsky contended minimized conflict and enabled a certain amount of rationality and self-corrective feedback, and it was those things that became the most popular targets of the reformers of the budgetary process. Although the goals of the reformers were said to be economy or efficiency, the changes advocated would result not only in alteration of the budgetary process, but would spell major changes in the political system.

Most reform proposals were based upon the concern that the entire budget was not examined as a whole; such examination would enable specific decisions to be made on their relative merits. Wildavsky contended that this view ignored the fact that there is no consensus in the ranking of values. Thus, he suggested that a normative theory of budgeting is incompatible with a pluralistic democracy.[78] A theory that forces men to ask what a government ought to do, or as Wildavsky suggests, "what ought to be in the budget," would result in the "end of conflict over the government's role in society."[79] He contended, therefore, that the organic budget resulted in the triumph of particular values.[80] It allowed for more alternative views to be expressed, and it minimized conflict. The comprehensive program budget, on the other hand, would exacerbate ideological differences and thereby prevent compromise. Wildavsky maintained, therefore, that "the study of budgeting is just another expression for the study of politics."[81] However, the practice of budgeting must remain separate from theory because he insisted that theory is part of the normative realm. The advocates of comprehensive budgeting who enter the normative realm thereby lose sight of the practice of politics.

In attempting to uphold the integrity of political decision-making, numerous critics have attacked the "scientific rationality" of comprehensive budgeting. "In the name of rationality, program budgeting has sought to eliminate politics from the decision-making process."[82] Another critic suggested that the techniques of program and comprehensive budgeting "may represent the even more disastrous triumph of economic rationality over the political and social

---

[77]"Budgeting as a Political Process," *Encyclopedia of the Social Sciences* 2 (New York: MacMillen, 1968), p. 192.

[78]Aaron Wildavsky suggested that if "a normative theory of budgeting is to be more than an academic exercise, it must actually guide the making of governmental decisions. The items of expenditures . . . must in large measure conform to the theory. . . . This is tantamount to prescribing that virtually all the activities of government be carried on according to the theory." This, it should be noted, was in the early editions of *The Politics of the Budgetary Process* (Boston: Little, Brown & Co., 1964), p. 128.

[79]Ibid., p. 129.

[80]Cf. ibid., pp. 165-167.

[81]Ibid., p. 126.

[82]Felix A. Nigro, *Modern Public Administration* (New York: Harper & Row, 1973), p. 350.

rationality which . . . belong in government decisions on resource allocation."[83] It appears therefore that in either case, as regards the contemporary
study of budgeting, there is no possibility of reconciling theory and practice.
On the one hand, when viewed within the framework of economic analysis,
budgeting prevents a consideration of political means; rather it is concerned
only with the technical means to ensure the end of efficiency. As Lionel
Robbins has noted, "there are no economic ends. There are only economical
and uneconomical ways of achieving given ends."[84] Such theory is unconcerned with the legitimacy of the ends to which it places the organizational
methods designed to ensure efficiency. On the other hand, the incrementalists
deny the rationality of ends on the assumption that theory (the normative
realm) can offer no guide to the practice of politics. Thus they are concerned
only with an analysis of the political process (or the means) that ensures the
successful operation of the system. To be sure, such a system accommodates
the numerous competing interests that are too complicated for rational understanding.[85] Both then deny however that the practice of politics can be informed by an understanding in which means and ends (or theory and practice)
are not separated.

PUBLIC SPENDING: FROM REGRESSIVE
TO PROGRESSIVE ACT

Budgeting as a practical matter has existed and will persist as long as resources
are limited and the appetites of men remain potentially limitless. The recognition of the necessity to impose restraints upon those public appetites was an
important consideration in the way in which the early generations of leaders
viewed public expenditures and public taxation. Both were regarded as inseparable from public debt. The public debt was considered not only economically
unsound but politically immoral. A government that does not habitually raise
sufficient revenues to cover its expenses soon becomes an extravagant and
irresponsible government.[86] It was a recognition of the limitations of what government could accomplish compatible with public welfare that imposed restraints upon the desire for greater public expenditure.

   When viewed as a practical activity, budgeting cannot be understood apart
from what the purposes of government should be. It was not that the importance

   [83]Ida R. Hoos, *Systems Analysis in Public Policy: A Critique* (Berkeley: University of California Press, 1972), p. 74.
   [84]Lionel Robbins, *An Essay on the Nature and Significance of Economic Science* (London:
Macmillan & Co., 1952), p. 145.
   [85]What remains, it appears, is that the two major schools of budgeting provide powerful support
of the neutrality (comprehensive budgeting) and the legitimacy (incremental budgeting) of the
liberal regime.
   [86]Adam Smith had recognized the tendency of government to seek to expand its activity and
suggested that they are "always and without any exception, the greatest spendthrifts in the society."
Wealth of Nations, Edwin Caanan edition (London: Methuen, 1922), vol. 1, p. 328.

of money was lost upon the founding generation; money was viewed as a principal means to accomplish ends that were themselves unrelated to money. Thus, the budget was not regarded as an economic document that, when used as a fiscal policy device, became a powerful tool of centralized administration in which the use of expenditure becomes an end in itself.

It is not surprising, therefore, that neither the Constitution nor the *Federalist* speaks of a budget. Hamilton did consider the importance of money to the accomplishment of the essential functions of government.[87] Of course, the early struggles between the Hamiltonians and the Jeffersonians concerned precisely the question of what those essential functions were. Hamilton believed that preservation of the public credit depended upon assumption of state debts and the domestically held public debt. He favored a funding system through which the portion of expenditures not covered by revenues would be converted into debt.[88] The establishment of a sound public credit contributed not only to government stability but set the standard for private behavior. "Public and private credit," he noted, "are closely allied if not inseparable."[89]

Hamilton's emphasis on the establishment of public credit reflected his desire to promote the growth of sound financial institutions in the national government and to ensure a sound economy.[90] The objection to his financial schemes, particularly the funding and assumption proposals, was that they were conducive to increased indebtedness, which was thought to contribute to moral degeneration.

Unlike Hamilton, Jefferson stressed the need for a minimal level of government activity and a reduction of the national debt. "I place economy among the first and most important of republican virtues, and public debt as the greatest danger to be feared."[91] But both Jefferson and Hamilton agreed that public expenditures should not exceed revenues in ordinary times. Thus the attitudes with respect to the federal budget and debt policy in the early period contained the following key elements:

> First, a low level of public expenditures was believed desirable. The smaller the revenues required, the less was the interference through taxation with the operation of the economy. Second, a balanced federal budget was the minimum goal deemed acceptable in times of peace. When deficits were incurred, they were neither con-

---

[87]"Money," Hamilton noted in *Federalist* No. 30, "is with propriety considered as the vital principle of the body politic, as that which sustains its life and motion, and enables it to perform its most essential functions." p. 188.

[88]Lewis H. Kimmel, *Federal Budget and Fiscal Policy* (Washington, D.C.: Brookings Institution, 1959), cf. pp. 8-13.

[89]*Second Report on the Public Credit*, cited in ibid., p. 9.

[90]Lewis H. Kimmel has suggested that "Hamilton's views on the federal debt and budget were neither narrow nor doctrinaire. To a remarkable extent . . . he was able to distinguish between the use and abuse of credit. In his view the public credit was an intangible asset of enormous value, not only because of possible emergency needs but also because it stood at the very center of the financial system. *Federal Budget and Fiscal Policy,* (Washington, D.C.: Brookings Institution, 1959) p. 12.

[91]Letter to William Plummer, Jr., 1816, cited in Kimmel.

doned nor rationalized. Third, when federal debt was outstanding, official policy called for its retirement. The latter idea . . . served for many years as a unifying principle in the management of the federal finances.[92]

Why was the public debt spoken of in moral terms and greatly to be feared? Perhaps it was because it was thought to represent an economic burden on the people and, as such, it was considered undemocratic.

The principal arguments against the public debt, arguments that were respectable throughout the nineteenth century were that (1) interest on the public debt was a burden on the working classes; (2) interest payment involved a redistribution of income in favor of the well-to-do; and (3) the capital freed from unproductive employment through debt reduction would find its way into productive uses.[93] In practice, therefore, the development and legitimacy of the philosophy of the annually balanced budget (except in extraordinary times) were augmented by the realization that a public debt was undemocratic. As a result, public expenditures must necessarily remain low. Although it enjoyed widespread acceptance in the political arena, the philosophy of an annually balanced budget was widely defended on economic grounds as well.[94]

The successful implementation of a budget system at the national level therefore required the legitimation of the opinion that the government had positive tasks to perform in the economic as well as the political realm.[95] But a prior assumption was also made that public expenditure could be made compatible with public welfare. In other words, public expenditures would have to be transformed from what has been considered a regressive act that created a burden on the economy and the working class, to a progressive act that could be used to alleviate that burden. In short, public finances would have to be democratized.

An important requirement that aided in the transformation of public taxation and expenditure from a burden to a potential device to ensure greater equality in the collection and dispersal of public funds was the progressive

---

[92]Ibid., p. 37.

[93]See Kimmel, pp. 301-305.

[94]According to Kimmel, the economists advanced the following reason for limiting public expenditure: "The principal economic reason advanced in support of the balanced budget was that an increase in public debt involves a draft on funds or savings that otherwise would be available for private capital expansion. Public borrowing slows economic progress because it impinges on the growth of capital. . . . With the development of the wage-fund doctrine, the principal economic arguments were in effect packaged into a unified anti-public borrowing philosophy. Public borrowing, it was reasoned, reduced the wages fund, thereby lowering the wage level and placing incidence of loans directly on the workers. Because of the regressive revenue system, a disproportionately large portion of the burden of debt service was borne by the working classes. Since only small amounts of government obligations were held by the lower-income groups, redistribution of income in favor of those with higher incomes was inevitable." Kimmel, p. 302.

[95]Jesse Burkhead has observed, "there can be no doubt that a budgeting system is implicit recognition that a government has positive responsibilities and that it intends to perform them. This assumption of responsibility required a concomitant organization of executive authority and an increase in the relative importance of governmentally organized economic power in relation to privately organized economic power." Government Budgeting, p. 29.

income tax. The adoption of the Sixteenth Amendment to the Constitution in 1913 prepared the way for the eventual acceptance and the successful implementation of a national budget system.[96] The income tax necessitated increased administrative centralization, but it was not incompatible with the competitive market system, that rewarded individual initiative. As Joseph Pechman suggests, " all successful income taxes depend upon central rather than local administration. Most importantly, perhaps, it [the income tax] does not involve direct intervention in free market activities."[97] But equally important, perhaps, it was reflective of the new view of government as a positive tool to ensure minimal conditions for the achievement of social justice.

THE EXECUTIVE AND BUDGET REFORM: IMPLEMENTATION OF A NATIONAL BUDGET SYSTEM

The usefulness of budget-making as a tool available to the executive in the national government was not realized until it had become effective in the political arena at the local level.[98] Budget reform was part of a political reform movement, the success of which had ensured its status as a nonpartisan device. The concern for economy and efficiency in government, as well as a desire for "good government," resulted in early attempts at budget reform. Those who were most outspoken in regard to budgetary reform were those who wanted reform generally. They viewed government in its present form as irresponsible, immoral, and much in need of accountability.[99] The "hostility to doing business in the dark," to "boss rule," to "invisible government," became the "soil in which the budget idea finally took root and grew."[100] The budget was conceived as a major weapon for instilling responsibility into the governmental structure by ensuring that government would be conducted in the open, thus destroying secrecy and the control of the party bosses.[101] It would also, like cabinet government, ensure accountability by institutionalizing the budget in the executive.

[96]It was "appropriate public policy to moderate economic inequality," says Joseph A. Pechman, "and taxation of personal incomes at progressive rates is an efficient method of promoting this objective." "Income Tax," in *Encyclopedia of the Social Sciences,* vol. 15, p. 530.

[97]Ibid., p. 530.

[98]See Martin J. Schiesl, *The Politics of Efficiency: Municipal Administration and Reform in America, 1800-1920* (Berkeley: University of California Press, 1977).

[99]"In place of the people controlling their service organ—the government," wrote Frederick Cleveland, an early reformer, "we have boss rule." "Popular Control of Government—Three Schools of Opinion in the U.S. with Respect to Budget-Making," *Political Science Quarterly,* 34 (June 1919), p. 248.

[100]Frederick Cleveland, "Evolution of the Budget Idea in the United States," *The Annals* (November 1915), p. 22.

[101]"But the making is," Cleveland suggests, " a process in the operations of the mechanism of popular control over government." "Popular Control of Government," p. 248.

Nearly all the early reformers agreed that "the ideal that government exists to serve is a fundamental principle of democracy."[102]

If the budget idea was itself an outgrowth of an intellectual movement (Progressivism) to ensure a positive role for government, it was soon transferred to the political arena where it became a powerful tool in the rhetoric of reform, appealing to conservatives and liberals alike. Although a tool of the executive, budgeting, like administration, once instituted does not itself serve political purposes. Once the ends of government are clearly seen, the means of ensuring those ends require the employment of a neutral mechanism to secure economy and efficiency. Executive budgeting was one way in which the methods of government could be reconciled to the demands of modern life.[103]

If in the early period effective budgeting was prevented as a result of a political system that encouraged decentralization and legislative control, finally it could be based on reliable principles.[104] It was the growing expectations of what the tasks of government should be and the "expansion in the economic sphere which pointed up the inadequacy of traditional budget principles." As Kimmel has observed, "those principles were formulated with legislative control in mind." But the new conditions directed attention "to budget principles designed from the point of view of the chief executive."[105] Not only should the executive control the finances of government but also the entire executive administration as well.

However, the first attempts at control of the administration were made in the legislative branch. It was on March 2, 1887 that "Senator Francis Marion Cockrell introduced his resolution, which conducted in 1887 and 1888 the first comprehensive legislative inquiry into administration."[106] Along with the subse-

---

[102]Cleveland, "Popular Control of Government," p. 239. As Dwight Waldo has observed: "the budget movement was a part of Progressivism and its leaders were leaders of Progressivism. . . . They were sensitive to the appeals and promise of science, and put a simple trust in the discovery of facts as a way of science and as a sufficient mode for solution of human problems. They accepted— they urged—the new positive conception of government, and verged upon the idea of a planned and managed society." *The Administrative State* (New York: Ronald Press Company, 1948), pp. 32-33.

[103]How did public finance, like administration, come to occupy a central position in modern government? Leonard White suggests that "the source is a new social philosophy, growing out of the industrial revolution and its many social, economic, and political implications. . . . The industrial revolution has necessitated . . . a degree of social cooperation in which laissez-faire has become impossible; and gradually the new environment is building up in men's minds a conception of the role of the state which approximates the function assigned it by the conditions of modern life. These new ideas involve the acceptance of the state as a great agency of social cooperation, as well as an agency of social regulation." *Introduction to the Study of Public Administration* (New York: Macmillan Co., 1926), p. 8.

[104]As Smithies noted: "it is essential to realize that traditional budgetary procedures have grown out of efforts by the Congress to control the Executive through the device of highly specific appropriations, rather than by consideration of the requirements of an effective budgetary process." *Budgetary Process*, p. 49.

[105]Kimmel, *Federal Budget*, p. 284.

[106]Oscar Kraines, "The Cockrell Committee: First Comprehensive Congressional Investigation into Administration," *Western Political Quarterly*, 4 (December 1951), p. 583.

quent Dockery Committee investigations, it was assumed that accountability of administration rested with the legislature.[107] Taken together:

> The Dockery–Cockrell investigation strengthens the feeling that Congress would examine and reorganize the executive branch. It was not expected . . . that investigations to follow would be initiated by the President asserting that administration was accountable to the executive.[108]

Nonetheless, by 1905 with the investigations of the Keep Commission appointed by Theodore Roosevelt (the first reorganization committee to report to the president instead of Congress), the ascendancy of the opinion of executive leadership of administration had become a dominant reality.[109] The merging of the opinion of the "experts" with that of the president proved to be an irresistible force. The Commission report "led to Congressional acceptance of Roosevelt's view that administrative reorganization was an executive responsibility and led to Congress' appropriations of funds to enable the Taft Commission to operate."[110]

THE TAFT COMMISSION ON ECONOMY AND EFFICIENCY

The Taft Commission on Economy and Efficiency (1908–1912) provided the tools for and the justification of the concept of a managerial presidency that would enable presidential control of the executive branch.[111] The Commission was chaired by Frederick A. Cleveland and included W. F. Willoughby and F. J. Goodnow as members. The report was submitted to Congress in June 1912 under the title "The Need for a National Budget."[112] It called for an assumption of responsibility by the president for financial planning and management of the administration of government. It indicated the necessity of a competent staff to be located in the Bureau of the Budget, which would report to the president and become the center of information concerning all executive operations.[113] The creation of the Bureau of the Budget and staff was indicative of the importance

---

[107]Oscar Kraines has observed, "the Cockrell Committee paid no attention to and did not even consider the concept of accountability of administration to the executive." *Congress and the Challenge of Big Government* (New York: Brookman Associates, 1958), p. 107.

[108]Kraines, *Congress and the Challenge of Big Government*, p. 107.

[109]As Harold T. Pinkett has observed, "the Keep Commission . . . represented a clear shift of leadership in a long movement for federal administrative reform from the legislative to the executive branch of the United States government." Prior to the Commission, "standing and select Committees of Congress often directed their attention to administrative practices of the executive branch." "The Keep Commission, 1905-1909: A Rooseveltian Effort for Administrative Reform," *The Journal of American History*, 52 (September, 1965), pp. 297-298.

[110]Pinkett, p. 312.

[111]Cf. Herbert Emmerich, *Federal Organization and Administrative Management* (University: University of Alabama Press, 1971).

[112]*House Document No. 854*, 62nd Cong., 2nd sess., 1912.

[113]Of course, the control of the preliminary estimates of the departments would be in the hands of the executive.

of managerial research and executive branch organization to the control of the activities of government.

President Taft enthusiastically supported the establishment of a national budget system as an instrument of executive management and control.[114] Taft indicated that the object of the Commission

> was to suggest a method whereby the President, as the constitutional head of the administration, may lay before Congress, and the Congress may consider and act on, a definite business and financial program; to have the expenditures, appropriations, and estimates so classified and summarized that their broad significance may be readily understood.[115]

In his message to Congress, transmitted as "Economy and Efficiency in the Government Service," he stated that "the Constitutional purpose of a budget is to make government responsive to public opinion and responsible for its acts."[116] Taft sought to follow the advice of the Commission and attempted to institute an executive budget for the 1913 fiscal year. But a strong bloc of both Democrats and Progressive Republicans opposed the attempt and insisted that the heads of departments and agencies submit their appropriation requests at the time and in the manner required by the existing law. The consequence was that "heads of departments and agencies therefore undertook to prepare two sets of appropriation requests—one in accordance with the requirements of the Congress, and the other in accordance with the requirements of the President as set forth in the Commission's report."[117] Congress ignored Taft's attempt and a national budget system was postponed until after the world war. (Taft lost the election that year and Congress still reflected the opinions of an earlier time.)

Perhaps the major problem that the Commission faced was constitutional: how to fit a budget into a government organization in which the powers were divided? William Riker has argued that a government in which the legislative branch is supreme cannot endure a budget.[118] To solve this problem, the Commission stole an idea expressed in Wilson's essay on "The Study of Administration" that for a truth to be made acceptable it must first be made commonplace. The Constitution became, by analogy, a trusteeship. As Burkhead notes:

> The government is the trust instrument; government officials are the trustees. Citizens, in their sovereign capacity, are the beneficiaries and creators of the trust. The President as the principal government official must be responsible for the budget. He should submit the budget message and the summary statement.[119]

---

[114]For Taft's view of the Commission, see "The Boundaries Between the Executive, the Legislature, and the Judicial Branches of the Government," *Yale Law Journal*, 25 (June 1916), p. 612.

[115]"The Need for a National Budget," in House Document No. 854, 2nd Cong. 2d sess., 1912.

[116]*House Document No. 458*, 62nd Cong., 2d sess., 1912.

[117]Burkhead, *Government Budgeting*, p. 12.

[118]Prior to 1921, of course, the U.S. government worked without a budget. Cf. Riker, *Democracy in the United States* (New York: Macmillan Company, 1975), who suggested that when budgeting was introduced, it transferred financial control to the budget-maker. See pp. 203-219.

[119]Burkhead, *Government Budgeting*, p. 20.

The members of the Commission considered a budget system to be a means of adapting the governmental process to the changing needs of the people. It was thought to be a necessary innovation that would ensure the continuation of political progress. The report noted that the budget provided the method "whereby the Government may be kept in constant adjustment with the welfare needs of the people; a means also whereby the economy and efficiency of administration may be regularly brought to a test."[120]

In spite of the fact that the report of the Commission on Economy and Efficiency led to no immediate legislation, "it had tremendous long-run value. The prestige of the Commission and its backing by the President made budgeting an issue of national significance."[121] It stimulated a large volume of writing on the subject of budget reform and led to increased demands for such reform at state and local levels. Perhaps most importantly, business groups, even the National Chamber of Commerce, came to support the concept of executive budgeting as a means to ensure economy and efficiency.[122] Its appeal was widespread and included intellectuals, who were impressed with the growing success of the methods of the positive sciences—for those methods could be adapted to the purposes of administration. It was attractive to those who admired the practice of business for the clarity of its ends and the economy of its means—which in the administrative realm could be translated into the desire to attain those ends of economy and efficiency.

But a practical difficulty remained that threatened the successful implementation of an executive budget system at the national level. It was the inability to dislodge the prerogatives and power of the legislature. The means of overcoming that obstacle entailed the necessity to attack the Constitution itself (with its separation of powers) as the bulwark of tradition that served to prevent reform and the modernization of government.[123] The cry for reform (from civil service to budget reform) was made in the name of a moral regeneration that sought to return government control from the partisans of special interests and the invisible government of the party bosses to the rightful heirs—the people.[124]

In the final analysis, the major obstacle to the development of a national

---

[120]"The Need for A National Budget," n. 116 *supra*, p. 132.

[121]Burkhead, *Government Budgeting*, p. 21.

[122]As Charles Wallace Collins noted, "the business interests of the country today are practically a unit for this reform by the federal government." *The National Budget System* (New York: Macmillan Co., 1917), p. 136.

[123]Cf. Vile, *Constitutionalism*, p. 272.

[124]Cf. Frederick C. Mosher, *Democracy and the Public Service* (New York: Oxford University Press, 1968). From the first, the president was in the vanguard of the moral regeneration, as can be seen in the controversy for civil service reform. Paul S. Van Riper suggests that Theodore Roosevelt's well-known support of civil service was a "recognition of the administrative phase of the progressive movement [which] identified with the movement for more effective political machinery and organization as well as with the pressure for moral political men." *History of the U.S. Civil Service* (Evanston: Row-Peterson, 1958), p. 181.

budgeting system was the separation of powers.[125] The division between the executive and the legislative authority in the Constitution and the accepted practice of legislative control of the purse strings had resulted in a fragmented budgetary process. As Richard A. Musgrave has observed:

> It must be recognized that the struggle for a centralized and comprehensive budget, beginning with Alexander Hamilton's defeat in this quest, was not only a drive for efficient budget planning. More important, it was a struggle between executive and congressional control over expenditure policy.[126]

The establishment of a budget system, it was thought, required a change in the structure of government in order to achieve a harmonious relationship within the political branches of government. First, however, a change in thinking about the organization and purposes of the government itself was required. As a result, much of the debate that occurred in intellectual and academic circles involved the attempted justification of the proposed alteration in the organization of government.

> The Congress has for more than a century exercised complete control over all phases of the financial program. . . . Now it is proposed to supplant the present system by a national budget system. . . . The budget system ordinarily advocated involves, as its prime factor, the relinquishing of the initiative in financial legislation to the executive by the Congress. . . . We have always clung to the constitutional theory of separate and coordinate government powers. . . . How then could we reconcile the apparent giving over to the executive a part of the legislative power with our traditional theories of a constitutional government? Now here is the point of contact with the budget system. It involves a closer application of party responsibility in the particular field of public finance. Recognize the party as the working unit in legislation and legalize the position of the executive as party leader in financial legislation.[127]

Its critics saw executive budgeting as a dramatic shift toward party government and away from the fundamental American form of representative government with its separation of powers. "It proposed a shifting of the center of gravity of our government. Its tendency is toward autocratic executive power. It would achieve this change in government as a by-product to the budget scheme."[128] The Speaker of the House Joseph Cannon objected on similar grounds. He

[125]Dwight Waldo has noted "the traditional separation of powers became the *bete noir* of American political science, and exaltation of the powers of the executive branch its Great White Hope." *The Administrative State*, p. 36.

[126]*Public Finance: In Theory and Practice* (New York: McGraw-Hill, 1973), p. 36.

[127]Charles Wallace Collins, "Constitutional Aspects of a National Budget System," *Yale Law Journal*, (March 1916), p. 380, 384-385.

[128]Edward A. Fitzpatrick, *Budget Making in a Democracy* (New York: Macmillan Co., 1918), p. 292.

insisted that, "when Congress consents to the Executive making the budget it will have surrendered the most important part of a representative government. . . ."[129]

However, the critics of budget reform were in retreat before the bill was debated on the floor of Congress. The orthodoxy of the new opinion was established with the legitimacy of the new science of administration and the nonpartisan goals (economy and efficiency) it sought to achieve.[130] In fact, both parties, in their 1916 platforms, had favored an executive budget system.[131] Indeed, even the intervening shift in political control from one party to the other "had no particular influence on the course of the debate. The matter was not treated as a partisan issue, and final voting reflected virtual unanimity on the essential features of the law."[132]

From the end of the World War to the passage of the Budget and Accounting Act, the voices of the early reformers were lost in the outcry for economy and efficiency.[133] If the academic arguments revolved around the relationship of the executive and the legislature, the debate in Congress concerned the necessity of reducing tax burdens. In 1919 the House appointed a Select Committee on the budget, which followed the lead of the Taft Commission and reported favorably on an executive budget system. The House took favorable action on the report in October 1919; the Senate, preoccupied by the debate on the Versailles Treaty, did not act. It was not until the next session of Congress (May 1920) that the House and Senate both completed action on the bill. There was wide agreement that the budget constituted a means of reducing expenditures and thereby taxes.

The budget measure would have gone into effect in 1920 except for a single difficulty. President Woodrow Wilson, long an advocate of a national budget system, vetoed the bill. It was ironic that Wilson who insisted that the Constitu-

---

[129]Cannon insisted that "when we create a budget committee we should keep it in Congress and as far as possible in the House of Representatives, which is directly responsible to the people on the basis of population. . . . The heads of departments want to make the budget of expenditures and compel Congress to levy taxes according to their plans for expenditure. The pharaohs had that kind of a budget system, and so have the Czars of Russia. It was not the system embodied in the American Constitution. . . . Taxation without representation brought this nation into being, and I think we had better stick pretty close to the Constitution with its division of power well defined and the power close to the people." J.D. Cannon, *The National Budget* (Washington, D.C.: Government Printing Office, 1919), p. 28.

[130]Two recent historians have suggested "the pressure for the adoption of an orderly procedure in the expenditure of public money was essentially not political. . . . Indeed, it did not originate among politicians." Eugene P. Trani and David C. Wilson, *The Presidency of Warren G. Harding* (Lawrence: Regents Press of Kansas, 1977), p. 61.

[131]Cf. Frederick A. Cleveland and A. E. Buck, *The Budget and Responsible Government* (New York: Macmillan Co., 1920), p. 358.

[132]Fritz Morstein Marx, "The Bureau of the Budget: Its Evolution and Present Role," *American Political Science Review*, 39 (August 1945), p. 656.

[133]Burkhead noted that "the arguments for strengthening the executive functions as a means of strengthening popular government, the case for the budget as an instrumentality of responsible and responsive government—these arguments were heard less often." *Government Budgeting*, p. 26.

tion must be adapted to changing times could not abide a statutory change that appeared to diminish executive authority. As part of the reform Congress had incorporated into the act the establishment of a General Accounting Office headed by a Comptroller General. The law allowed the Comptroller General to be appointed by the president, but prohibited the president from removing him. On the constitutional ground that the appointment and removal power could not be separated, Wilson exercised his veto power.[134] In placing the Budget Bureau under executive direction and the General Accounting Office under legislative control, Congress had attempted to distinguish between the executive and legislative aspects of fiscal management.

It was not until the following year, 1921, with Warren G. Harding in the White House that the Budget and Accounting Act was ensured passage (in nearly the same form as the vetoed bill of Wilson). "On June 10, marking an end to a 130-year dispute over the meaning of the separation doctrine and the spending prerogative, Warren G. Harding signed the Budget and Accounting Act."[135]

How did such a significant reform gain acceptance with so little partisan controversy? It was commonly recognized at the time as a major reform: President Harding himself, on presenting the first budget, suggested this system was "the beginning of the greatest reformation in governmental practice since the beginning of the Republic."[136] What appeared to pave the way for such a reform was the shift in the respectability of the opinion that the president had a positive responsibility for the conduct and control of the administration.[137] As W. F. Willoughby noted in his testimony in Congress:

> The fundamental principle at issue is that of establishing definite responsibility upon some offices of the government for the formulation of a budget . . . . It seems

---

[134]In his veto message he claimed, "it has always been the accepted construction of the Constitution, that the power to appoint officers of this kind, carries with it, as an incident, the power to remove. . . . I cannot escape the conclusion that the vesting of this power of removal in the Congress is unconstitutional and therefore I am unable to approve the bill." *House Document No. 804*, 66th Cong. 2d sess., 1920, p. 2.

[135]Louis Fisher, *President and Congress*, p. 103.

[136]Cited in Samuel McCune Lindsay, "Our New Budget System," *The American Review of Reviews*, 65 (January 1922), p. 64. One might object that such presidential rhetoric might simply reflect the excitement of the moment—but the passage of time only strengthened this view. Willoughby, writing in 1930 (*Encyclopedia of the Social Sciences*, Edwin R. A. Seligman, ed. [New York: Macmillan, 1930]), p. 42, noted "it has brought about a greater change in the character of the office of president than any which has occurred since the first organization of the government." And Herbert Emmerich, writing in the 1960s, called the Budgeting and Accounting Act "the greatest landmark of our administrative history except for the Constitution itself." *Federal Organization*, p. 40.

[137]This shift, prepared by the Keep Commission and nurtured by the Taft Commission, was reflective of the acceptance of an increased role of government—and established the legitimacy of the claim that the administration is accountable to the executive. It was the beginning of a long period of congruence between the "enlightened" opinion reflected in the Commission and the majority opinion represented by the president.

to me that there can be no doubt that the responsibility must necessarily be placed upon the President. He is the only officer of the administration or executive branch of the Government that is elected, and therefore in a position to be held rigidly accountable by the people, but he is the only officer who represents the Government as a whole as opposed to the parts.[138]

[138]*Hearings Before the Select Committee on the Budget,* House of Representatives, 66th Cong., 1st sess., 1919, pp. 78-79.

Chapter 3

Reorganization and Reform: The Institutionalized Bureaucracy and the Legacy of Liberalism

> Between the idea
> And the reality
> Between the motion
> And the act
> Falls the shadow
>
> *T. S. Eliot,*
> *The Hollow Men*

POLITICS AND ECONOMICS: THE END OF NORMALCY

Woodrow Wilson and the leaders of the Progressive movement placed great faith in the capacity of executives to overcome the inertia caused by the separation of powers. To the extent that government would have positive purposes to pursue, the president as leader of the party would articulate those purposes. In addition, executives would preside over the structures created to administer the new functions of government. At the heart of the debate concerning a positive role for government were budgets and control of the bureaucracy. It was not until the 1930s that this debate was decided in favor of a greater role for government: an outcome shaped largely by Franklin Roosevelt.[1] Roosevelt is often considered the first modern president, the father of the institutionalized

---

[1]Sidney Milkis and Michael Nelson have suggested that "as Americans increasingly came to regard the presidency as the preeminent source of moral leadership, legislative guidance, and public

presidency.[2] The fight over the attempt to develop an administrative capacity within the White House occurred after FDR's reelection in 1936. By this time, it was clear that public spending, or budgets, were a key to the growth of an administrative state.

The full impact of the budget's significance as a social and economic instrument had not been realized immediately upon adoption of a national budget system. The Bureau of the Budget, which had been placed in the Treasury Department, was largely viewed as a device for efficiently managing the money costs of government. As such, it was concerned only with public finance. The new machinery embodied in the Budget and Accounting Act did not lead directly to initiation of the concept of the managerial presidency immediately because the tools were useless without a purpose and a consensus. If the idea of the positive use of governmental power had been made respectable in the Progressive era, particularly in the realm of government regulation through the use of administrative agencies and commissions, a justification for the use of the budget as an economic tool was not forthcoming until the 1930s. The Great Depression provided the conditions for increased expenditure and Roosevelt's reelection in 1936 provided a consensus that enabled the consolidation of those programs into an administrative apparatus to ensure their permanence.

Harold Smith, FDR's director of the Budget Bureau, subsequently noted the importance of the budget as a device to serve the people. He distinguished the prevailing (post-Roosevelt) view of the budget from that of an earlier period:

> If a budget had existed as such 150 years ago, it would have been a small budget, consistent with the precept that "that government is best which governs least." But that conception no longer obtains. We now seem to operate under the precept that "that government is best which serves most. . . ." Certainly government today is a great service enterprise which not only gives protection . . . to individuals, but also undertakes to influence the business cycle in such fashion as to minimize the impact upon our citizens. The budget is the most accurate measure of the significant transition in the responsibility of government.[3]

Smith could have been speaking not only of the budgets of Jefferson or Jackson but of Warren G. Harding or Herbert Hoover as well. The use of the budget as an instrument of social and fiscal policy was a product of the 1930s. Prior to the

---

policy, pressure mounted to increase the size and professionalism of the president's staff. . . ." Roosevelt's "two-year battle for comprehensive administrative reform wrote a new chapter in the longstanding struggle between the executive and the legislature for the control of administration." *The American Presidency: Origins and Development, 1776–1990*, (Washington, D.C.: Congressional Quarterly Press, 1990), pp. 267–268.

[2] See for example, Fred I. Greenstein, ed., *Leadership in the Modern Presidency* (Cambridge, Mass.: Harvard University Press, 1988).

[3] *The Management of Your Government* (New York: McGraw-Hill Book Co., 1945), p. 73.

New Deal "the traditional function of the budget—expenditure control—had not yet become an adjunct of economic management."[4]

Throughout the 1920s the use of the Bureau of the Budget was compatible with the view that budgeting was an activity separate from politics. It was an administrative tool to secure the goals of economy and efficiency. As Charles G. Dawes, the first budget director (appointed by Harding) observed:

> One must remember that the Bureau of the Budget is concerned only with the humbler and routine business of government. Unlike cabinet officers, it is concerned with no question of policy, save that of economy and efficiency.[5]

In his first message to the agencies, Dawes demanded that "the Budget Bureau must be impartial, impersonal and non-political."[6] The emphasis was on economy for the sake of efficiency, and both parties throughout the 1920s campaigned under this banner. The orthodoxy, both political and intellectual, was that increased public expenditures should be avoided. Rather than becoming a primary tool of government intervention, the budget remained a mechanism for the good management of the revenues at hand.

But economy and a low level of public expenditures had been defended not only on the grounds of efficient management but on moral grounds as well. Calvin Coolidge was perhaps the last Republican president to defend the maintenance of the distinction between the political and economic realm as necessary for the preservation of individual liberty. As a result, economy was not merely a technical problem but a moral problem. As he noted in his Inaugural address:

> The policy that stands out with the greatest clearness is that of economy in public expenditures with reduction and reform of taxation. The principle involved in this effort is that of conservation. I favor the policy of economy, not because I wish to save money, but because I wish to save people. [Those] who toil are the ones who bear the cost of the Government. . . . Economy is idealism in its most practical form.[7]

The questions of taxation and expenditures, Coolidge noted,

> involve moral issues. . . . We need not concern ourselves much about the rights of property if we faithfully observe the rights of persons. Under our institutions their rights are supreme. . . . The very stability of our society rests upon production and conservation. For individuals or for government to waste and squander their resources is to deny these rights and disregard these obligations. The result of economic dissipation to a nation is always moral decay.[8]

---

[4]Aaron Wildavsky, *Budgeting, A Comparative Theory of Budgetary Processes* (Boston: Little Brown & Co., 1975), p. 254.

[5]*The First Year of the Budget of the United States* (New York: Harper & Bros.) p. xi.

[6]Cited in Vincent J. Browne, *The Control of the Public Budget* (Washington, D.C.: Public Affairs Press, 1949), p. 92.

[7]March 4, 1925, J. D. Richardson, ed., *Messages and Papers of the Presidents* (New York: Bureau of National Literature, 1926), vol. 18, p. 9486.

[8]Ibid., p. 9487.

It was becoming increasingly difficult to regard problems of economy and individual liberty in this manner. The Republican Party was not unanimous in its commitment to a system of free enterprise (especially in unrestricted form). Nor was there agreement concerning the absence of any governmental role in the economy. The split in the party's views concerning the role of government in the society could be seen in the controversy occasioned by the appointment of Herbert Hoover to the cabinet of Warren G. Harding.[9] Hoover's appointment as Secretary of Commerce exacerbated differences between the "old guard" (Senators Lodge and Penrose) and the new elements of the party represented by Hoover. The "old guard" considered Hoover a liberal and the split was indicative of the antagonism between the new managerial and progressive view, which was not incompatible with the new scientific spirit, and the old belief in laissez-faire.[10]

But Hoover's liberalism must not be judged by the same criteria as the later liberalism that was decisively altered by the New Deal. What distinguished Hoover's liberalism was his opposition to centralized administration. He was fearful of the coercive capacity of big government as well as big business. As he noted in his last speech of the 1928 election campaign:

> Every step of bureaucratization of business in our country poisons the very roots of liberalism—that is political equality, free speech, free assembly, free press and equality of opportunity. It is the road not to more liberty but to less liberty. Liberalism should be found not striving to spread bureaucracy but striving to set bounds to it.[11]

But the moral authority upon which the old system of free enterprise rested was curiously neutralized by the managerial conception that lay at the heart of Hoover's view. The individualism was no longer absolute, nor was the freedom.[12]

> The conservatism of the Old Guard centered on a faith in the old, entrepreneurial, laissez-faire doctrine. The liberalism of Hoover was founded on a new conception of industrial development. This conception rested on a commitment to stability in the

[9] Hoover had noted as early as 1920 that government regulation of public utilities was "proof of the abandonment of the unrestricted capitalism of Adam Smith." Cited in Herbert Stein, *The Fiscal Revolution in America* (Chicago: University of Chicago Press, 1969), p. 7.

[10] Herbert Stein suggests, "Hoover was the most important representative of the belief in the deliberate application of thought to social problems." Ibid. For other views of Hoover's use of scientific organization and management, see Barry D. Karl, "Presidential Planning and Social Science Research: Mr. Hoover's Experts," in *Perspectives in American History*, vol. 3, pp. 397–409; Otis Graham, *Toward a Planned Society* (New York: Oxford University Press, 1976), pp. 3–8; and Richard Rose, *Managing Presidential Objectives* (New York: The Free Press, 1976), pp. 38–39.

[11] "The New Day" speech delivered October 22, 1929, cited in Henry S. Commager, *Documents of American History*, 8th ed. (New York: Appleton-Century-Crofts, 1963), p. 224.

[12] As Hoover expressed it, "the very essence of equality of opportunity and of American individualism is that there shall be no domination by any group or combination in this republic, whether it be business or political. On the contrary, it demands economic justice as well as political and social justice. It is no system of laissez-faire." Ibid., p. 224.

economy, fostered through cooperation between the business sector and government.[13]

Peri Arnold goes so far as to suggest that Hoover, not Franklin Roosevelt, "is the father of modern public policy. . . . He provided the official rationale and organization for a public policy that brought government into areas once deemed wholly private. He . . . became the father of big government." Hoover's conception required a voluntarism among competing interests that was to be the hallmark of a later pluralism. As Arnold suggests:

> He viewed government as threatening evil because it was coercive. The ultimate democratization of government would be the minimization of that coercive capability of government. Hence his commitment was not to the limitation of the role of government but to controlling government through functional representation within the bureaucracy. He sought a system whereby those interests affected by public policy would have a major role in its formulation.[14]

Hoover was a technocrat and, like Alfred Sloan of General Motors, he considered himself a manager. Above all, good management required a smoothness in operation of the machinery of government and the economy.[15] His policy was based on a partnership between government and private groups.[16] Hoover's dislike of the coercive aspect of government prompted him to mistrust the harsh reality of the use of power. In this regard he was not too dissimilar from the liberals of a later time.[17]

If Hoover believed that the government had a positive role in minimizing tensions by fostering a stability in the economy through the cooperation of the business sector and the government, he could not take the decisive step of creating a large public sector. The old view that public expenditure is harmful to the public welfare was still powerful. Unlike the liberals of a later period, Hoover did not attempt to disguise the use of governmental power under the guise of "doing good things." His skepticism concerning the use of power prevented the leadership in the executive branch that would be decisive in the

---

[13]Peri Ethan Arnold, "Herbert Hoover and the Continuity of American Public Policy," *Public Policy*, 20 (Fall 1972), p. 526.

[14]Ibid., p. 536.

[15]Arnold suggests that Hoover "represented a new stage of industrial capitalism. . . . The great drive was toward the minimization of competition and the maximization of stability and order." Ibid., p. 529.

[16]He was, says Arnold, "a pluralist *par excellence*, and he sought to weld government to group interests through the structure of policy formation," Ibid., p. 527.

[17]This can be seen in an interesting exchange concerning the *End of Liberalism;* Harvey C. Mansfield, Jr., in his review of the Theodore Lowi book of that title, noted: "In plainer language [liberals] need a disguise for the harsh reality. . . . This is Lowi's most interesting point to see why liberalism is compelled to disguise its use of power." Lowi replied: "Disguises and deceits are for those who seek to use government coercively yet maintain consent. [Liberals are those who] do not want to use government coercively and who operate on faith that coercion can be avoided. . . . The mark of the modern liberal is displacement, not deceit. . . . They only want to achieve good things." Mansfield, review in *Public Policy*, 18 (Fall 1970): 618, 620; and Lowi in *Public Policy*, 19 (Winter 1971), p. 207.

creation of a large public sector.[18] Hoover presented the spectacle of a man fatally drawn to the new sciences that undercut the authority of the old morality and left in its place a neutrality that, when confronted with a situation in which there was no guide to action, could not justify any action.[19]

Calvin Coolidge, not Herbert Hoover, was the last president to attempt to maintain a distinction between the political and the economic realm. He considered the separation of powers to be necessary for the maintenance of political freedom, and the separation of politics and economics to be necessary for individual liberty.

> When we contemplate the enormous power, autocratic and uncontrolled, which would have been created by joining the authority of government with the influence of business, we can better appreciate the wisdom of the fathers in their wise dispensation which made Washington the political center of the country and left New York to develop into its business center. They wrought mightily for freedom.[20]

Coolidge, unlike Wilson or Hoover, did not regard the laws of science or history as of decisive importance. Rather, he noted in his inaugural address: "We must realize that human nature is about the most constant thing in the universe. . . . We must frequently take our bearings from these fixed stars of our political

[18]Hoover's contribution to the implementation of the managerial presidency occurred in his role as chairman of the Hoover Commission, in which he played a leading part in legitimizing that view and obtaining for it a bipartisan support. Peri Arnold notes that he "was able to depoliticize the office by equating the president's role with any other essentially managerial function. The presidency . . . became an organizational problem and was thus disassociated from the ideological problems of the New Deal." Arnold cites budget director James Webb's memorandum to Truman: "Based on my relation with Mr. Hoover, I believe there is now a possibility of getting the last Republican President to urge you to accept an implementation of an organization for executive responsibility that the Republican party has historically denied to Presidents.", p. 60. Arnold suggests that "through Hoover . . . the whole Republican party was brought to share the assumption and grant the legitimacy of the expansive, institutionalized Presidency". "The First Hoover Commission and the Managerial Presidency", *Journal of Politics,* 38 (February 1976), p. 64. See also Peri Arnold, *Making the Managerial Presidency* (Princeton: Princeton University Press, 1986) especially Chapter 5.

[19]From a post-Keynesian perspective, it could be argued that Hoover's insistence on a balanced budget was not unreasonable. It was the growth of the public sector itself with the increased use of government expenditures that provided a rationale for the development of fiscal policy. James R. Schlesinger subsequently noted, "the case for the annually balanced budget is at its strongest when the public sector accounts for a fairly small proportion of national income, for under such circumstances it may be argued that the nation's fiscal policy will have slight effect on economic conditions . . . and balancing of the budget is the most appropriate policy. As the size of the public sector increased, the case for attempting to an annual balancing of the budget weakens while the case for compensatory finance grows correspondingly stronger. For, in periods of recession when aggregate demand is already declining, the attempt to balance the budget either through the reduction of government expenditures or through the increase of tax rates tends to bring further diminution of aggregate demand. "Emerging Attitudes Toward Fiscal Policy," *Political Science Quarterly,* 77 (March 1962), pp. 3–4.

[20]Coolidge observed that "the great cities of the ancient world were seats of both government and industrial power, . . . in the modern world . . . political life and industrial life flow on side by side, but practically separated from each other." Cited in Paul A. Carter, *Another Part of the Twenties* (New York: Columbia University Press, 1977), p. 175.

universe."[21] The political star from which Coolidge appeared to take his bearing
was Lincoln. "To me," he said, "the greatness of Lincoln consisted very
largely of a vision by which he saw more clearly than the men of his time the
moral relationship of things. His great achievement lay in bringing the different
elements of his country into a more truly moral relationship."[22] For Coolidge,
political progress did not depend upon new institutions or new social theories,
but on the firm foundation of individual character and the security of individual
liberty.[23] If Coolidge was content to remain within the moral horizon of Lincoln,[24] his successor, Franklin Roosevelt, sought to create a new moral horizon.
Consequently, he used executive leadership and a new electoral majority to
establish a new moral purpose based not so much on the character of the individual nor even upon the character of the leadership, but on the commitment to
a common purpose that grew out of a common need.[25]

In subsequent years, the necessity of centralized economic planning to secure economic liberty—and ensure social justice—led to the creation of a large
public sector that tended to obscure the distinction that was central to liberalism, the distinction between the public and private realms, or between the state
and society. Indeed, the poet Archibald MacLeish would write:

> We live . . . in a revolutionary time in which the public lip has washed in over the
> dikes of private existence as sea water breaks over into the fresh pools in the spring
> tides till everything is salt. . . . The public world with us has become the private
> world, and the private world has become the public.[26]

It would become increasingly difficult to maintain a distinction between the economic and political realm as well. At the heart of economic liberty lies private
property. At the center of political liberty (limited government) is the separation
of powers with its checks and balances, but the two must be mutually reinforcing.
It is doubtful that the separation of powers could remain a viable means of
preserving individual liberty in the absence of a significant private sector.

> The most meaningful detail . . . for a balanced power arrangement lay outside the
> Constitution. . . . The Constitution did not specify how economic power was to be

---

[21]*Messages and Papers,* p. 9481.

[22]Ibid., p. 9367.

[23]"Character is the only secure foundation of the States; without it," Coolidge suggested, "all
plans for improving the machinery of government, all measures for social betterment fail. . . . The
moral force of Lincoln is with us still." Lincoln Day Speech. Ibid., pp. 9378–9379.

[24]He noted that "the essence of a republic is representative government" and he looked to
Congress as primary in the security of the rights and interests of the people. Ibid., p. 9488.

[25]As he noted in his first Inaugural Address, "We now realize as we have never before, our
interdependence on each other; that we cannot merely take, but we must give as well; that if we are
to go forward we must move as a trained and loyal army willing to sacrifice for the good of a
common discipline. . . . We do not distrust the future of essential democracy. The people of the
United States have not yet failed. In their need they have registered a mandate that they want direct,
vigorous action. They have asked for discipline and direction under leadership. They have made me
the present instrument of their wishes." *The Public Papers and Addresses of Franklin D. Roosevelt,*
compiled by S. I. Rosenman (New York: Random House, 1938), vol. 2, pp. 14–15.

[26]Archibald MacLeish, *A Time to Speak* (Boston: Houghton-Mifflin Co. 1941), pp. 62, 88.

distributed. . . . Whether they [the Framers] wanted the future to be ruled by commercial and industrial interests or by small farmers, they all agreed that the private person and not the state was to organize production and distribution.[27]

The end of liberalism would occur when the distinction between the public and the private was completely abandoned.

A NEW DEAL

Shortly after he was elected president in 1932, and prior to his inauguration, Franklin Roosevelt spoke of his conception of the presidency:

> The Presidency is not merely an administrative office. . . . It is more than an engineering job, efficient or inefficient. It is pre-eminently a place of moral leadership. All the great Presidents were leaders of thought at times when certain historic ideas in the life of the nation had to be clarified. Isn't that what the office is—a superb opportunity for reapplying in new conditions, the simple rules of conduct to which we always go back? Without leadership alert and sensitive to change, we are all bogged up or lose our way.[28]

What historic idea did Roosevelt seek to embody through his leadership and control of the Democratic Party? He proclaimed the moral problem in his first Inaugural Address as the failure of vision of a generation of self-seekers:

> And when there is no vision the people perish. The money changers have fled from their high seats in the temple of our civilization. We may now restore that temple to the ancient truths. The measure of the restoration lies in the extent to which we apply social values more noble than mere monetary profit.[29]

That idea in its germinal form had been expressed in his acceptance speech, from which his administration derived its name. "I have described the spirit of my programs a 'new deal' which is plain English for a changed *concept* of the duty and responsibility toward *economic* life"[30] (emphasis added). If Roosevelt did not know in the beginning what the best course of action would be to accomplish a renewed responsibility to economic life, he was at least willing to act.[31] In attempting to commit the national government to a positive role in the

---

[27]Sydney Hyman, *The American President* (New York: Harper & Brothers, 1954), p. 242.

[28]Roosevelt noted that "Washington personified the idea of Federal Union. Jefferson practically originated the party system as we know it by opposing the democratic theory to the republicanism of Hamilton. Two great questions of our government were forever put beyond question by Lincoln. . . . Theodore Roosevelt and Woodrow Wilson were both moral leaders, each in his own way, and for his own time, who used the Presidency as a pulpit." *New York Times,* 13 November 1932, section 8, p. 1.

[29]*The Public Papers,* vol. 2, p. 12.

[30]Ibid., vol. 1, p. 782.

[31]Roosevelt insisted that "the country needs and, unless I mistake its temper, the country demands bold persistent experimentation." Quoted in William E. Leuchtenburg, *Franklin Roosevelt and the New Deal* (New York: Harper & Row, 1963), p. 5.

economic life of the nation, Roosevelt sought to extend the authority of the people against the defilers of the temple of liberty. He, like Wilson, regarded leadership as necessary to provide the principles that could legitimize the authority of the party, through which he sought not only to rule the government, but to lead and shape the opinion of the majority.

In the early years of his administration, Roosevelt had no guide, either intellectual or political, for the means to attain his goal. His actions were tentative, relying on the accepted truths of the necessity of a balanced budget and the demands imposed by an extraordinary situation.[32] Roosevelt had yet to discover what Burkhead has called "one of the most important aspects of a public budget . . . its use as an instrumentality in the management of a nation's economy."[33] But the increase in activity of government and the concomitant growth in public expenditures soon indicated that public finance and public budgeting provided greater possibilities for management and control than mere disbursement of funds through the Treasury Department. "The emergence of the term fiscal policy is generally attributable to the relative and absolute growth of the public sector."[34]

This distinction between public finance and fiscal policy "is a direct product of the anti-depression experience of governments in the 1930s and the writings and influence of John Maynard Keynes."[35] Keynes had argued that a nation could suffer as much from an absence of effective demand as from a lack of adequate supply.[36] Practically all modern depressions in advanced countries are due to a failure in demand—"goods without a buyer."[37] Keynes attempted to give an adequate explanation of the "paradox of poverty in the midst of plenty" in *The General Theory of Employment, Interest and Money,* in which he argued that aggregate economic activity can be controlled by the proper use of government power.[38]

---

[32]Cf. Lawrence Pierce, *The Politics of Fiscal Policy Formation* (Pacific Palisades: Goodyear Publishing Co., 1971).

[33]Burkhead, *Government Budgeting,* p. 59.

[34]Ursula Hicks, *British Public Finance* (London: Oxford University Press, 1954), p. 141.

[35]Burkhead, *Government Budgeting,* p. 60.

[36]He observed that "if our poverty were due to famine or earthquake or war—if we lacked material things and the resources to produce, we could not expect to find the means to prosperity except in hard work, abstinence and invention." But, he suggested, "our predicament is notoriously of another kind." J. M. Keynes, *The Means to Prosperity* (New York: Harcourt, Brace & Co., 1933), p. 3.

[37]Ibid., p. 136.

[38]The failure of demand could be remedied and "the propensity to consume"—the effective demand from consumption—could be greatly increased by a transfer of funds from the rich to the poor. Harlan McCracken notes that "public policy, from the progressive income tax, to welfare, unemployment benefits . . . tend to increase the effective demand of the poor." *Keynesian Economics in the Stream of Economic Thought* (Baton Rouge: Louisiana State University Press, 1961), p. 138. But one problem to be solved was the high rate of savings, which resulted from the emphasis in the United States on individualism. The necessity to remain self-sufficient resulted in an unnecessary savings, which hindered consumption. Modern social legislation (such as old-age pensions, sickness and accident benefits, etc.) relieves the individual of savings against a rainy day.

The link to the establishment of government as an economic force was the use of fiscal policy, public expenditure, and the national budget as stabilizing devices in the economy as a whole.[39] It could be said that the primary political objective was the creation of a significant national or public economic sector—as a counterweight to the private sector—in order to secure a balance.[40] The means of establishing the public sector as a significant force was through the expanded use of the federal budget.[41] The budget

> is the nerve center of the public economy. Its role can be compared with that played by the market place in the private sector of the economy. In the private sector decisions about what goods and services are to be produced . . . are determined by the actions of the people in their capacity as consumers, workers, entrepreneurs, and financiers. . . . In the public sphere, decisions about what goods and services are to be produced, who will receive benefits, and who will pay for the goods and services are largely made by the political mechanism.[42]

The free market of Adam Smith, it was argued by the New Dealers, had forever disappeared, if it had ever existed. "The cat is out of the bag," Rexford G. Tugwell noted. "There is no invisible hand. There never was. . . . We must now supply a real and visible guiding hand to do the task which that mythical, non-existent invisible agency was supposed to perform, but never did."[43]

It was recognized from the beginning that the formulation of fiscal policy could be a potential source of great division, or a powerful tool for executive centralization and planning, for it was both a technical device and an important means to ensure social goals.[44] In 1938, in the midst of the struggle to reorganize Roosevelt's government, Pendleton Herring noted that

> the formulation of fiscal policy lies in the dead center of democratic government. It is the very essence into which is distilled the conflict between the haves and the

---

McCracken notes, as a result "more dependence is placed on the state than on individual savings and thrift. Therefore the propensity to consume would appear to have shifted upward." Ibid., p. 139.

[39]See Gerald Colm, "Fiscal Policy and the Federal Budget," in *Essays in Public Finance and Fiscal Policy* (New York: Oxford University Press, 1955), p. 192.

[40]William Leuchtenburg has noted that "the word that appears most frequently in the writings of the New Deal theorists is 'balance'. . . . They believed that the best society was one in which no important element held preponderant power." *Franklin Roosevelt*, p. 35.

[41]Arthur N. Holcombe noted that Budget Director Harold Smith "repudiated the 'watchdog of the treasury' view of the Bureau's function. . . . The new role of the executive budget, he believes, should be to implement democracy." *Public Administration Review*, 1 (Spring 1941), p. 225.

[42]Gerald Colm, "The Government Budget and the Nation's Economic Budget," in *Essays in Public Finance*, pp. 258–259.

[43]Rexford G. Tugwell, *The Battle for Democracy* (New York: Columbia University Press, 1935), p. 213.

[44]Among the uses of fiscal policy, George Galloway noted, are "the determination of the source, volume, and forms of public revenues and (expenditures); . . . the smoothing out of the inequalities of wealth in the community and expenditures as instruments of economic and social policy." *Planning for America* (New York: Henry Holt, 1941), p. 617.

have-nots. Utterly divergent economic forces are seeking to control the financial machinery of government to promote their own ends.[45]

Fiscal policy was not merely an economic tool devoid of political and social consequences. Even Keynes had indicated that a political purpose lay at the base of his economic doctrine; it was "to combine three things, economic efficiency, social justice, and individual liberty."[46] It is not surprising, even in the so-called revolutionary work *The General Theory,* that Keynes returns in the final chapter to those three things.[47] Moreover, Keynes was aware of the power of ideas in accomplishing political objectives.

> Soon or late, it is ideas, not vested interests, which are dangerous for good or evil. . . . The ideas of economists and political philosophers are more powerful than is commonly understood. Indeed the world is ruled by little else. I am sure that the power of vested interests is vastly exaggerated compared with the gradual encroachment of ideas.[48]

Those ideas went far in legitimizing political purposes under the guise of scientific and technical neutrality.

ROOSEVELT AND REORGANIZATION: THE SCIENCE OF MANAGEMENT

Prior to the election of 1936, the practical conduct of government affairs had provided Roosevelt with sufficient experience in economic matters to seek a new and positive course, but he needed a mandate from the electorate to embark the country upon that course. He was not likely to propose a radical change—which would entail a collision with Congress—with a slender majority. A large electoral victory in that year seemed essential to ensure his purpose.[49] Paul Conklin has suggested this election

> came as close to a plebiscite as any other in American history. Roosevelt was clearly the issue. . . . With more success than any preceding politician, he convinced most of those who voted for him that he was for the people. . . . His programs were their programs; his enemies their enemies.[50]

[45]Pendleton Herring, "The Politics of Fiscal Policy," *Yale Law Journal,* 47 (March 1938), p. 728.

[46]"Liberalism and Labor," (1926); quoted in Hyman P. Minsky, *John Maynard Keynes* (New York: Columbia University Press, 1975), p. 147.

[47]*Collected Writings of John M. Keynes* (London: Macmillan Co. 1973), vol. 7, p. 372. This chapter was titled "Concluding Notes on the Social Philosophy Towards Which the General Theory Might Lead."

[48]Keynes, *Collected Writings,* vol. 7, p. 384.

[49]Paul Conklin, a historian of the New Deal, has suggested that "Roosevelt's 1936 campaign could be compared only with that of Jackson in 1832. . . . He announced no dramatic new policies or programs. It was a highly personal appeal, in which he asked voter approval primarily for himself. . . . He played on old fears, capitalized on immediate gratification, exploited future hopes. *The New Deal* (New York: Thomas Y. Crowell, 1975), p. 81.

[50]Ibid., p. 82.

In the wake of this huge electoral victory, Roosevelt thought it politically feasible to begin the task of consolidating the purposes of the "new deal." By 1936, Roosevelt "finally understood that reorganization was the key to governmental effectiveness."[51] If the electoral mandate was deemed a fulfillment of the requirement of consent, it was thus necessary to use the tools of management to bring the administrative apparatus under executive control. Roosevelt's "decision to reorganize the structure of government signified that mammoth growth was over. By 1936, he wished to consolidate what had already been done."[52] His commitment to reorganization stemmed from his experience in the Wilson administration.

Since Theodore Roosevelt, nearly every president had asked for authority to reorganize the government. FDR, like the rest, had considered this an executive task. But unlike the others who sought to achieve economy as the primary goal of reorganization, Roosevelt did not. "We have got to get over the notion that the purpose of reorganization is economy," he told Louis Brownlow. "The reason for reorganization is good management."[53] Roosevelt knew that a restrictive view of government activity prevented the acceptance of the role he had come to assume concerning the use of the public budget and fiscal policy, and the expanded necessity of centralized planning in the economy.[54] Roosevelt, on the one hand, wanted to embody his political objectives in the governmental machinery itself; on the other, he wished to provide them with a neutrality and a stable authority, which would have the effect of blunting partisan criticism and lessening the institutional tension imposed by a strict adherence to the theory of the separation of powers. In looking to administration, Roosevelt had come to accept Woodrow Wilson's criterion of efficiency as the key to such neutrality. The survival of democratic government might depend upon the extent to which efficiency could be made compatible with constitutional government. As Louis Brownlow observed, "At the root of the distrust of democratic institutions . . . is the fear that popular government cannot hope to be efficient."[55]

The success of the New Deal could be dependent upon the extent to which executive leadership could be institutionalized on the neutral ground of administration; this would ameliorate the fragmentizing tendencies created by the sepa-

[51]Otis Graham, *Toward a Planned Society* (New York: Oxford University Press, 1976), p. 60.

[52]Richard Polenberg, *Reorganizing Roosevelt's Government* (Cambridge: Harvard University Press, 1966), p. 191.

[53]Louis Brownlow, *A Passion for Anonymity* (Chicago: University of Chicago Press, 1958), p. 382.

[54]Polenberg suggests that "what distinguished Roosevelt's conception of reorganization from that of his predecessors was his objective rather than the means he employed. Other presidents had considered reorganization an executive responsibility, but their aim had consistently been the reduction of expenditures. Roosevelt disagreed. He believed that the true purpose of reorganization was improved management, which would make administration more responsive to the national interest and better able to serve that interest." *Reorganizing Roosevelt's Government*, p. 7.

[55]*The President and the Presidency* (Chicago: Public Administration Service, 1949), p. 136.

ration of powers.[56] The means of reducing this fragmentation involved a rigidity of interpretation concerning constitutional doctrine. Public administration is regarded as exclusively the province of the executive branch "where the work of government is done."[57] Politics and administration are regarded as separate functions, "the combination of which cannot be undertaken within the structure of administration without producing inefficiency."[58] Efficiency is to be the single overriding and unifying goal of organization and administration. As Luther Gulick noted, "Efficiency is thus axiom number one in the value scale of administration. This brings administration into apparent conflict with the value scale of politics, whether we use that term in its scientific or popular sense."[59] But the conflict is only apparent; when there is broad agreement concerning the ends of politics, the means become the dominant focus. The orthodox theory of scientific management considered the "execution of policy to be a matter for professional, technically trained, nonpartisan career managers."[60] The administrative realm, strengthened and centralized under a unified executive authority, offered a means of overcoming the fragmentary effect of the separation of powers. Not only would a centralized administration allow unified political control, it would provide a means whereby nonpartisan expertise and the tools of scientific management could be used to legitimize its activity. The result would be the subordination of practical political judgment to the technical and theoretical authority of the social sciences.[61]

The "use of social intelligence in the determination of national policy"

[56]Harold D. Smith (FDR's Budget Director) believed that the problem was that "the relationship between the legislative and executive branches largely determines the success or failure of democratic government." "The Budget as an Instrument of Legislative Control and Executive Management," *Public Administration Review,* 4 (Summer 1944), p. 181.

[57]Luther Gulick, "Science, Values and Public Administration," in Luther Gulick and L. Urwick, eds., *Papers on the Science of Administration* (New York: Institute of Public Administration, 1937), p. 191.

[58]Ibid., p. 10.

[59]Ibid., p. 192.

[60]Harold Seidman, *Politics, Position and Power,* 2nd. ed. (New York: Oxford University Press, 1975), p. 6.

[61]The consequence of that subordination, in the discipline of political science, was to reduce the constitutional arrangements to the status of mere formality; the substance of politics and power was said to adhere in the realm of the psychology of decision-making (cf. Chester Barnard, Herbert Simon) and in the informal systems and processes of government and the interplay of social forces (parties and pressure groups). As Gulick noted, "Whether an act is executive or legislative or judicial in character, it is purely an institutional concept, and grows out of the nature of the thing done." A "political act" or a "nonpolitical act" cannot be discovered with reference to the act itself, "but only by an examination of that act in relation to social psychology." Under the guise of concentrating on the facts of politics rather than law, attention was shifted away from the role of the constitutions. As Vile notes, "The general attack upon political theory, which suggested that it was merely the expression of opinion . . . tended to depreciate those theories that historically had been strongly empirical in content. The concern of political studies with the role which political parties and groups play . . . makes it impossible any longer to discuss a theory like that of separation of powers purely in terms of the formal institutions of government." Luther Gulick, "Politics, Administration, and the New Deal," *Annals of the American Academy of Political and Social Science,* 169 (September 1933), p. 62; and Vile, *Constitutionalism,* p. 20.

brought to bear the precepts of the new science of administration upon the practical conduct of government.[62] The separation of politics and administration from Wilson's time onward had at its basis the neutrality of administration, which made it adaptable to the use of scientific techniques and nonpartisan administrators.[63] The goal of that study is efficiency; the means to attain it is good management, and the key to good management is unity in the executive.

THE PRESIDENT'S COMMITTEE
ON ADMINISTRATIVE MANAGEMENT

Roosevelt was primarily a practical man. However, the long-term success of his New Deal required a clarification and justification of his views that would begin a process of informing and shaping public opinion. To accomplish this, he turned once more (as had Theodore Roosevelt and Taft) to the use of a presidential commission to add the authoritative opinion of the academic and scientific community to his endeavor. It appears that Roosevelt was more concerned with the political effects of their counsel than with the truth of their opinions.[64]

Roosevelt's goal was to consolidate the activities of government under executive authority. He hoped to legitimize that goal by using authority and techniques that could establish the neutrality of his management. He appointed the membership of the Committee in March 1936 with Louis Brownlow as chairman and Charles Merriam and Luther Gulick as members.[65] Prior to the election, he was careful to avoid the appearance of having any influence upon the contents of the report. However, in seeking the opinion of experts in the academic disciplines of Political Science and Public Administration, Roosevelt was careful to make clear that he wanted the report to reflect and reinforce his purposes. The Committee could be useful in legitimizing his position by grounding it in an "intellectual opinion" that might be crucial to the implementation of a change in public opinion. In his meetings with Brownlow and Merriam prior to the appointment of the Committee, Roosevelt emphasized that a

[62]"The indispensable condition of success of the New Deal," wrote Charles Merriam, "is effective and unified planning," which would encourage the use of "social intelligence in the determination of national policies." Quoted in Polenberg, *Roosevelt's Government*, p. 16.

[63]"Upon the shoulders of the bureaucrat," Pendleton Herring observed, "has been placed in large part the burden of reconciling group differences." *Public Administration and the Public Interest* (New York: McGraw-Hill Co., 1936), p. 7.

[64]As Richard Neustadt later surmised, "the group was in effect a White House 'chosen instrument.' The committee urged what Roosevelt wanted. They wrote, he edited. In the election year of 1936 he gave them a 'nonpolitical' assignment, administrative management. After his reelection they couched their response in appropriate terms . . . with 'administration' set apart from 'policy' and 'politics.' Roosevelt thought it politic that they should do so. But he took care that their proposals met his purposes which were emphatically . . . political. He wanted to enhance his own capacity to rule. . . ."Approaches to Staffing the Presidency," in Thomas E. Cronin and S. E. Greenberg, eds., *The Presidential Advisory System* (New York: Harper & Row Co., 1969), p. 12.

[65]Under authorization of the First Deficiency Appropriation Act, 1936; see W. B. Graves, *Basic Information on the Reorganization of the Executive Branch* (Washington, D.C.: Commission on Intergovernmental Relations, 1949), pp. 129–204.

broad disagreement between them might jeopardize his whole attempt at reorganization.[66] He made certain that there was agreement on general principles before allowing the Committee to proceed.

Generally speaking, Roosevelt was concerned that the Committee reflect his view that the aim of reorganization was to restore the original constitutional role of the executive as head of the administration. Had he deliberately chosen partisans to undertake this task, it could not have been better. Rather, they brought to their task an authority, the scientific underpinnings of their disciplines, which could rationalize the partisan sentiments of their sponsor. If Roosevelt wanted consent to his proposals, the Committee in its report showed that efficiency was prior to, and the basis of, such consent.[67] Consent requires that the will of any majority must be the foundation for action. If the majority is to rule, its will must be embodied in the machinery and reflected by and administered in the most efficient way. The report states:

> With us the people's will is not merely an empty phrase, it denotes a grave and stern determination in the major affairs of our Nation, a determination which does not intend to be baffled in its basic plans and purposes by any cluttering or confusion in the machinery for doing what it has been deliberately decided to do.[68]

If majority rule is legitimate because it is democratic, so too the legitimacy of the Chief Executive derives from the fact that he is the leader and embodiment of the majority.[69] The Committee viewed the presidency, as had Wilson, as the best instrument to ensure progress by adapting and adopting the opinion of the majority to the conditions and purposes to be achieved at various times.[70] The report suggested that in order to understand the purposes of reorganization it is necessary to look at its ends.

> Too close a view of the machinery must not cut off from sight the true purpose of efficient management. . . . There is but one grand purpose, namely, to make democracy work today in our National Government; that is, to make our government an up-to-date, efficient, and effective instrument for carrying out the will of the

[66]Cf. Polenberg, *Roosevelt's Government*, pp. 11–20.

[67]"The efficiency of government," they wrote, "rests upon the two factors, the consent of the governed and good management." *The President's Committee on Administrative Management* (Washington, D.C.: Government Printing Office, 1937) p. 3. Vincent Ostrom has suggested "the President's Committee indeed affirms the essential theses in Wilson's theory of administration." *Intellectual Crisis*, p. 35.

[68]*President's Committee*, p. 1.

[69]The Committee noted that "the President is indeed the one and only national officer representative of the entire Nation. . . . He is an instrument for carrying out the judgment and will of the people of the nation. . . . He combines the elements of popular control and the means for vigorous action and leadership—uniting stability and flexibility." *Ibid.*, pp. 1–2.

[70]The report noted that "throughout our history we have paused now and then to see how well the spirit and purpose of our Nation is working out in the machinery of every day government with a view to making such modifications and improvements as prudence and the spirit of progress might suggest. Our government was the first to set up in its formal Constitution a method of amendment, and the spirit of America has been from the beginning of our history the spirit of progressive changes to meet conditions. Ibid., p. 2.

Nation. It is for this purpose that the Government needs thoroughly modern tools of management.[71]

Efficient government, therefore, "must be built into the structure of government, just as it is built into a piece of machinery.[72] The principles of efficiency were distilled by the Committee into "canons of efficiency" that required "the establishment of a responsible and effective chief executive as the center of energy, direction, and administrative management."[73] The establishment of appropriate managerial and staff agencies as well as a complete fiscal system was also thought to be necessary.[74] Efficiency is the technology of human choice; it is unconcerned with origins or ends apart from efficiency itself.

The effect of the recommendations, as Richard Neustadt noted, was that the president's Committee "heralded a major innovation in our constitutional arrangements: substantial staffing for the President distinct from other parts of the Executive establishment, in Edwin Corwin's phrase an 'institutional presidency'."[75]

The Committee report suited Roosevelt's purposes well; any changes that were made had been made on his recommendation. On seeing the final copy he commented, "This is grand."[76] In his message transmitting the Committee findings to Congress in January 1937, he stated what he considered to be the justification for increased presidential power:

> In these troubled years of world history a self-government cannot long survive unless that government is an effective and efficient agency to serve mankind and carry out the will of the Nation. A government without good management is a house built on sand. . . . If we have faith in our republican form of government and in the ideals upon which it has rested for 150 years, we must devote ourselves energetically and courageously to the task of making that Government efficient. The great stake in efficient democracy is the stake of the common man.[77]

He wanted to give the executive branch those modern tools of management and an up-to-date organization that would enable it to go forward efficiently. "We

---

[71]Ibid., p. 4.

[72]Ibid., p. 3.

[73]Ibid.

[74]The Report recommended expansion of the White House Staff. In addition, "the managerial agencies of the Government, particularly those dealing with the budget, efficiency research, personnel, and planning, should be greatly strengthened and developed as arms of the Chief Executive. The merit system should be extended upward, outward, and downward to cover all nonpolicy determining posts. The whole Executive Branch of the Government should be overhauled and the present 100 agencies reorganized under a few large departments in which every executive activity would find its place. The fiscal system should be extensively revised in the light of the best governmental and private practice, particularly with reference to financial records, audit, and accountability of the Executive to Congress." *President's Committee*, p. 4.

[75]Neustadt, in Gronin and Greenberg, eds., *The President Advisory System*, p. 11.

[76]Polenberg, *Roosevelt's Government*, p. 21.

[77]*President's Committee*, p. iii.

can prove to the world that American government is both democratic and effective."[78]

Roosevelt was aware that these proposals would be construed as an attempt to increase the powers of the president and, by a revolutionary means, subvert the principle of the separation of powers. He insisted, however, that

> this program rests solidly upon the Constitution and upon the American way of doing things. There is nothing in it which is revolutionary, as every element is drawn from our experience either in government or large-scale business. . . . What I am placing before you is not the request for more power, but for the tools of management and the authority to distribute the work so that the president can effectively discharge those powers which the Constitution now places upon him.[79]

In an important way, Roosevelt assumed that the liberty of the individual was tied to the national government's capacity to provide for the economic welfare of the individual. He did not speak so much of individual freedom as the freedom of "self-government" or the necessity of "national self-government" to ensure that the will and welfare of the majority were well administered. He wished to establish a public authority on a scale commensurate with those few private wills that had embodied themselves in the large-scale financial and industrial corporation. Although Roosevelt implies that government and administration are nearly synonymous, he does not go so far as to suggest that administration is merely a technical problem. "Reorganization," he said, "is not a mechanical task, but a human task, because government is not a machine, but a living organism."[80]

What Roosevelt's message underscored was the fact that the machinery of government, its organization and capacity for good management, was as important to the survival of self-government as the limitations upon the power of government in an earlier period were to individual liberty. As a consequence, the machinery of government itself was increasingly important to the welfare of the majority. The institutions, particularly the executive establishment, were seen as the vehicle for ensuring the welfare of the people. Consequently, the personal motives of the leaders of government were not viewed in a suspicious manner, because they were thought to be beyond reproach. It is not accidental that from FDR to JFK the president was presumed to be the embodiment of what was good in the American system.

In submitting the Committee report to Congress, Roosevelt made it clear

---

[78]Ibid., p. v.

[79]Ibid.

[80]Consequently he noted: "in striving to make our Government more efficient, you and I are taking up in our generation the battle to preserve the freedom of self-government which our forefathers fought to establish and hand down to us. They struggled against tyranny, against nonrepresentative controls, against government by birth, wealth, or class, against sectionalism. Our struggle now is against confusion, against ineffectiveness, against waste, against inefficiency. This battle, too, must be won, unless it is to be said that in our generation national self-government broke down and was frittered away in bad management." Ibid., p. iii.

that he wanted no modification.[81] He did not approach any Congressman in advance to gain support for his proposals. Congress greeted the plan with "sullen silence." Its members were "shocked," "flabbergasted," and "knocked breathless" by its daring nature.[82] Only the proposed plan to pack the Supreme Court some weeks later prevented consideration of the plan. It was not until April 1938 that the plan came to a vote. In the interim it generated a great deal of controversy concerning the proper relationship between the branches of government. At first the plan appeared to be received satisfactorily in the press at large,[83] but when reorganization stalled in Congress public opinion gradually turned against it. When the vote came,

> more than one hundred Democratic Congressmen deserted President Roosevelt to defeat the Executive Reorganization Bill by a vote of 204-196. The defeat of this bill followed six weeks of bitter debate in the House and Senate. The opposition centered on the fact that reorganization would create a presidential dictatorship.[84]

Luther Gulick, a Committee member, was baffled by the failure of Congress to accept these proposals. It was not, he said, "a daring new and original compound of untried theories"; this was the essence of ideas "proven and respectable in the study of Public Administration for a half century."[85]

The failure of the reorganization attempt was not, however, a repudiation of the new science of Public Administration, nor was it a repudiation of Roosevelt's social philosophy. It was the practical operation of the principle of separation of powers that produced the institutional clash. Public opinion is crucial as a support of the president because if it appears that he has the support of the majority, he is in the best position (as the only nationally elected leader) to speak for the majority. If, on the other hand, there appears to be no consensus, the interests of the organized groups are likely to prevail. In the long run, however, the power of those who form opinion may be decisive.[86]

[81]Polenberg, *Roosevelt's Government*, p. 42.

[82]*Ibid.*, p. 28.

[83]This was due largely to Roosevelt's presentation of his views at a press conference on January 11, 1937, which lasted several hours. Polenberg notes that Roosevelt had thoroughly mastered the Committee recommendations, and "in his most engaging manner . . . anticipated the objections he knew would be raised and tried to dispel them. . . . He presented the plan as one consistent with the best American traditions of efficiency." Ibid., p. 29.

[84]Ibid., p. vii.

[85]Ibid., p. 3.

[86]The importance of the Committee to Roosevelt could be seen in the extent to which enlightened opinion could be used to legitimize the political purposes of the New Deal. The authority of those opinion leaders should not be underestimated. As Neustadt observed: "A quarter-century ago, members of our profession dealt with staffing the Presidency as a problem in management. . . . Those students of administration and that politician [FDR] . . . [found themselves in agreement on the premise] that both democratic theory and constitutional prescription put the president, by right, in charge of the Executive establishment as though it were a business corporation and he its chief executive." In Cronin and Greenberg, eds. *The Presidential Advisory System*, Neustadt, p. 24. As a consequence of the report, Otis Graham wrote: "There was a crucial pivot in the American governmental experience, and in the evolution of liberalism itself." Graham, *Planned Society,*

The extent to which authoritative opinion would be decisive could be seen in the response in Congress to the president's proposals. The opposition in the Senate produced its own report. The Byrd Committee Report[87] reflected what the "enlightened opinion" had accepted in principle—the neutrality of administration and the efficacy of efficiency as the end of administration. Its main point of opposition to the president's Committee was that it favored greater use of independent commissions—an implicit recognition that efficiency and technical neutrality could replace partisanship and political control.[88] The argument against executive centralization, though often made as a defense of the principle of the separation of powers, did not involve the strengthening of the legislature, but a greater use of administrative agencies that would be further removed from all political control.

At the bottom of the dispute between the president and Congress, and reflected in the differences between the president's Committee and the Congressional Select Committee, was the trust or mistrust of the power of the majority.[89] The president sought by an articulation of a common purpose to use the majority as a vehicle to ensure that purpose. On the other hand, those who did not share his opinion looked to the legislature and the constitutional separation of powers as a restraint upon presidential power.[90]

---

p. 59. It marked the beginning of mutually reinforcing collaboration between those disciplines and the presidency until the end of the 1960s when the president appeared to desert the liberals in favor of the majority.

[87]This report was compiled by the Brookings Institution; it was titled *Report of the Select Committee to Investigate the Executive Agencies of the Government.*

[88]The report stated that "the movement for executive centralization of administration in the interest of efficiency has gained much headway; but, along with it, the feeling has grown that such centralization may not be altogether safe unless emphasis is given . . . to the protection of the administration from personal or partisan manipulation." *Report of the Select Committee,* p. 10.

[89]Historic ideas in the life of the nation periodically need to be clarified and adapted to changing times, but the legitimacy of those ideas is not ensured by large majorities. Even in the wake of the massive electoral victory in 1936, Roosevelt was unable to ride roughshod over Congress. The separation of powers goes a long way toward ensuring that a majority, to be legitimate, must be constitutional, which is to say it must be reasonable. In the institutional struggles that occur and test that reasonableness, the political rhetoric usually pits the rule of law (as it is articulated in the statutes—or in a rigid Constitutional interpretation concerning the separation of powers) against the legitimacy of the idea embodied in the representative of the majority. The importance of opinion is crucial in such a struggle because acceptance of the legitimacy of that opinion brings about the possibility of success. The separation of powers serves as a practical means of reconciling majority rule—or consent—with animating principles of the regime by tying the legitimacy of the opinion to the forms of the Constitution itself. Majority opinion cannot be separated from an attitude toward equality from which individual liberty derives and from which the legitimacy of majority rule itself derives. Roosevelt viewed the election as having provided a consensus upon which his party could rule; the opposition to that rule embodied itself in the legislature. Ultimately, Roosevelt's success was dependent upon legitimizing his majority with reference to the principle of equality.

[90]Polenberg suggested that "Roosevelt's crusade for executive reorganization enlisted the support of a group of professional administrators and political theorists who shared his social philosophy. . . . They wished to strengthen the Chief Executive and weaken the power of Congressional committees and interests groups to block proposals for federal reorganization. Roosevelt's original effort at reorganization failed—because it did not attract the support of the American people. On the

The organized groups and the Congress only succeeded in blocking the president's plan in a direct confrontation. Despite the failure of 1938 and his partial success in Congress in 1939, after the controversial features of the reorganization bill were removed, Roosevelt's "imaginative use of the limited powers granted in 1939 confounded his critics and gave convincing proof of his administrative genius."[91] In the creation of the Executive Office of the President—by Executive Order 8248—Roosevelt was able to accomplish many of the purposes he had previously intended. It was his view that the presidency needed some managerial resources and an institutionalized capability to accomplish its goals. As a result, the Bureau of the Budget was transferred to the Executive Office (from the Treasury Department) and six administrative assistants were added to the White House Staff.

Luther Gulick considered Executive Order 8248 a "nearly unnoticed but none the less epoch-making event in the history of American institutions."[92] "It is virtually impossible," Clinton Rossiter observed, "to conceive of the Presidency without the Executive Office, so essential has this nexus of administrative machinery become to its proper functioning."[93] It has given an "entirely new cast to the question of executive management in the national government."[94] According to Rossiter, the institutionalized presidency has saved the Constitution from "oblivion" by providing "the only solution to the problem of an eighteenth-century Constitution in a twentieth-century world."[95] The managerial capability of the Executive Office converts the presidency into "an instrument of twentieth-century government."[96]

The creation of the Executive Office of the President is often considered the beginning of the "institutionalized presidency." As a result, it appeared that the president not only began to usurp the prerogatives of the legislature,[97] but also to intervene in economic affairs. As a critic subsequently noted:

In Executive Order 8248, Roosevelt set this country on a completely unchartered course. Other presidents were happy enough to follow his . . . lead. . . . Great and

---

other hand, most pressure groups attacked the plan because it threatened their influence over the government bureaucracy." *Roosevelt's Government*, p. 191.

[91]Ibid., p. 192.

[92]"The Executive Office of the President: A Symposium," *Public Administration Review*, 1 (Winter 1941), p. 101. See also George A. Graham, "The President and the Executive Office of the President," *Journal of Politics*, 12 (November 1950), pp. 599–621.

[93]"The Constitutional Significance of the Executive Office of the President," *American Political Science Review*, 43 (December 1949), p. 1207.

[94]Ibid., p. 1209.

[95]Ibid., p. 1216.

[96]"It assures us," Rossiter insists, "that the presidency, and with it the Constitution of 1787, will survive the advent of the service state." Ibid., pp. 1212–1213.

[97]Robert E. Sherwood suggested that the Executive Office was part of Roosevelt's effort to free himself from congressional scrutiny. *Roosevelt and Hopkins* (New York: Harpers, 1948), p. 258.

infamous events alike have stemmed from this power, including fundamental contri-
butions to our burgeoning apparatus of nonmarket control over economic life.[98]

Nonetheless, the authoritative ratification of Roosevelt's view concerning the
relationship of government and the economy occurred in the legislative branch.
In 1946, Congress passed the Employment Act. This act mandated an economic
planning capacity in the executive branch by creation of the Council of Economic Advisors—and the requirement of the president's annual Economic Report. "This law," Jonathan Hughes suggests, can be categorized as "revolutionary." Unlike the New Deal legislation, "the Employment Act accepts direct
federal responsibility for the level of employment and economic growth. The
responsibility of the Federal Government [is] . . . to promote maximum employment, production and purchasing power. . . . It is the legislative line which
divides modern government of the United States from its past.[99]

Roosevelt's "clarification of the historic idea in the life of the nation" had
involved the necessity of reconsidering the relationship of the "duty and responsibility of Government toward economic life." The partisan and ideological
controversies that subsequently emerged derived from an affirmation or denial
of the legitimacy of that idea. Liberalism and conservatism had come to revolve
around greater or lesser state intervention into the economic and private relationships of individuals.[100] Walter Lippman had noted earlier, in the middle of
the debate over centralized economic planning, that "the first principle of liberalism . . . is that the market must be preserved and perfected as the prime
regulator of the division of labor. . . . When the collectivist abolishes the market place, all he really does is to locate it in the brains of his planning board."[101]
Ultimately, it was a difference concerning the meaning of equality and its implication for liberty that distinguished the older liberals from the new. As Milton
Friedman has argued:

> The nineteenth-century liberal regarded an extension of freedom as the most effec-
> tive way to promote welfare and equality: the twentieth-century liberal regards
> welfare and equality as neither prerequisites of or alternatives to freedom. In the
> name of welfare and equality the twentieth-century liberal has come to favor a
> revival of the very policies of state intervention and paternalism against which

---

[98]Jonathan Hughes, *The Governmental Habit: Economic Controls from Colonial Times to the
Present* (New York: Basic Books, 1977), p. 198.

[99]Ibid., pp. 197–198.

[100]Eric Voeglin has observed this changing relationship. He noted that "in the American political vocabulary liberal generally means, not the European liberalism of the nineteenth century,
which today is considered conservative, but, on the contrary, a politically progressive attitude. Thus
in America the Republican Party is called conservative, but, the Democratic Party, liberal-progressive.
But what is conservative in the Republican Party is its liberalism in the older sense—that is, its
opposition to socialism to excessive state intervention . . . while the Democratic Party is liberal
insofar as its program tends towards the welfare state, state capitalism, and a decided emphasis
upon the interests of the labor unions." "Liberalism and Its History," *Review of Politics,* 36 (October 1974), p. 507.

[101]*The Good Society* (Boston: Little Brown & Co., 1937), pp. 174–175.

classical liberalism fought. . . . The nineteenth-century liberal favored political decentralization. Committed to action and confident of the beneficence of power . . . the twentieth-century liberal favors centralized government.[102]

It was a skepticism concerning the motives and the capacity of men to govern the details of life that prompted the earlier liberals to prefer the free market.

> The attempt to regulate deliberately the transactions of a people multiplies the number of separate, self-conscious appetites and resistances. To establish order among these highly energized fragments . . . a still more elaborate organization is required—but this elaborate organization can be operated only if there is more intelligence, more insight, more discipline, more disinterestedness, than exists in any ordinary company of men. This is the sickness of an over-governed society and at this point the people must seek relief through greater freedom if they are not to suffer greater disasters.[103]

But it was not until the "Great Society" that Lippman's observation in the *Good Society* would be tried and truly tested.

THE NEW ECONOMICS AND THE NEW CLASS

The changes brought about by the New Deal itself had transformed the majority into what was thought to be a middle-class democracy. But a new class was in the process of forming, "a new class," Daniel Moynihan noted, "which is to say persons with a new economic function."[104] This class was both a product of the economic orthodoxy characteristic of the New Deal and the focus of the attempt to radicalize it. It was, said Moynihan,

> at base a technological phenomenon. A post-industrial society needs progressively fewer farmers, fewer factory workers, fewer technicians, proportionate to the available work force; whilst simultaneously it educates an ever larger proportion of its youth at possibly declining . . . levels of competence. Work has to be found, and in the main it is government work, or work paid for by government, or subsidized (as through tax exemptions) by government.[105]

This new class was committed to what Robert Nisbet has called "a conception of equality . . . [which entails] a substantial, even massive and revolutionary, redistribution of income, property, power, status—virtually the whole range of what social scientists call primary social and economic goods."[106] When the increasingly affluent middle class abandoned its commitment to economic and

---

[102]*Capitalism and Freedom* (Chicago: University of Chicago Press, 1962), p. 6.

[103]Lippman, *Good Society*, pp. 39–40.

[104]Moynihan, "Social Policy: From Utilitarian Ethic to Therapeutic Ethic" in Irving Kristol and Paul Weaver, eds., *The Americans: 1976* (Lexington, Massachusetts: Lexington Books, 1976), p. 43.

[105]Ibid., p. 46.

[106]"The Costs of Equality," in Michael Mooney and Florian Stuber, eds., *Small Comforts for Hard Times, Humanists on Public Policy* (New York: Columbia University Press, 1977), p. 34.

social justice, it in turn was abandoned by the new class. The traditional liberal support for the strong presidency was part of a larger commitment to democratizing government and centralizing social reform.

It was the increasing growth of the "affluent society" itself that prompted the demand for a more powerful public sector to attempt to equalize economic conditions. John Kenneth Galbraith in a highly influential book in 1958 provided a solution to the dilemma:

> The community is affluent in privately produced goods. It is poor in public services. The obvious solution is to tax the former to provide the latter. . . . By making private goods more expensive public goods are made more abundant.[107]

Galbraith suggested that "the line which divides our area of wealth from our area of poverty is roughly that which divides privately produced goods from publicly rendered services."[108]

The decade of the 1960s was among the most massive governmental attempts in history to wipe out the "area of poverty in publicly rendered services."[109] The new bureaucratization rested on the assumption that social justice could be achieved by the equalization of the economic, educational, political, and cultural realms.[110] It was dependent for its success on a new administrative class. It was thought that the growth of the welfare state would usher in the truly egalitarian society, i.e., the classless society.[111] The new equality was an attack on liberalism, particularly that of John Locke, which sought to maintain a distinction between the public and private sphere.

In America the desire for the classless society necessarily had to focus on economic inequality because social class distinctions were primarily derivative from wealth and often, therefore, from one's labor. Consequently, it took the form of an assault upon the competitive, capitalistic society that had, by the retention of the principle of natural equality, laid the foundation of social inequality. The social and economic equality demanded by the new class was oblivious to the freedom of the individual, which accompanied the traditional view of equality. It rejected the view that an individual is responsible for and

---

[107] *The Affluent Society* (Boston: Houghton-Mifflin, 1958), p. 315.

[108] Ibid., p. 251.

[109] That it was not concerned with wiping out poverty itself could be seen in Daniel P. Moynihan's book, *Maximum Feasible Misunderstanding: Community Action in the War Against Poverty* (New York: Free Press, 1969).

[110] Cf. Eugene J. McCarthy, "A Note on the New Equality," *Commentary,* 64 (November 1977), p. 53.

[111] Henry Steel Commager recognized this necessity before the "new frontier" or the "great society." "It is inevitable," he noted in 1959, "that there will be an immense growth of the welfare state. . . . The national government will necessarily take on ever larger responsibilities in the realm of conservation, education, science, public health, urban rehabilitation . . . and so forth. The dividing line between "private" and "public" and between "local" and "general" already blurred, will become all but meaningless. Finally, an affluent society, universal education, the welfare state, and a growing awareness of and respect for world opinion should go far to bring about truly classless society in the United States." "Brave New World of the Year 2000," *New York Times Magazine* (November 1, 1959), p. 24.

has the right to the fruits of his own labor. In looking at a society based on the principle of equality it could see only inequality.[112]

This inequality, resulting from the equality of opportunity and resting upon natural distinctions that led to unequal reward in the private sphere, was the most objectionable. As John Rawls noted, "There is no more reason to permit the distribution of income and wealth to be settled by the distribution of natural assets than by historical and social fortunes. No one deserves his greater natural capacity nor merits a more favorable starting place in society."[113] A meritocracy, said Rawls, "follows the principle of careers open to talents and uses equality of opportunity as a way of releasing men's energies in the pursuit of economic prosperity and political domination."[114] It was not merely that the equality of opportunity characteristic of democratic societies supported "the competitive capitalistic spirit"; rather, as John Schaar complained, "it opened more opportunities for more people to contribute more and more energies toward the realization of a mass . . . privatized . . . consumption-oriented society."[115] It was the transformation of the "bourgeois citizen into the bourgeois consumer," that "has dissolved that liberal-individualist framework which held the utopian impulses of modern society under control."[116]

The problem had become one in which political equality as the basis of legitimacy in society led to social inequality. Its effects would persist as long as government rested on the consent of the governed or majority rule. The solution to the problem was to substitute "inequality as the basis of equality in the making of the law."[117] Unlike equality, inequality is not dependent upon consent as an organizing principle to maintain its legitimacy; it depends upon the proper use of force.[118] Consequently that most elaborate rationalization of bureaucratic power, Rawl's *Theory of Justice,* is dependent upon the massive use of govern-

---

[112]Tocqueville has noted: "When inequality of conditions is the common law of society, the most marked inequalities do not strike the eye; when everything is nearly on the same level, the slightest are marked enough to hurt it. Hence the desire of equality always becomes more insatiable in proportion as equality is the more complete." Tocqueville, *Democracy in America,* vol. 2, p. 147.

[113]*A Theory of Justice* (Cambridge: Harvard University Press, 1971), pp. 74, 102. Michael Young, too, had argued, in his *Rise of the Meritocracy* (London: Thames and Hudson, 1958) that the theory of equal opportunity justifies a continuation of a class system that is objectionable because it bases rewards upon productivity and merit, distributed in the private realm. It is a system that is unusually capable of generating wealth. Lester G. Thurow has insisted that such a system not only generates wealth, but inequality as well. Cf. *Generating Inequality* (New York: Basic Books, 1975).

[114]*Theory of Justice,* p. 107.

[115]"Equality of Opportunity and Beyond," in James R. Renrock and John W. Chapman, eds., *Nomos IX, Equality* (New York: Atherton Press, 1967), p. 231.

[116]Moynihan, "Social Policy," in Kristol and Weaver, eds., *Americans,* p. 49.

[117]Wilfred Desan, "Inequality as a Basis of Equality in the Making of the Law," *Philosophy Today,* 20 (Fall 1976), p. 227.

[118]Thus, as Desan has suggested, "in the world of the future there should be no room for *majority rule.* We shall move beyond Locke." Ibid., p. 234.

mental force to accomplish the end of justice, which is primarily the redistribution of wealth and status.[119]

That this newest respectable opinion is inegalitarian at its core can be seen in its denial that consent (and majority rule) plays any part in legitimate government. Majority rule is surely the only organizing principle that is compatible with the rights of individuals, that is, derivative of their natural equality. Although consent is necessary it is not sufficient; its denial, however, is tantamount to the denial of the principle of equality itself. Indeed, it is for this reason that the "right of revolution" had nearly disappeared as a subject of political discourse in America.[120] The reason is clear; "only after establishing the need for government by consent of the governed does the Declaration state the right of revolution."[121]

The destruction of those individual rights that lay at the heart of the distinction between the public and private (which was the hallmark of liberalism) would surely destroy the essence of a constitutional system that, by limiting the power and authority of the government, sought to ensure the autonomy of the individual. The new equality attempted to substitute coercion for consent on the basis of a new kind of political inequality. Moreover, by the denigration of the private, the public is elevated—as the only legitimate source of authority. Every distinction in society is distributed in the public realm. As Rawls proposed, "All social primary goods—liberty and opportunity, income and wealth and the basis of self-respect—are to be distributed equally unless an unequal distribution of any of all these goods is to the advantage of the least favored."[122] The new class was apparently not animated by a democratic passion but by what Tocqueville called an aristocratic passion—successful implementation of which would lead to despotism.

The new class commitment to social justice has placed it unequivocally behind the maintenance of the bureaucratic state, not only as a result of its opposition to a free economy, but also because of its opposition to middle-class morality. Insofar as middle-class values remained strong, there was a reluctance to support excessive public spending. But increasingly, the gulf between the middle class and the new class—which was practically reflected in differences concerning public spending—resulted from a difference in their opinions con-

---

[119]As Robert Nisbet has observed: "the 'new equalitarian' is under no illusion that we will reach the New Equality through representative democracy. . . . It is no doubt for a similar reason that John Rawls does not include majority representation among the central tenets of his equalitarian doctrine of justice." "Costs of Equality," in Mooney and Stuber, eds., p. 44.

[120]As Harvey C. Mansfield, Jr., has noted, "in the two most sophisticated recent restatements of liberal democratic political philosophy [John Rawls' *Theory of Justice* and Robert Nozick's *Anarchy, the State and Utopia*], the right of revolution does not appear at all." "The Right of Revolution", *Daedalus*, 105 (Fall 1976), p. 151.

[121]Ibid., p. 153.

[122]Rawls, *A Theory of Justice*, p. 303.

cerning equality. The one view was compatible with consent and individual rights, the other with coercion and centralized administration.[123]

> Redistribution of income and property is increasingly viewed as the prime purpose and task of government, and this, more than anything else, explains the spectacular growth in domestic public expenditures over the past two decades. To redistribute through the political process the rewards and punishments of the market has become the foremost goal of those who do not believe that a man is entitled to the value of his product, who feel that the allocation of natural talents—of intelligence, inventiveness, judgment, drive, aspiration, persistence— is basically unfair to those less endowed and must be overruled and revised in a more egalitarian direction.[124]

PUBLIC SPENDING AND THE GROWTH
OF THE PUBLIC SECTOR

In viewing the growth of public expenditures in the period during and after the New Deal, it is necessary to distinguish between the acceptance of the legitimacy of increased spending in the public sector and the partisan distinctions that grew out of disputes concerning the purposes of that spending. Opponents of the growing public sector had viewed the line between public and private spending as the dividing line between coercive governmental authority and individual freedom. Consequently, they attempted to keep decision-makers from expanding the public sector at the expense of the free market and the private sphere.[125] If private relations are characterized by the freedom to engage in contracts, the public realm must be distinguished by its coercive necessities. Thus it rests not only on authority, but on the legitimacy of that authority. The New Deal succeeded in destroying the legitimacy of the opinion that private solutions to economic problems were intrinsically preferable to public ones.[126] It enabled,

---

[123]Daniel Moynihan noted at the time that in the twenty years after the publication of Galbraith's work, the public sphere grew dramatically. "Increasingly," he observed, "this has become a world of public affluence and private squalor. Anyone living off the public sector lives well. The professors in local . . . state university branches go abroad for the summer. The state troopers fly to their fishing vacations. The school teachers have good houses and pensions . . . In the meantime, the small farms close down, the filling station attendants live week to week . . . the "bench workers" in local mills worry about tariffs. . . . Any building associated with government is painted and trim; the others tend to sag." Moynihan, "Social Policy," in Kristol and Weaver, eds., *Americans,* p. 47.

[124]Roger Freeman, *The Growth of American Government: Morphology of the Welfare State* (Stanford: Hoover Institution Press, 1975), p. 152.

[125]Gerhard Colm has noted that "the public realm is distinguished by the fact that it rests on authority and, if necessary, even on compulsion, while private relations rest on contract." "Theory of Public Expenditures," *The Annals of the American Academy of Political and Social Science,* 183 (January 1936), p. 1.

[126]Daniel Bell has observed that the New Deal also made "legitimate the idea of group rights and the claim of groups, as groups rather than individuals, for government support. Thus unions

therefore, the creation of a legitimacy for that authority in the public realm. Consequently, "once the principle of positive government in an indeterminable but expanding political sphere was established, criteria arising out of the very issue of principle itself became irrelevant."[127]

William Henry Chamberlain in 1960 attempted to characterize the distinction between the freedom of the marketplace and the coercion characteristic of government (and implicitly the distinction between the public and the private solution to economic problems) as the crucial dividing line between conservatism and liberalism. He suggested that "the level of government spending is perhaps the most clear-cut battlefield between American conservatives and liberals."[128] It was not, however, the level of spending that distinguished them, but the purposes of that spending. After the New Deal, hardly anyone denied the legitimacy of increased public spending. By the end of the 1960s, Chamberlain's statement could have been qualified somewhat to read "the levels of government spending in domestic affairs for social services is the most clear-cut battlefield between liberals and conservatives." Conservatives considered the use of public expenditures in the defense of the nation as a proper use of federal power compatible with individual freedom; social spending was another matter.

But the growth of social spending was not simply a product of the New Deal. Even at the end of the New Deal the greatly increased scope of federal power had been used in a manner not inconsistent with traditional functions of government. Rather, "federal involvement in public services and benefits prior to 1952, including the New Deal of the 1930s, had been relatively small."[129] If the Roosevelt revolution provided the legitimacy of an increased public sector, the increase in the level of public activity was confined to those traditional areas of federal expenditure.[130] The most significant change in the nature of federal expenditures seemed to have occurred in the period between 1952 and 1972.

---

won the right to bargain collectively and, through the union shop, to enforce a group decision over individuals; the aged won pensions, the farmers gained subsidies; the veterans received benefits; the minority groups received legal protection. . . . Similarly, the government has always had some role in directing the economy. But the permanently enlarged role . . . created a vastly different set of powers in Washington than ever before in American history." *The End of Ideology* (Glencoe: The Free Press, 1960), pp. 62–63.

[127]Theodore J. Lowi, *The End of Liberalism: Ideology, Policy and the Crisis of Public Authority* (New York: W. W. Norton, 1969), p. 57.

[128]"State vs. Individual," cited in Freeman, *Growth of American Government*, p. 154.

[129]Ibid., p. 109.

[130]As Roger Freeman observed: "In 1902, 87% of the federal expenditures went for what may be called the traditional federal functions: national defense, international relations, post office, veterans services and benefits, interest on the general debt, financial administration, and general control. All other outlays accounted for a mere 13% of the budget." Half a century later, after two world wars, the Great Depression, and the New Deal, "the share of the other outlays had grown very moderately to 19%." In other words, says Freeman, "until about twenty years ago, the dominant functions of the national government were as they had been for over 160 years—national defense and related programs, ministerial activities . . . and general and financial administration." Ibid., p. 111.

From the creation of the Department of Health, Education, and Welfare to the consolidation of the programs of the Great Society and beyond, those "other outlays" had come to account for a majority of federal spending. By 1972 53% of the federal budget was devoted to income redistribution and the provision of services, largely in the area of social welfare.[131]

In this period (1952-1972) the presidency vacillated between the parties, but the Congress was consistently Democratic. Incumbents were becoming increasingly immune to defeat at the polls. The crucial election that appeared to legitimize the purposes of the new social spending was the election of 1964.[132] If FDR had viewed the 1936 election as a mandate that created the possibility of providing executive leadership in economic affairs, the 1964 election was regarded by Johnson as the mandate to use the entire executive bureaucracy to attain the goal of greater economic equality.[133] This was accomplished, curiously enough, by the large-scale introduction of experts or nonpartisans into the government to set the standards for the Great Society.

The growth in the power of the bureaucracy was not as a result of an increase in the size of the federal bureaucracy, but in its increased ability to set the standards for all levels of government. The real growth in the power of the national administration, consequently, has resulted from an increased centralization.[134] This growth has not appeared primarily in greater numbers of employees in the federal government, nor wholly as a consequence of a significant increase in the functions assumed by the national government. It has occurred through an administrative centralization that mandated an increase of employment at the state and local levels in response to federal directives reinforced by federal grants.[135] The growth in the size of the public work force occurred at the state and local level. The number of persons on the federal payroll declined by nearly one million between 1952 and 1972, while those on state and local payrolls increased by more than six million.[136] By the mid-1970s there was one

---

[131]As Freeman has stated: "Between 1952 and 1972 the national government came to play not only a larger role than it ever had before but also a far different role. Social services and income redistribution, previously of minor significance or unknown, have become the major and controlling elements in the budget and thereby the core function of the United States government." Ibid.

[132]Cf. Philip Converse, Aage Clausen, and Warren Miller, "Electoral Myth and Reality: The 1964 Election," *American Political Science Review*, 59 (June 1965), pp. 321-326. Also, Gerald Pomper, who argued that the 1964 campaign provided a turning point in the growth of public concern with policy questions. "From Confusion to Clarity; Issues and American Voters," *American Political Science Review*, 66 (June 1972), pp. 415-428.

[133]See George Reedy, *Twilight of the Presidency* (New York: The World Publishing Co., 1970), p. 66.

[134]Big government, it seems, is more a phenomenon of the mid-sixties than of the New Deal. It has also become more difficult to distinguish the public and private sphere. Government has developed close relationships with private corporations; see David Guttman and Barry Willner, *The Shadow Government* (New York: Pantheon Books, 1976).

[135]Cf. William Lilley III and James C. Miller III, "The New Social Regulation," *The Public Interest*, 47 (Spring 1977), pp. 49-61.

[136]Freeman, *Growth of American Government*, p. 42.

person working in government for every four in private industry.[137] As Freeman
has observed:

> The 16 million persons drawing their wages from public sources possess, with their
> families, a significant voting power, which they use to exercise influence on pay
> decisions by the legislative and executive branches of the governments they serve.
> It becomes increasingly difficult for officials to vote against higher pay for public
> workers.[138]

In the years following the New Deal and particularly since the Great Society it
has become clear that it was not the executive branch alone that benefited from
increased public expenditures. "One of the features of the period after the
Second World War has been inflation throughout the free world. Another has
been the constant increase in government budgets." William Riker suggests that

> these two phenomena are related to each other through the medium of legislator's
> motives. Reelection depends on taking positions, especially on redistributive issues.
> As a result, the output of contemporary legislatures involved a tremendous increase
> in expenditures, with legislatures giving goodies to everybody in the hope of keep-
> ing their seats.[139]

The old moral authority that had restrained public appetites had been overcome
by a new legitimacy and a new apparatus to conquer the social and economic
effects of inequality. Governments needed no longer to fear inflation; indeed,
inflation may ease the problems of government finance.[140] If increased public
spending grew out of a reconsideration of the necessity for an increased governmental role in the economy, the result of that spending and the administrative
apparatus created by it decisively changed American politics.

The growth of an administrative bureaucracy has transformed the self-
interest of the governed as well as of the governors. The full scope of centralized regulation's profitability is difficult to assess; "the conventional, but still
important example, of the large corporation which fights to be regulated federally" is instructive. Moreover:

> It is no longer true that inflation hits all. Many, who are not necessarily debtors,
> profit from this most common means of financing administrative centralization;
> many workers—especially government workers and elected officials—and all Social
> Security recipients have pay scales that over-anticipate the rise of the cost of living.
> Treasury receipts swell out of proportion with the inflation rate because of fixed,
> progressive income and property tax rates. Also, there are industries, e.g., envi-

---

[137]Ibid.

[138]Ibid., p. 41. This could be seen in the ease with which Congress in 1974 overrode Ford's
decision to postpone federal pay hikes.

[139]Riker, "The Politics of Economics," in Robert Blattberg, ed., *The Economy in Transition*
(New York: New York University Press, 1976), p. 67.

[140]See Sir John Hicks, *A Theory of Economic History* (London: Oxford University Press,
1969), pp. 97–99.

ronmental impact reporting, whose life blood is regulation. No doubt, increasing numbers will profit from national bureaucratization.[141]

This transformation of the self-interest of Americans, as a consequence of the increased federal spending that sustains the bureaucracy, resulted in the "inversion of the New Deal order." Since the mid-1960s "there has been an inversion of the relationship of class to electoral choice from that prevailing in the New Deal era. . . . Groups at the top are more supportive of positions deemed liberal and more Democratic than those at the bottom." Along with the more highly educated—who provided the intellectual attack on middle class values— "the more prosperous strata . . . [are] the most resistant to such changes."[142] The new class that emerged has a vested interest in change and the technology that sustains it.[143]

But the upper class (and the new class that benefits from increased spending) does not sustain a similar hardship in the support of those social programs financed by federal spending as does the middle class. As Everett Carl Ladd suggests,

> the top does not pay a much higher share of its income in taxes than does the lower middle, even though it has much more of a cushion, and the burden of an expanding role for the state has in one sense been borne disproportionately by the lower middle cohorts.[144]

Even labor itself, long the heart of the old Democratic coalition, is split in its support of increased federal spending and greater bureaucratic control.[145] Had the growth in domestic expenditures and the increased bureaucratization been the result of a partisan appeal of the Democratic Party which, according to Lyndon Johnson, had provided such a consensus in the election of 1964? Or had the use of fiscal policy and budgeting techniques obscured the costs of such services to the majority? Since the end of the Coolidge administration in 1929, no American president has, over the period of tenure in office, experienced a net surplus in the federal budget. As Senator Carl Curtis (R-Nebr.) observed:

> We reordered priorities to provide the services of a welfare state, while depriving the voters of the right to assess the costs of those services to them, either in terms of taxes or inflation. Had the increased federal role in the field of social services

[141]John A. Wettergreen, "The American Voter and his Surveyors," *The Political Science Reviewer*, 7 (Fall 1977), p. 224.

[142]Everett Carl Ladd, Jr., "Liberalism Upside Down: The Inversion of the New Deal Order," *Political Science Quarterly*, 91 (Winter 1976–1977), pp. 577, 591.

[143]Cf. Kevin Phillips, *Mediacracy: American Parties and Politics in the Communications Age* (Garden City: Doubleday & Co., 1970). Phillips notes the extent to which the new "knowledge industry" is supportive of social change.

[144]Ladd, "Liberalism Upside Down," p. 591.

[145]Wettergreen suggested, "this is a conflict between those unions whose members' interests are more dependent upon federal spending and those less dependent; that is, between those [who] enjoy a demand for their labor which is relatively independent of government spending and those . . . [who] would not work apart from such spending." "The Free Society After Watergate," *Leviathan*, 1 (February 19, 1975), p. 6.

been financed by equivalent boosts in taxes, the American people would have been fully aware of what was happening. . . . But the primary methods of financing the multiplication of social benefits and services, to the extent to which the added expenditures have exceeded the automatic growth of revenues from economic advance, were (a) budgetary deficits, that is inflation, and (b) a cut to less than half in the share of resources allocated to national security. Deficits incurred in this way carry the false message that we can get something for nothing. Our appetite for private goods is disciplined by the necessity of paying for them. Public services financed by deficits appear to be for free. No wonder government prefers deficit-induced inflation to taxation.[146]

The bureaucracy, like the new class and the Congress itself, has developed a stake in the greater social spending that grew out of the Great Society. "It would be naive to suppose that growth has been impartial: the national bureaucracy is disproportionately Democratic, and no Republican president, however popular, has been able to change this."[147] And the members of Congress have become increasingly dependent upon its continued existence. The Democratic dominance of the legislature, as a result, has come to rest more on providing services for constituents and less on partisan appeals.[148] This has changed the function of the legislature from that of representative of constituencies in the legislature to ombudsman, or pleader of special-interest supporters, against the requirements of bureaucracy.[149] Regardless of party, the legislature has developed a self-interest in the maintenance of the bureaucracy and greater levels of public expenditure as the best means to ensure reelection.[150]

The perpetuation of the Democratic congressional majority closely allied with the Republican minority, which rests on and gives support to the executive bureaucracy, has resulted in distortion of the function of representation in the national government. Consequently, the object of congressional attention has been the satisfaction of electorally decisive minorities. As Gary Orfield has indicated:

During the 1950s and the 1960s while the country confronted a social revolution, two divisive wars, three changes in party control in the White House, dramatic

[146]"Controversy over Proposed Mandatory Balancing of the Federal Bank," *Congressional Digest*, 55 (March 1976), p. 76.

[147]Wettergreen, "American Voter," p. 222.

[148]A number of reforms have made this dominance more convenient, including the increase in congressional staff and campaign resources, the new rival budget system, and sophisticated redistricting techniques.

[149]Samuel Huntington noted that "explicit acceptance of the idea that legislation was not its primary function . . . would legitimize and expand the functions of constituent service and administrative oversight, which in practice, already constitute the principal work of most congressmen." "Congressional Responses to the Twentieth Century," in David Truman, ed., *The Congress and America's Future*, (Englewood Cliffs: Prentice Hall, 1965), p. 30.

[150]The problem is, as Kevin Phillips has noted, that "Congress has continued to 'conserve' the liberal interest rooted in the expansion of the sixties. As was true forty years ago, a shift in popular thinking can capture the presidency before it can dominate a House and Senate with 535 bases of election. During the 1970s, Congress is likely to be the branch most responsive to interest group liberalism." *Mediacracy*, p. 226.

economic swings, and numerous technological and cultural changes—there was rarely an election when even a tenth of the House incumbents were defeated. . . . Such a grave "distortion" in Congressional representation comes from the extraordinary difficulty of defeating incumbents and the great dependence [of Congressmen] upon interests with very specific legislative objectives.[151]

Why have Congressmen gradually developed more and more security of tenure?[152] Perhaps "as a result of their own efforts in increasing the amount of money spent by the federal government in campaigning for them, and putting more and more restrictions on money available to their opponents for purposes of campaigning against them." Bureaucracies continue to grow, Gordon Tullock suggest, because "the factor suppliers are permitted to vote . . . and to exercise political influence in many ways." Consequently, "incumbent members of Congress, with rapidly growing resources at their disposal, do what they can to entrench themselves personally in their districts."[153]

David Mayhew has shown the extent to which every feature of Congress—committees, staff, party organization—is shaped to aid members' chances at the polls. Coupled with the growth of a bureaucracy that has enabled incumbents to base their appeals on noncontroversial activities, all incumbents benefit from the social pork barrel and the performance of nonpartisan constituent services, such as helping voters deal with administrative agencies.[154] As a result, there has been a decline in citizen voting on the basis of party affiliation in Congressional elections.[155] Nor has there been an increase in "issue voting"; rather, "incumbency voting" has replaced party voting at the Congressional level. Thus,

incumbent members of Congress of both political parties have become increasingly invulnerable to defeat in their districts and more or less regardless of the fate of their party's candidates for other offices in the same election. . . . It seems clear

[151]*Congressional Power: Congress and Social Change* (New York: Harcourt, Brace & Jovanovich, 1975), p. 306.

[152]The advantage of incumbency has become an enormous asset to reelection. Cf. Morris P. Fiorina, "The Case of the Vanishing Marginals: The Bureaucracy Did It," *American Political Science Review*, 71 (March 1977), pp. 177–181; David R. Mayhew, "Congressional Elections: The Case of the Vanishing Marginals," *Polity*, 6 (Spring 1974); pp. 295–317; also Walter D. Burnham, *Critical Elections and the Mainsprings of American Politics* (New York: W. W. Norton, 1970), pp. 100–106.

[153]Gordon Tullock, "What Is to Be Done," in Thomas E. Borcherding, ed., *Budgets and Bureaucrats: The Sources of Government Growth* (Durham: Duke University Press, 1977), pp. 283, 285.

[154]*Congress: The Electoral Connection* (New Haven: Yale University Press, 1974); See also Morris Fiorina, *Representatives, Roll Calls, and Constituencies* (Lexington: Lexington Books, 1974); John A. Ferejohn, *Pork Barrel Politics: Rivers and Harbors Legislation 1947–1968* (Stanford: Stanford University Press, 1974).

[155]John A. Ferejohn, "On the Decline of Competition in Congressional Elections," *American Political Science Review*, 71 (March 1977), pp. 166–176.

that electorally decisive minorities of voters have increasingly been voting for incumbent representatives as incumbents during the past two decades.[156]

The result has been an increase in ticket splitting,[157] a near-certainty that incumbents will be reelected, and the dire prediction that "the party's over."[158] As the authors of *The Changing American Voter* suggested, we may be entering a postpartisan era.[159]

The bureaucracy, which was the creation of a partisan majority, became the key to the decline of partisanship in the United States.[160] The overwhelming superiority of the Democratic Party at the Congressional and state level and the acceptance of the legitimacy of the goals of the Great Society as the ultimate consensus among intellectuals had created a disjunction between presidential electoral politics and politics at lower levels.[161]

> Parties as national electoral organizations must decline out of disuse in proportion to the rise of a national, centralized bureaucracy as the chief instrument of government ("conflict resolution") and the chief governmental source of private or local benefits. Agencies are the new, stabilizing "political structures" for the resolution of social conflicts. Therefore, disjunction between particular private or local interests, which are administered to individually and not legislated for nationally, and the national or public interest, which is articulated by presidents or aspiring presidents, is likely to continue.[162]

Consequently, the rise of the bureaucracy itself and the demise of parties further destroyed the capacity of the majority to rule by denying the element of consent.

The consequence of bureaucratization has been an increased tension between the executive and the legislature regardless of party and the increasing apathy of the electorate. This is so because most important political decisions will be made in Washington by an executive administration that is not clearly accountable to the elected chief executive. Also, the interest of the legislature will be closely allied with—and committed to the perpetuation of—an executive

---

[156]Walter Dean Burnham, "Insulation and Responsiveness in Congressional Elections," *Political Science Quarterly*, 90 (Fall 1975), p. 412–413.

[157]See Walter DeVries and V. Lance Tarrance, *The Ticket-Splitters: A New Force in American Politics* (Grand Rapids; W. B. Erdmans Publishing Co., 1972).

[158]Cf. David S. Broder, *The Party's Over: The Failure of Politics in America* (New York: Harper & Row, 1972).

[159]Norman H. Nie, Sidney Verba, and John R. Petrocik, *The Changing American Voter* (Cambridge: Harvard University Press, 1976), pp. 345–356.

[160]As a result, any partisan or "principled" appeal will occur at the presidential electoral level and is likely to be an attack or defense of the administrative bureaucracy. Because the bureaucracy is seen to embody the moral authority of the New Deal and rests at bottom on a certain view of equality—as the embodiment of social justice and the classless society—the moral appeal of the candidate attacking Washington is diminished by being deprived of the authority on which partisanship itself (and parties) originally derived—that is, the principle of equality.

[161]Cf. Warren Miller and Teresa Levitin, *Leadership and Change: The New Politics and the American Electorate* (Cambridge: Winthrop Publishers, 1976), p. 39.

[162]John Wettergreen, "American Voter," p. 223.

administration; thus the bureaucracy (cloaked in the mantle of nonpartisanship) will retain effective power when backed by Congress. Walter Dean Burnham observes that

> as party erodes both in the electorate and in the House, divergence in the electoral coalitions of President and Congress increasingly reinforce the separation of powers; incumbents tend increasingly to be protected or insulated. . . . The responsiveness of the representational system to electoral change declines; and abstention from the polls become the largest mass movement of our time.[163]

But it seems unlikely that separation of powers is reinforced or even sustained to the extent that the president is unable to control the administration or force it to conform to the demands of a new majority. Rather, the president, with the party, remains impotent, the symbol of an impotent majority. In the absence of crisis, or without a need for a national consensus, the rule of a political executive appears unnecessary.

> This state of affairs has led one observer to conclude: The only two real and enduring parties in American politics are the presidential versus the congressional. . . . Without patronage or party, a president must deal with Congress by showing he is president of all the people . . . but all the people are none of the people. While Congress, with its allies in the bureaucracy, and its close associations with every known interest group represents something more potent than all the people; it represents the organized people.[164]

Deprived of the ability to legitimize party with reference to the opinion of equality—which has animated great parties—the president is left only with his legal powers and a dependence upon a numerical majority.[165]

The disjunction between the presidential and congressional majority has resulted in the disjunction between the enlightened opinion of a national elite (which sees the bureaucracy as the best repository for the attainment of social justice and economic equality) and the majority which sees it as a threat not only to liberty but to a conception of equality which is compatible with the requirement of consent.[166]

---

[163]Burnham, "Insulation and Responsiveness," p. 430.

[164]Nicholas von Hoffman, "Winner Take Nothing," *The New York Review of Books,* 24 (August 4, 1977), p. 4.

[165]*Ibid.,* but as Hoffman has noted, Nixon, "who tried to govern relying on little else than the presidency's legal power, discovered it couldn't be done."

[166]Wettergreen has suggested that "this disjunction is politically difficult. No presidential, i.e., national, majority is likely to be authoritative, because presidents can no longer command the administrative budget, nor even the administration itself in many cases. On the other hand, the basis of congressional majorities cannot be publicly articulated, because they are private spirited or self-interested; such majorities result from the ombudsmen's logrolling. The difficulty could dissolve, if the presidential majority were harmonized with the congressional. That is, if the centrally organized bureaucrats and their clientele composed a constitutional majority capable of electing a president, the bureaucracy could enjoy the authority of a national majority's support. But, first, such a majority would have to be formed around the public opinion that a bureaucratized political order is best for the country." "American Voter," pp. 223-224.

PLANNING AND SOCIAL REFORM: THE IMPACT
OF ADMINISTRATIVE CENTRALIZATION

Since the New Deal, much of American politics has revolved around the attempt to extend the social progress of the welfare state to its furthest point, i.e., the classless society. At that point, politics and administration would be indistinguishable: politics would be administration. The opposition to the extension of that power and that vision has attempted to restrain the bureaucratization of society or the neutralization of power—the conduct of government by experts or technicians—in order to retain the freedom of the individual. In the election of 1960, Richard Nixon insisted that the choice between the parties was a choice between the free society and the bureaucratic society. Nixon noted:

> Our differences . . . arose over how best to solve the problems [unemployment, discrimination, medical care, etc.]. . . . Kennedy would do it by primary emphasis on huge and costly Federal government programs—which would have to be paid for right out of the pockets of the people he was trying to help. . . . I proposed to solve them with a necessary minimum of government action, but with primary emphasis on and encouragement of individual initiative and private enterprise. The great gulf of difference between us . . . was that of a bureaucratic society versus a free society.[167]

With the election of John Kennedy in 1960, it would appear that the choice of a bureaucratic society had been ensured.

The liberal presidency and the institutionalized bureaucracy reached the zenith of legitimacy and strength in the mid-1960s.[168] It was the culmination of the progressive idea that the presidency offered the best institutional perch to ensure social justice, and that social science provided the technical means of making it a practical reality.[169] The intellectual, particularly, had created for himself an almost indispensable role in the entourage of the liberal presidency. As Irving Kristol noted:

> Whatever the eventual terms and conditions of their role, it is quite clear that the intellectuals are in American politics to stay. None of the major programs of the Great Society is workable without their participation. The economists on the Council of Economic Advisors, the scientists and social scientists in the Pentagon, sociologists and psychologists in the Office of Economic Opportunity, the city planners in the new Department of Urban Affairs—these are very much the signs of the times. Indeed, those government departments which have not yet "intellectualized"

---

[167]Richard Nixon, *Six Crises* (Garden City: Doubleday & Co., 1962), p. 339.

[168]As James MacGregor Burns noted, "the stronger the exertion of presidential power, the more liberal and internationalist it will be because of the make up and dynamics of the presidential party." *The Deadlock of Democracy* (Englewood Cliffs: Prentice-Hall, 1963), p. 264.

[169]As Samuel Huntington has observed, "since Theodore Roosevelt . . . the Presidency has been viewed as the most popular branch of government and that which is most likely to provide the leadership for progressive reform. Liberals, progressives, and intellectuals have all seen the Presidency as the key to change in American politics, economics and society." "The Democratic Distemper," *The Public Interest*, 41 (Fall 1975), p. 25.

themselves—such as Commerce and Agriculture—are finding their political power dwindling, their status in the public eye diminishing and their very existence being questioned.[170]

It marked the almost perfect merging of politics and administration. The means and ends were so widely shared as to be nearly indistinguishable; the problems themselves were not regarded as political problems but technical problems.[171] As John F. Kennedy, the most popular president among intellectuals since FDR, stated in May 1962,

> Most of us are conditioned to have a political viewpoint—Republican or Democrat, liberal, conservative, or moderate. The fact of the matter is that most of the problems that we now face are technical problems, are administrative problems.[172]

If administration itself was not considered a part of the partisan or even political realm, but merely regarded as a technical problem, technology too obscured a concern with ends by concentrating solely on means.[173] As Carl Schmitt observed, "The plausibility of today's widely held belief in technology depends upon another belief, i.e., that technology is absolutely and finally neutral ground."[174] Bureaucracy, it would seem, is an integral part of progressive liberalism.

The mechanism of reform introduced into the federal government in the 1960s was based on the legitimacy of the claim that the problems of government were no longer partisan and political, and that the means were at hand to provide a rational solution to those problems. It was not that power had ceased to be a concern, but it had been purified and made to do only good things.[175] Nearly all the reforms attempted to strengthen centralized executive leadership,

---

[170]"The Troublesome Intellectuals," *The Public Interest*, 2 (Winter 1966), p. 5.

[171]See Henry Fairlie, *The Kennedy Promise: The Politics of Expectation*, especially "The Displacement of Politics," (Garden City: Doubleday & Co., 1973), pp. 319–344. Carl Schmitt had earlier observed, "The Movement in which the modern mind has attained to its maximum effectiveness, liberalism, is in fact characterized by the *negation* of the political." *The Concept of the Political*, trans. George Schwab (New Brunswick: Rutgers University Press, 1976), p. 82 [emphasis in the original].

[172]Cited in Thomas Cronin, "The Presidency and Politics," in Charles W. Dunn, ed., *The Future of the American Presidency* (Morristown, N.J.: General Learning Press, 1975), p. 272.

[173]Martin Heidegger noted that "the essence of technology is by no means anything technological, thus we shall never experience our relationship to the essence of technology as long as we merely conceive and push forward the technological. . . . We remain unfree and chained to technology . . . but we are delivered over to it in the worst possible way when we regard it as something neutral; for this conception of it . . . makes us utterly blind to the essence of technology." "The Question Concerning Technology," in David F. Krell, ed., *Basic Writings* (New York: Harper & Row, 1977), pp. 287–288.

[174]Schmitt, *The Concept of the Political*, p. 100.

[175]Allen Schick noted that "the constant concern with power was masked by the celebrated dichotomy between politics and administration. . . . The dichotomy provided for the ascendancy of the administrative over the political; efficiency over representation; rationality over self-interest." "The Trauma of Politics: Public Administration in the Sixties," in Frederick C. Mosher, ed., *American Public Administration: Past, Present, Future* (University, Ala.: University of Alabama Press, 1975). p. 152.

for it was found that "far from being antagonistic to the working of pluralism, executive leadership was the glue that held the process together."[176] Not surprisingly, the budget became a crucial focus of centralized planning and control within the executive establishment.[177] As one economist noted at the time:

> To a significant extent the federal establishment and Washington, D.C. revolve around the "budget cycle." . . . People involved in public decisions—Congressmen, bureaucrats, President, budgeters, lobbyists—are rational strugglers each trying to further his personal interest. . . . They are viewed as maximizing only one thing; their own personal net gain, their own personal utility. . . . It would not miss the mark by far to claim the public policy maker [is] a rational, calculating, pain-pleasure machine.[178]

A public interest, it was thought, could be calculated by economists rationally, without reference to politics by procedures like cost–benefit analysis.[179] They became institutionalized in the federal bureaucracy as Planning Programming Budgeting Systems (PPBS). The program budget, Melvin Anshen observed, "is a neutral tool. It has no politics."[180] Rather, "the PPB system is the vehicle chosen by the federal government to institute comprehensive application of economic analysis to public spending alternatives."[181] This form of analysis

> implies the challenging of every policy proposal with the question, "do the gains to the people exceed the sacrifices required of them?" If the answer is affirmative, the

[176]Robert Dahl had discovered in New Haven (Who Governs) that an executive-centered coalition "welded together the various power centers into a cohesive structure." The enthronement of pluralism, Schick noted, "occurred during a period marked by the ascendancy of executive leadership." It was not accidental, therefore, as Schick observed, that Public Administration, "in the name of efficiency and rational government . . . promoted the augmentation of executive power through a succession of reform instruments; the short ballot, administrative reorganization, the executive budget." Schick, Public Administration, pp. 152, 154.

[177]The need for administration centralization was concomitant of the utopian character of both modern science and modern liberalism. As Michael Oakshott observed, "From this politics of perfection springs the politics of uniformity; a scheme which does not recognize circumstance can have no place for variety. . . . If the rational solution for one of the problems of a society . . . has been determined, to permit any relevant part of society to escape from the solution is . . . to countenance irrationality." Rationalism and Politics (New York: Basic Books, 1962), pp. 5–6.

[178]Robert H. Haveman, The Economics of the Public Sector (New York: John Wiley, 1970), pp. 140–141.

[179]Political scientists had long rejected the notion of a public interest in the name of systems analysis, group process, or mere irrationality. As Joseph Schumpeter wrote, "though a common will or public opinion of some sort may be said to emerge from the complex jumble of individual and group-wise situations . . . actions and reactions of the democratic process, the result lacks not only rational unity but also rational sanction." Capitalism, Socialism and Democracy (New York; Harper & Brothers, 1942), p. 253. Lasswell (Psychopathology and Politics) considered the public interest as a means of rationalizing the displacement of private motives onto public objects; David Truman simply states, "We do not need to account for a totally inclusive interest, because one does not exist." The Governmental Process (New York: Knopf, 1951), p. 51. The scientific study of politics had the effect of undercutting the autonomy and rationality of the practical understanding of politics, paving the way for the distinction between political rationality and economic rationality.

[180]In David Novick, ed., Program Budgeting: Program Analysis and the Federal Budget (Cambridge: Harvard University Press, 1967), p. 370.

[181]Haveman, The Public Sector, p. 171.

proposal should be adopted; if it is negative, the proposal is not in the public interest.[182]

The systematic attempt to apply cost–benefit analysis to public sector expenditures occurred in the Johnson White House. "PPBS and cost-effectiveness analysis are designed to solve problems by finding the most effective and most efficient solution on the basis of objective criteria."[183] In the summer of 1965 Lyndon Johnson ordered the departments and agencies to institute this "revolutionary new system." He suggested that this system

> would identify our national goals with precision and on a continuing basis . . . search for alternative means of reaching those goals most effectively at the least cost . . . inform ourselves not merely of next year's cost, but on the second and third, and subsequent years' cost of our programs.[184]

As Haveman noted, PPBS "implies a significant departure from traditional federal budgetary procedures and a major step toward developing a rational decision-making process."[185] Program budgeting "is manifestly concerned with policy politics, and not much concerned with partisan politics."[186] But it was not difficult to see its attraction. As Wildavsky noted, it "contains an extreme centralizing bias. Power is to be centralized in the presidency (through the Budget Bureau) at the national level, in super departments."[187]

In tracing the origins of PPBS, Wildavsky claims it emerged from at least "three distinct but closely related strains" of development.

> These strains—economic development planning, the administrative reforms of the early decades of this century, and management of national economies to control cyclical fluctuation—all rest on . . . the optimistic confidence in the power of intelligence to order man's environment and improve human welfare.[188]

Science proved to be the model. "When implemented successfully the new methods would permit the planner, policy-maker, and administrator to achieve the same objective control of government, economy and society as could, theoretically, be attained in a laboratory.[189] So, too,

> the administrative reforms of the early years of this century aimed at purifying government by taking politics and personality out of it. . . . PPBS, by merging the

[182]Ibid., p. 150.
[183]Charles Schultz, *The Politics and Economics of Public Spending* (Washington, D.C.: The Brookings Institute, 1968), p. 2.
[184]Cited in Haveman, *The Public Sector*, p. 169.
[185]Ibid., p. 170.
[186]Wildavsky, *Budgeting*, p. 328.
[187]Ibid. Jesse Burkhead, too, had suggested that the program budget "becomes a technique, not for management at the operating level, but for the centralization of administrative authority." Burkhead, "Review of *Program Budgeting*," David Novick, ed., *American Economic Review*, 56 (September 1966), p. 943.
[188]Wildavsky, *Budgeting*, p. 237.
[189]Ibid., p. 274.

long-term perspective of planning with the systematic analytic methods of economics in the name of administrative reform is thus but the latest of a long chain of proposals to introduce a greater rationality into the process of government.[190]

But it was clear that the reforms were in keeping with the political purposes of the Great Society. They rested on a conception of equality that was compatible with a certain view of democratic pluralism. They attempted to extend the benefits of society to every element in that society.[191] As Allen Schick noted:

> Many Great Society programs were designed to rest political power in disadvantaged groups by opening up the administrative process to their participation. . . . The strategy was to give power to the poor. . . . This required a tearing down of any barrier between political and administrative practice. Election, representation, advocacy—the heart of the political process—were to be introduced into the administrative arena. Federal assistance programs were proliferated in order to give the poor their own programs and their own administrative units in the same manner that "interest group liberalism" customarily provided political and administrative power to the advantaged sectors of the American polity.[192]

In the federal system, the national executive had come to be preferred over the legislature. In the states, the city governments were preferred to the state governments because the Chief Executive and city mayors (important parts of the New Deal coalition) were most receptive to liberal and minority interests. If, as Lyons suggests, "the interest group system itself [was] institutionalized and strengthened by the structure of Congress,"[193] it had been necessary for the president to open up the federal bureaucracy to the new claimants. The abandonment of the presidency did not occur until nearly every significant element in society had obtained access to the administrative bureaucracy. The "executive-centered coalition" represented a transition from partisan politics to bureaucratic politics.

The implicit premise of the bureaucratic state is the recognition of the fact that a "diminution of political liberty" may be necessary to continue "the social progress of the welfare state."[194] If the majority would not succumb to the abandonment of the liberal or constitutional state when given a clear choice, it was in the interest of the supporters of the bureaucracy to obscure the political character of the bureaucratic state. Rather, its humanitarian and equalitarian goals were emphasized. Thus, as Hubert Humphrey noted in the 1976 presidential electoral campaign, "candidates who make an attack on Washington are making an attack on government programs, on the poor, on blacks, on minori-

---

[190]Ibid., p. 274.
[191]Gene M. Lyons observed, "it is through the President . . . that groups ill-organized to operate in the interest group system can gain effective access to the political process." "The President and his Experts," *The Annals of the American Academy of Political and Social Science,* 394 (March 1971), p. 38.
[192]Schick, "Trauma of Politics," in Mosher, ed., p. 149.
[193]Lyons, *The Annals of the American Academy,* p. 38.
[194]Cf. Wettergreen, "Free Society," p. 6.

ties, on the cities. It is a disguised new form of racism, a disguised new form of conservatism."[195] Not only had the moral authority of the New Deal come to reside in the bureaucracy (and the traditional supporters of the Democratic Party), it had become the means of implementing a view of equality that was identical to that of the new class.

In discussing the presidency, Stephen Hess pointed to the distinctive characteristics that animated the view of presidential power in this period:

> During the period from 1933 through 1964, when the majority view was that social progress is best achieved through a strong presidency, social scientists and others concentrated on finding ways to support a President's natural instincts for doing good. This involved identifying the forces that were frustrating presidential efforts, devising mechanisms to overcome those frustrations, and providing a President with the means—people and money—to do his job.[196]

The obstacle to presidential fulfillment of the goals of social progress was the deadlock imposed by the separation of powers and an obstructionist Congress.[197] "Effective government," a noted political scientist wrote, "requires that what the Founding Fathers separated—President and Congress—we must put together."[198]

The question that would not be answered until the end of the Nixon presidency was whether the liberals' attachment to the presidency was as a result of an attachment to majority rule or whether it was a partisan attachment to the majority consensus created by the New Deal. In any case, by the end of the decade it was apparent that the opinions that animated the majority had diverged from those of the intellectuals. The intellectual, nurtured on the assumption that the presidency was the best vehicle for ensuring social justice, had come to recognize an identity between the personal power of the president and the public interest.[199]

Nixon's hostility to the bureaucracy was not simply expedient; it was part of his hostility to the old coalition of FDR that, with modification in the New Frontier and Great Society, had created the bureaucratic state.[200] It was a parti-

[195]*New York Times,* 25 March 1975, p. 31.

[196]*Organizing the Presidency* (Washington, D.C.: The Brookings Institution, 1976), p. 1.

[197]Some conceived of the party—with the president as its leader—as the mechanism to overcome this deadlock. Cf. V. O. Key, Jr., *Politics, Parties, and Pressure Groups* (New York: Thomas Crowell, 1964), p. 656.

[198]Michael D. Reagan, "Toward Improving Presidential Level Policy Planning," in Cronin and Greenberg, eds., *The Presidential Advisory System,* p. 259.

[199]See Richard Neustadt, *Presidential Power* (New York: John Wiley, 1960), pp. 181–185.

[200]Thomas Cronin has revealed compelling reasons for the abandonment of the presidency during the Nixon era. In comparing FDR and Richard Nixon, Cronin notes, "both were masters at the accumulation of power in the presidency. But in marked contrast to Roosevelt, who strove to use the power for social reform and redistributive ends, Nixon nearly always used his power for the mere accumulation of enhanced powers apparently elevating his means to ends unto themselves." "The Presidency and Politics," p. 282. Cronin, nurtured on the principles of the New Deal, could not understand that the accumulation of power was not a mere accumulation for its own sake, but the attempt to divest the bureaucracy, which had been the product of a previous consensus of the

sanship based on principle. Quoting Albert Beveridge, Nixon remarked at the dedication of the LBJ Memorial Library:

> Partisanship should only be a method of patriotism. He who is a partisan merely for the sake of spoils is a buccaneer. He who is a partisan merely for the sake of a party name is a ghost of the past among living events. . . . But he who is a partisan of principle is a prince of citizenship.[201]

Nixon expressed, on this occasion, his own view of partisanship and of the presidency. He noted:

> A partisan of principle—that is what our political system is all about; that is what transforms ordinary disputes into those great debates that illumine for years to come the issues confronting the nation, in which men of principle test their principles and the nation achieves a deeper understanding of itself. It also is what holds us together on those great questions on which our unity has kept us free.[202]

Nixon's massive victory in 1972 appeared to offer the kind of electoral mandate necessary to begin the process of dismantling the bureaucracy and neutralizing the power of the experts precisely by politicizing the bureaucracy. The bureaucracy had been erected and sustained because of an implicit agreement as to what constituted the purposes for which political power was to be used. Once those ends were put into doubt, the question of means could not be viewed merely as a matter of utilizing the proper technique—or ensuring greater efficiency. The primary feature of Nixon's "new American revolution" was the reorganization of the federal government to begin the process of managing the bureaucracy in order to attempt its dismantling, and a decentralization that, by returning power to the localities and the people, would revitalize the individual's role in self-government. Nixon "showed that he was prepared to alter the structure and direction of federal welfare policies that had not been seriously challenged, let alone by the White House, since the New Deal" with the result that "it would be difficult for a future liberal president to undo [that policy's] consequences and recover the lost powers of the federal government to shape nationwide social policies."[203] Nixon's attempt to politicize the bureaucracy and the budgetary process created the greatest crisis of modern presidential-congressional relations.

---

authority that made it immune to control by the contemporary majority. Bureaucratic authority rested on the legitimacy of the opinion that the achievement of social justice was the necessary and sufficient condition of bureaucratic rule. In denying that opinion, Nixon sought to rest his claim to legitimacy on the majority's right to rule. His attack on the bureaucracy and his defense of middle-class values against the new class and the intellectuals resulted in an attempt to delegitimize those opinions, which offered the most powerful support of the bureaucracy. The key to accountability and responsibility in the American government had come to reside in one crucial area—control of the bureaucracy.

[201]*A New Road for America: Major Policy Statements, March 1970 to October 1971* (Garden City: Doubleday & Co., 1972), p. 3.

[202]Ibid., p. 4.

[203]Dennis H. Wrong, "Watergate: Symptom of What Sickness?" *Dissent*, 21 (Fall 1974), p. 506.

Chapter 4

Reorganization and Reaction: The End of the Progressive Presidency?

Politics as a practice, whatever its profession, has always been the systematic organization of hatreds.

—Henry Adams, *The Education of Henry Adams*

A NEW AMERICAN REVOLUTION

The struggle between Congress and the president for control of budgets and the bureaucracy reached its peak in the administration of Richard Nixon. The bitterness of those battles derived from a disagreement concerning fundamental principles of government, both the legitimacy of the power of the federal government, and the organization and structure of the national government. Nixon was the first Republican president to question the legitimacy of the bureaucratic state. In political terms Democrats perceived it as an attack not only on the Great Society, but more importantly on the New Deal. The core of this attack appeared early in his tenure, during a televised address[1] in which he announced his "new federalism" program that became, subsequently, the "new American revolution."[2] It was a direct assault on what Nixon perceived to be the bureaucratic centralization and the "social experimentation" that had dominated the politics of the New Frontier and the Great Society and had rendered the bureaucracy immune to political control. He noted in this address:

> A third of a century of centralizing power and responsibility in Washington had produced a bureaucratic monstrosity, cumbersome, unresponsive, ineffective. A third of a century of social experiment has left us a legacy of entrenched programs that have outlived their time or outgrown their purpose.[3]

The struggle between the executive and legislative branch that ensued was not a party struggle "dominated by the same fundamental dispute over the role of government, that defined a new party alignment in the 1930s."[4] Rather, it was a struggle over the control of the bureaucracy in which the interests of the legislature and those of executive diverged regardless of party. Nixon's solution to the problem was the increased centralization of power in the White House and away from the permanent government. Such a strategy required a massive reorganization of the bureaucracy on the one hand, and the reversal of the flow of power to Washington and back to the localities on the other. Nixon suggested that it marked the first time in American history that the federal government had assumed powers and responsibilities that it was not well-equipped to handle.

---

[1]Nixon addressed the nation on August 8 1969. It may not have been coincidental that he announced his intention to resign the presidency on this same day, August 8, 1974, if he believed his assault on the bureaucracy was responsible for his downfall.

[2]Raymond Price, Nixon's speechwriter, has suggested, "What Nixon sought to bring about was indeed a revolution. This Nixon revolution set out not only to reverse a forty-year trend in domestic social policy, but also to give primacy to a hierarchy of values that paid the same respect to Main Street that it did to the Main Line. If this revolution succeeded, it would shake the snobbish assumption of natural superiority that lay in the fashionable east. For years the custodians of fashion—including most of the national media—had made fun of traditional middle-class values. In striking back in behalf of the equal right of those values to a decent respect, [he] touched deep chords of response . . . but he also won the contempt of the self-consciously fashionable." *With Nixon* (New York: The Viking Press, 1977), p. 118.

[3]Richard Nixon, *Setting the Course, the First Year: Major Policy Statements of President Nixon* (New York: Funk & Wagnalls, 1970), p. 49. The need for decentralization resulted from the necessity to strengthen the role of the individual in society. Quoting Abraham Lincoln, he noted, "The legitimate object of Government is to do for a community of people whatever they need to have done, but cannot do at all, or cannot do so well, for themselves, in their separate and individual capacity. In all that the people can individually do as well for themselves, government ought not to interfere. This philosophy underlies the efforts of my administration to strengthen the role of the individual in American society. It is a cornerstone of the New Federalism." *Historic Documents* (Washington, D.C.: Congressional Quarterly Inc., 1975), p. 108.

[4]James Sundquist, "Whither the American Party System," *Political Science Quarterly*, 88 (December 1973), p. 580.

THE DOMESTIC COUNCIL AND REORGANIZATION

In his first term, Nixon attempted to work with Congress to achieve his goals, and he achieved a significant victory in his Reorganization Plan No. 2 of 1970.[5] The Plan had originated in the recommendations of the Ash Council (headed by Roy Ash, later director of the OMB); its most important objective was the creation of a management capacity in the executive branch and a policy-making one in the White House. On July 1, 1970, the Plan took effect; the Office of Management and Budget replaced the Bureau of the Budget and a Domestic Council was established in the White House.

The Domestic Council was considered to be "the key institutional innovation in domestic affairs during the first Nixon administration."[6] It reflected Nixon's view that the "silent majority did not speak out, were not represented, and were badly served by the existing interest groups."[7] Consequently, the Domestic Council was designed to serve the President. It was to be a means of developing policy, to "say what would be done—the Office of Management and Budget, how it would be done."[8] The Council was to be the domestic equivalent of the National Security Council (in which Henry Kissinger had achieved some success in rivaling the State Department bureaucracy from the White House). John Ehrlichman, who had succeeded by the middle of 1969 in replacing Moynihan and Burns as the dominant White House Assistant for Domestic Affairs, was to head the Council. Its purpose was seen to be that

> of reducing the influence of the federal government in people's lives. This took many forms such as support of the state and local government, the simplification of federal process and grants . . . and the reduction of federal planning control over local decisions in all fields.[9]

The primary means of controlling the bureaucracy was thought to be through the budget.[10] The perspective would not be merely one of ensuring greater efficiency and neutral competence, but the reintroduction of a partisan and political perspective.[11] In the annual budget review, Domestic Council per-

---

[5]Cf. William D. Carey, "Reorganization Plan No. 2," *Public Administration Review,* 30 (November/December 1970), pp. 631–4. For a broad treatment of the OMB and the Presidency, see Larry Berman, *The Office of Management and Budget and the Presidency, 1921–1979,* (Princeton, N.J.: Princeton University Press, 1979).

[6]Raymond J. Waldmann, "The Domestic Council: Innovation in Presidential Government," *Public Administration Review,* 36 (May-June 1975), p. 260.

[7]Ibid.

[8]Ibid., p. 262.

[9]Ibid., p. 265.

[10]As John Kessel noted, "the Domestic Council [is] to be the vehicle through which the departments and OMB fight their budget battles." *The Domestic Presidency, Decision-Making in the White House* (North Scituate, Mass.: Duxbury Press, 1975), p. 98.

[11]Cf. Hugh Heclo, "OMB and the Presidency—The Problem of Neutral Competence," *Public Interest,* 38 (Winter 1975), pp. 80–98.

sonnel participated as "presidential representatives bringing to the OMB table a political perspective."[12]

In attempting to implement the Reorganization Act, the administration was made aware of the extent to which the interests of the bureaucracy had resulted in independent alliances with Congress and outside interest groups. "The capability of the Bureau to function effectively in a presidential role was impaired by the close identification of many examiners with the agencies they were assigned to review."[13] Even the Budget Director, Robert Mayo, appointed by Nixon, opposed the plan on the grounds that the Budget Bureau was made up of nonpartisan civil servants. Its success was the result of the Budget Bureau's lack of support among significant interest groups, and the apparent hostility in Congress to those Bureau personnel who had failed to support favored legislation. As one critic suggested:

> The Ash Council succeeded because the Bureau's popularity with Congress was at the all-time low. . . . The reorganization marked the victory of a presidential "interest" to improve the management processes of the Executive Office of the president through the reorganization of the Budget Bureau.[14]

It was inevitable that a rigorous attempt to manage the executive branch would ultimately result in a collision with the organized interests and their allies in Congress. This would have been so even if the president had substantial support for the aims of the programs enacted, which Nixon did not. "The Nixon administration was guided by a desire to reduce the level of government activity wherever possible. Since many Democrats did not share these views, the Nixon administration faced principled as well as partisan opposition."[15] The Domestic Council, too, was soon confronted with the "triple alliance . . . the mutually supportive relationship of interest groups, bureaus, and the relevant committees on the Hill."[16] As John Whitaker, former Under Secretary of the Interior, has argued, "This iron triangle—composed of the vested interests, select members of Congress, and the middle-level bureaucracy—runs the federal government."[17] Even the political leadership of the executive branch, the Cabinet members themselves, were often co-opted by the departments and

---

[12]Waldmann, *Domestic Council*, p. 264.

[13]Allen Schick, "The Budget Bureau That Was," *Law and Contemporary Problems*, 35 (Summer 1970), p. 533. Consequently, as Roy Ash noted, "one of the biggest problems in trying to convert the Bureau of the Budget to the Office of Management and Budget, the pocket of greatest resistance, of political resistance, was the BOB. . . . Some of those guys went up the Hill to sabotage that thing and to really turn the screws up on some of them." Quoted in Larry Berman, "The Office of Management and Budget That Almost Wasn't," *Political Science Quarterly*, 92 (Summer 1977), p. 299.

[14]Berman, *Office of Management and Budget*, pp. 300–301.

[15]Kessel, *Domestic Presidency*, p. 50.

[16]Ibid., p. 71.

[17]Quoted in Price, *With Nixon*, p. 197.

agencies and were soon captive of particular interests.[18] This was reinforced at lower levels by assistant secretaries who saw their loyalty to the Secretary and not the president.[19] In the final analysis, it became a question of whose priorities would be decisive.[20] It was not, however, until Nixon's reelection that the full potential of the management strategy embodied in the Domestic Council would become apparent, in what has been called the "administration presidency."[21]

By the end of his first administration, Nixon had come to believe that the problems of domestic government could not be solved by the leadership of the national government. Moreover, that leadership and its creation, the administrative machinery, had undermined the ability of the people to govern themselves, by weakening the character of the individual. The view that government was good in itself because it was concerned with the welfare of the people could no longer be taken for granted. In addition, such an opinion would almost certainly reintroduce the problem of the motives of the leaders of government, in a manner unlike anything since the New Deal. It could no longer be assumed that the government, or its leaders, was simply well-intentioned. The problem of government had become the machinery of government itself, which, though enshrouded in the humane purposes of the New Deal and the Great Society, had obstructed an essential element of democracy—the responsiveness of government to the people. Unlike Roosevelt, Nixon suggested that

> the major cause of the ineffectiveness of government is not a matter of men or money. It is principally a matter of machinery. . . . Good people cannot do good things with bad mechanisms. But bad mechanisms can frustrate even the noblest aims.[22]

The primary obligation of the president in domestic affairs was the reorganization of the executive branch so that it could become responsive to political

---

[18]Nixon noted after the 1972 election that "It is inevitable when an individual has been in a Cabinet position . . . after a certain length of time he becomes an advocate of the status quo, [and] rather than running the bureaucracy, the bureaucracy runs him." *New York Times*, 28 November 1972, p. 40.

[19]Cf. Dom Benafede, "White House Staffing: The Nixon-Ford Era," in Thomas Cronin and Rexford G. Tugwell, eds., *The Presidency Reappraised* (New York: Praeger Publishers, 1977), p. 163.

[20]John Kessel has suggested that "Congressmen and cabinet members had the luxury of advocating programs popular with their constituencies or departments. But at some point in the policy process [Domestic Council] decisions had to be made that certain proposals were going to become part of the administration's legislative programs, and other programs were not." *Domestic Presidency*, p. 92.

[21]Subsequently, the Council made policy "through administrative change by Executive Order, budget decision or agency head directive" (Waldmann, *Domestic Council*, p. 264). It involved the politicization of the so-called neutral bureaucracy.

[22]*A New Road for America, Major Policy Statements of President Nixon* (Garden City, NJ: Doubleday & Co., 1972), p. 409.

leadership and accountable to the demands of the contemporary majority. He noted:

> In my view that obligation now requires us to give more profound and more critical attention to the question of government organization than any single group of American leaders has done since the Constitutional Convention adjourned in Philadelphia in September of 1787. As we strive to bring about a new American Revolution, we must recognize that central truth which those who led the original American Revolution so clearly understood, often it is how the government is put together that determines how well the government can do its job.[23]

Nixon's plans to reorganize the executive branch had been detailed in his State of the Union message of 1971.[24] He proposed to abolish the constituency- and clientele-oriented Departments of Agriculture, Labor, Commerce, HUD, Interior, HEW, and Transportation and consolidate their functions among four "goal-oriented" super-departments. The new departments were to be Human Resources, Natural Resources, Community Development, and Economic Affairs. He spelled out in greater detail the rationale of his reform plans in his Reorganization Message to Congress two months later, on March 25, 1971.[25] At that time, Nixon suggested that "we must rebuild the executive branch according to a new understanding of how government can best be organized to perform effectively."[26] The key to that understanding is that the executive branch should be organized around the basic goals to be achieved rather than constituencies to be served. The first task of government organization is to bring discipline into the bureaucracy in order to make it responsive to political control. Thus, Nixon noted, "As we reflect on organizational problems one seems to stand out above all others; the fact that the capacity to do things—the power to achieve goals and to solve problems—is exceedingly fragmented and

---

[23]Ibid., p. 410.

[24]In this message, Nixon offered his reasons for attempting to manage the bureaucracy: "the further away government is from the people, the stronger government becomes and the weaker people become. . . . The idea that a bureaucratic elite in Washington knows best what is best for people everywhere and that you cannot trust local government is really a contention that you cannot trust the people to govern themselves." Ibid., pp. 12–13. Consequently, he noted, "I shall ask not simply for more new programs in the old framework, but to change the framework itself—to reform the entire structure of American government so we can make it fully responsive to the needs and wishes of the American people." Ibid., p. 7.

[25]Nixon made it clear in the subsequent message that it was better political control, rather than a more efficient administration, that was his prime concern. "It was obvious from the outset," however, "that Congress would never enact this measure because its committee structure is closely tied to the departmental structure of the executive branch," and the legislation just languished in committee. "An effort to sell the reorganization bill . . . proved to be a monumental failure." The White House could not "overcome the opposition of vested interests on the Hill which were determined enough to resist all . . . attempts at persuasion, influence and bargaining." John Hart, "Presidential Power Revisited," *Political Studies*, 25 (March 1977), p. 58. See also Hart's *The Presidential Branch* (New York: Pergamon Press, 1987).

[26]Nixon, *A New Road*, p. 417.

broadly scattered through the federal establishment."[27] The consequence of this fragmentation is that responsibility is scattered and agencies of government become the servants of various special interests. "Problems are defined so that they will fit within established jurisdictions and bureaucratic conventions." As a result, he said, "the role of a government department . . . is fundamentally compromised by the way its mission is defined. The narrower the mission, the more likely it is that the department will see itself as an advocate within the administration for a special point of view."[28] Nixon implied, consequently, that not only had the executive administration ceased to be responsive to the Chief Executive as a means to solve common problems, it had become in many cases an adversary of the president. "When any department or agency begins to represent a parochial interest, then its advice and support inevitably become less useful to the man who must serve all the people as their President."[29]

The proliferation of the executive bureaucracy had led to a contradictory situation. On the one hand, power had become increasingly fragmented within the departments and agencies at the federal level; at the same time, it was becoming increasingly centralized as a result of bureaucratic momentum that necessitated the creation of new levels of bureaucracy to solve jurisdictional disputes. Government became more invisible at the level at which the important decisions were made—and where the problems had originated there was no authority to solve them. Important decisions were made by faceless, nameless bureaucrats. This scattered responsibility also contributed to the overcentralization of public decision-making.

> Because competing offices are often in different chains of command, it is frequently impossible for them to resolve their differences except by referring them to higher authorities. In an attempt to provide a means for resolving such differences and for providing needed coordination, an entire new layer of bureaucracy has emerged at the interagency level. Last year, the OMB had counted some 850 interagency committees.[30]

The concentration of decision-making in the executive branch of the national government also undermined the authority of the lower levels of government.[31] But the most important consequence of the new administrative centralization was that it had prevented elected leadership from being praised or blamed for a particular policy. "In our political system," Nixon noted,

> when the people identify a problem they elect to public office . . . [those] who promise to solve that problem. If these leaders succeed, they can be reelected; if

[27]Ibid., p. 412.
[28]Ibid., p. 413.
[29]Ibid.
[30]Ibid., p. 414.
[31]Nixon suggests, "Inefficient organization at the federal level also undermines the effectiveness of state and local governments. Mayors and Governors waste countless hours and dollars touching base with a variety of federal offices." Ibid.

they fail, they can be replaced. Elections are the people's tool for keeping government responsive to their needs.[32]

Nixon suggested that the bureaucracy was capable of setting itself above the will of the majority:

> This entire system rests on the assumption . . . that elected leaders can make the government respond to the people's mandate. Too often this assumption is wrong. . . . When the lines of responsibility are as tangled and as ambiguous as they are in many policy areas, it is extremely difficult . . . for the president to see that intentions are carried out. . . . There is frequently no single official—even at the Cabinet level whom the President or the Congress can hold accountable for the government's success or failure in meeting a given need. No wonder bureaucracy has sometimes been described as "the rule of no one." When elected officials cannot hold appointees accountable for the performance of government, then the voters' influence on the behavior of government is also weakened.[33]

Nixon's reorganization attempts in 1971 were doomed to failure. As Dwight Ink has suggested,

> A strong presidential move to manage the Executive branch will send out waves of alarm to hundreds of special interest groups, who in turn will move at once to sensitize each of their supporters in Congress to the threat the dictatorial presidential plans pose to the favorite programs of that particular congressman.[34]

But more importantly, reorganization faced one hurdle that turned out to be insuperable; the congressional committee structure was geared to the old organization. Reshuffling committees would mean tampering with the seniority positions of committee members. It would also break up the cozy arrangements committee members and committee staffs had with the old departmental bureaucracies.[35] The problem of the federal government, according to Nixon, was that it responded well to the organized interests and organized minorities but had become increasingly unconcerned with the public interest and the interests of the national majority. Consequently, after his Inauguration in January 1973, he made clear his intention in his second term when he declared, "I am going to stand for the general interest."[36] As a result, Price suggests, Nixon "tried to achieve administratively what he had not been able to get approved legislatively."[37]

[32]Ibid., p. 415.

[33]Ibid.

[34]"The President as Manager," *Public Administration Review,* 36 (September/October 1976), p. 511.

[35]Price, *With Nixon,* p. 197.

[36]Cited in Richard P. Nathan, *The Plot that Failed: Nixon and the Administrative Presidency* (New York: John Wiley, 1975), p. 85.

[37]Price, *With Nixon,* p. 197.

THE ADMINISTRATIVE PRESIDENCY

The key to Nixon's attempt to manage the executive branch, and the core of the administrative presidency, was unveiled two weeks before the Inauguration on January 5, 1973.[38] Nixon had criticized Congressional inaction on the reorganization he had requested and detailed in his State of the Union Message and the Executive Reorganization Message of 1971. He maintained on this occasion that if the actual integration of fragmented department operations required Congressional action, the "broadening of policy perspectives on the part of top managers and advisors can be achieved at once."[39] His purpose, he maintained, was to "integrate and unify policies and operations throughout the executive branch . . . and to bring about better operational coordination and more unified policy development."[40] This strategy, according to Richard Nathan, was aimed "at the functional subgovernments, particularly the bureaucracy, those personnel shifts involved not only Cabinet officials, but hundreds of sub-Cabinet and other top policy posts."[41] The management strategy of the second term, says Nathan, "represented an attempt to implement the philosophy and aims of the President's March, 1971, agency reorganization plans to the fullest extent possible *without legislation*"[42] (emphasis in the original). The president would put his own trusted appointees in positions to manage directly key elements of the bureaucracy without elaborate White House or Executive Office staff machinery to encumber their efforts. "The new appointees would be the President's men. They would be arranged so that there would be clear lines of authority. The bureaucracy would report to them; they would be held accountable."[43] Nathan suggests that Nixon and Ehrlichman came to the conclusion

> sometime in 1971 that in many areas of domestic affairs, *operations is policy.* Much of the day-to-day management of domestic programs—regulation writing, grant approval, and budget apportionment—actually involves policy-making. Getting control over these processes was the aim of the President's strategy for domestic government in his second term[44] (emphasis in the original).

The huge electoral victory of 1972 provided Nixon with what was thought to be the mandate that would enable him to gain control of the permanent

---

[38]Nixon's plans for his second term could be seen in his reorganization strategy, which was embodied in the six mini-messages of the State of the Union Address in 1973, and the national priorities reflected in his budget for fiscal 1974.

[39]*White House Press Release,* cited in Harold Seidman, *Politics, Position and Power* (New York: Oxford University Press, 1975), p. 212.

[40]Ibid.

[41]Nathan, *Administrative Presidency,* p. 74.

[42]Ibid., p. 61.

[43]Ibid., pp. 61–62.

[44]Ibid., p. 62.

government.[45] In his *Memoirs,* Nixon subsequently wrote, "This is going to be quite a shock to the establishment, but it is the only way, and probably the last time, that we can get government under control before it gets so big that it submerges the individual completely and destroys the dynamism which makes the American system what it is." He insisted that his "attempts at reorganizing or reforming the federal government . . . had been resisted by the combined and determined inertia of Congress and the bureaucracy." Such resistance was not only the result of partisan differences but also, he suggested, "because the plans and programs . . . threatened the entrenched powers and prerogatives that they had built up over many decades."[46] Nixon admitted that he could do nothing but accept the fact that no major reform would come from Congress in his first term. But, he wrote, "now, however, armed with my landslide mandate and knowing that I had only four years in which to make my mark, I planned to force Congress and the federal bureaucracy to defend their obstruction and their irresponsible spending in the open arena of public opinion."[47] Congress, Nixon observed, "had smothered my attempt in 1971 to streamline the government," so he asked "John Ehrlichman and Roy Ash to determine how much reorganizing I could legally do on my own." They advised "that I could in fact create by executive authority a system closely resembling the one I had requested in the 1971 reform proposal."[48]

In his first term, Nixon had attempted to appoint a Cabinet that would balance the various interests he wanted represented in his administration. However, by 1970 Nixon concluded that he needed to create a direct means of exercising authority over the domestic bureaucracy to achieve his New Federalism aims. As Nathan suggested,

> he appeared to have further decided that many of the men he had named to head the biggest spending domestic programs held points of view different from his own. The traditional strategy of a balanced Cabinet of distinguished men . . . of independent national reputation was not working.[49]

As a result, Nixon sought in his second term to place his trusted aides in the top

---

[45]Graham Allison and Peter Szanton have noted, "This permanent government is organized by department and agency, each with its separate professional career lines, protected by Civil Service regulations and now largely unionized, . . . which does most of the day-to-day business of government. . . . Because [it] often resists the initiatives of new administrations, political appointees are tempted to depend solely on small groups of trusted assistants, to circumvent or distract the bureaucracy. . . . Members of the permanent government resort to doing their business around and beneath appointed officials . . . working through Congressional or private allies." "Organizing for the Decade Ahead," in Charles Schultze, ed., *Setting National Priorities: The Next Ten Years* (Washington, D.C.: The Brookings Institution, 1976), p. 239.

[46]Nixon, *RN: The Memoirs of Richard Nixon* (New York: Grosset & Dunlop, 1978), pp. 761–762.

[47]*Memoirs,* p. 762.

[48]*Memoirs,* p. 767.

[49]Nathan, *Administrative Presidency,* p. 61.

agency posts. John Herbers of the *New York Times,* contrasting Nixon's second Cabinet with his first, noted: "Now high posts, with rare exceptions, are held by little-known loyalists who can be dismissed or transferred at will without creating a ripple in public."[50]

Nixon then proceeded to reorganize (without Congressional authority) the White House Office around five assistants: foreign affairs (Henry Kissinger), domestic affairs (John Ehrlichman), economic affairs (George Schultz), executive management (Roy Ash), and White House administration (Bob Haldeman). In addition, he appointed three Cabinet members to the position of "Counselor to the President"; their functions were policy coordination in a broad area that cut across existing Cabinet jurisdictions. These appointees were divided into the areas of human resources (Casper Weinberger), natural resources (Earl Butz), and community development (James Lynn).[51] Taken together, "Nixon's approach for running the government in his second term . . . was now decisively changed."[52]

Nixon had come to view the traditional Cabinet and its relationship with the departments and agencies and their clientele as a primary obstacle to the management of the executive branch. As a result he attempted to limit access to the president to these five Assistants, who in turn would be accessible to the Counselors. . . .[53] The Counselors would be informed and make judgments on budget matters; control key personnel positions and manpower strength; provide policy direction on legislation and legislative strategy; and review speeches, testimony, press releases, and internal policy statements. In effect,

> the President had converted the executive branch into a three-tiered structure with the Assistants to the President at the top and department and agency heads (other than those designated as Counselors) at the bottom. The clear intent was to transfer to the President's immediate staff effective control over executive branch policies and programs to reduce Cabinet officers to an essentially ministerial role.[54]

As John Ehrlichman observed, "There shouldn't be a lot of leeway in following the President's policies."[55]

In bypassing the Cabinet—and placing trusted aides in strategic positions— it was thought that direct control over the departments could be obtained.[56] The

---

[50]*New York Times,* 6 March 1973, cited in ibid., p. 73.

[51]Nathan suggested that "the three super secretaries were assigned responsibilities in a way that presumably put them in a position to pass on program action in areas that were formally the responsibility of the other Cabinet officers." *Administrative Presidency,* p. 69. Cf. Hart, *Presidential Power Revisited,* p. 58.

[52]Nathan, *Administrative Presidency,* p. 69.

[53]Ibid., pp. 68–69.

[54]Seidman, *Politics, Position and Power,* p. 117.

[55]*Washington Post,* 24 August 1972, quoted in Seidman.

[56]As Seidman noted, "White House control over the departments would be maintained directly through key deputies appointed by and reporting to Assistants to the President." *Politics, Position and Power,* p. 117.

Washington Post disclosed that over a hundred people formerly employed by the White House, OMB, and the Committee to Reelect the President had been reassigned to the departments and occupied strategic posts in HEW, Interior, and Transportation.[57] It was also claimed that

> politically endorsed appointees recruited by the Deputy Director of OMB and operating under his general supervision replaced the departmental Assistant Secretaries for Administration, most of whom had been in the career civil service. Assistant Secretaries for administration . . . with their control of budgets, management services, and personnel, were regarded as potentially powerful instruments of control.[58]

Taken as a whole, the organization strategy "developed after the 1972 election was aimed squarely at the vitals of bureaucratic power." Political appointees "too narrowly identified with programmatic and constituency interest, or with an independent power base were purged."[59] As a Panel of the National Academy of Public Administration (convened at the request of Senator Ervin's Select Committee on Presidential Campaign Activities) subsequently wrote: "In terms of top-level political appointees, the transition between the first and second Nixon terms was as extreme as most transitions from one party to the other."[60] What was the consequence of the reorganizational strategy? As a result,

> the bureaucracy was neutralized and isolated by leaving major departments "headless," by coopting the Secretaries as Assistants to the President and White House Counselors, thus preventing their "capture by the natives"; depriving it of resources through revenue sharing and impoundment; cutting lines of communication by interposing Regional Councils under White House and OMB control between departments and their agents in the field. The departments were to be allowed to wither away with the White House assuming direct operational responsibility.[61]

There could be no doubt that such an attempt would be severely contested, and in the final analysis, Congress had a greater interest in upholding the status quo.

> There were several overlapping power struggles. There was the one between the Congress, and the one between the White House and the executive departments, and the one between the "political" members of the executive branch—the President and his appointees—and the permanent bureaucracy. In these the Congress tended to be a natural ally of the bureaucracy against the political leaders, and of the departments that had grown up over the years between congressional committees and the various bureaus and their staffs within the executive departments.[62]

[57]*Washington Post*, 19 July 1973, quoted in Seidman.
[58]Seidman, *Politics, Position and Power*, p. 118.
[59]Seidman, Ibid., p. 118.
[60]*Watergate: Implications for Responsibility Government*, Frederick C. Mosher, Chairman (New York: Basic Books, 1974), p. 9.
[61]Seidman, *Politics, Position and Power*, p. 119.
[62]Price, *With Nixon*, p. 194.

Nixon's reorganization strategy to attempt the management and control of the bureaucracy was supplemented by his attempt to reorder national priorities. The key to such an attempt required control of the federal budget. In his second Inaugural Address, he set the tone for his second term. "I offer no solution of a purely governmental kind for every problem. We have lived too long with that false hope."[63] But, "the meaning of mandate for domestic affairs . . . was expressed not in the State of the Union message as is customary, but in Nixon's tightfisted budget for fiscal year 1974."[64] In his budget message of January 29, 1973, he expressed his disdain of the social programs—and their experts—that characterized the increased centralization of the 1960s.[65] He was aware that bureaucratization rested finally on the respectability of the opinion that the exercise of control of modern organizations derives ultimately from its technical knowledge and thereby its neutrality.[66] Bureaucratic control is increased inevitably as scientific expertise expands. Such expertise in the social sciences had provided important links between the professions and the bureaucracy which, it could not be ignored, were largely dominated by Democrats.

In placing his reliance on the "new federalism," Nixon expressed his confidence in the majority and common sense management of government. It required a change from a national perspective to a local perspective, from greater dependence upon "experts" to more dependence upon individuals.[67] The 1974 budget, Nixon announced, "proposes a leaner federal bureaucracy, increased reliance to carry out what are primarily State and local responsibilities, and greater freedom for the American people to make for themselves fundamental choices about what is best for them."[68] The "failure of the 1960s," he noted, "derived from the do something, do anything pressure for federal panaceas which led to the establishment of scores of well-intentioned social programs."[69] These programs had resulted in the linkage of social science professionals and the national bureaucracy.[70] They were dominated largely by Democrats and

---

[63]January 20 1973, in *Historic Documents* (Washington, D.C.: Congressional Quarterly Inc., 1974), p. 83.

[64]Nathan, *Administrative Presidency,* p. 70.

[65]After the budget was unveiled, House Speaker Carl Albert vowed that Congress "will not permit the President to lay waste the great programs . . . inaugurated by FDR and advanced and enlarged by every democratic President since then." *Historic Documents,* p. 171.

[66]Cf. Nathan, *Administrative Presidency,* p. 82–85.

[67]Price suggested that "the direction of change was clear; a shift from homogeneity and toward heterogeneity, from paternalism and toward individualism, from national direction and toward local option, from the bureaucratic process and toward the political process, in all its multiple forms. . . . For the armies of those who had grown accustomed to commanding the Washington heights and . . . directing the battles across the grand sweep of the national plain. . . . It would require a yielding of power by those grown accustomed to power." *With Nixon,* p. 130.

[68]*Historic Documents,* p. 175.

[69]Ibid.

[70]Nixon's attack on the sciences and social sciences resulted in the attempt to exert "a concerted and direct influence over specific areas of science and social sciences policy. . . . 'Federal science

served their interests.[71] Nixon's reorganization attempts and budget strategy—
an "administration spokesman conceded privately"—sought as a "major purpose" to break the "linkage of the professional groups and the bureaucracies."[72]

In the management of the government itself, the political strategy was away
from the professional bureau-clientele relationship; rather, it was to be replaced
by management by objectives (MBO) and goals.

> In introducing management by objectives the staff at OMB consciously reacted
> against the experience of the attempt to introduce PBB (Planning Programming
> Budgeting) eight years previously. MBO was not described as a scientific device for
> identifying or making choices.[73]

As Roy Ash (Director of OMB) remarked, "I think it is reasonably clear that
the approach we have taken is neither particularly new nor particularly profound. . . . Frankly, I would prefer to label it 'management by common
sense'."[74]

In attempting to downgrade the expertise that provided significant authority
to the bureaucracy as well as its neutrality, Nixon concluded his budget message
with a return to common sense. He noted:

> The respect given to the common sense of the common man is what has made
> America the most uncommon of nations. Common sense tells us that government

---

policy will no longer be made by top ranking elite scientists. Instead, policy is in the hands of bright
young Republican lawyers in the White House. . . . Also, an important shift in emphasis within the
social science budgets occurred in terms of the ideological perspective of the institutions receiving
funds.' Nixon preferred to fund conservative institutions." James Everett Katz, "Science, Social
Science and Presidentialism: Policy During the Nixon Administration," in Louis Horowitz, ed.,
The Use and Abuse of Social Science (New Brunswick: Transaction Books, 1975), p. 270. Nixon
also, in Reorganization Plan No. 1 of 1973, abolished the Office of Science and Technology, and
the NASA as units of the Executive Office. This was seen to be a "downgrading of our sciences
apparatus." Some, Seidman observed, "suspected it was motivated by a desire to punish the scientific community for its opposition to the Vietnam War." Seidman, *Politics, Position and Power*, pp.
240–241.

[71]Joel D. Aberbach and Bert A. Rockman have suggested that it was Nixon's view that "in the
main, services performed by these [social service agencies, particularly HEW, HUD, OEO] agencies are directed toward the Democratic party, in terms of electoral support. Moreover, the organized interest group clientele affected by most of the programs of these . . . social service agencies
are often professional associations and social cause organizations with informal but substantial ties
with the Democratic party nationally. "Clashing Beliefs Within the Executive Branch: The Nixon
Administration Bureaucracy," *American Political Science Review*, 70 (June 1976), p. 459.

[72]Seidman, *Politics, Position and Power*, p. 112.

[73]Richard Rose, "Implementation and Evaporation: The Record of MBO," *Public Administration Review*, 37 (January/February 1977), p. 67.

[74]Quoted in Rose, Ibid., p. 67. Under Nixon, the claim was made that "OMB had become an
advocate of policy rather than a politically neutral analytic tool. It was called a monolithic super-
agency imposing budgetary decisions based on political considerations on other federal agencies
and departments." David Boorstin, "Federal Fiscal Control," *Editorial Research Reports—The
U.S. Economy Under Stress* (Washington, D.C.: Congressional Quarterly Inc., 1975), p. 138.

cannot make a habit of living beyond its means. If we are not willing to make some sacrifices in holding down spending, we will be forced to make a much greater sacrifice in higher taxes or renewed inflation. . . . Common sense tells us that we must not abuse an economic system that already provides more income for more people than any other system by suffocating the productive members of the society with excessive tax rates. Common sense tells us it is more important to save tax dollars than to save bureaucratic reputations. . . . It is hard to argue with these common sense judgments; surprisingly, it is just as hard to put them into action. . . . Two years ago, I spoke of the need for a new American Revolution to return power to the people and put the individual *self* back in the idea of *self*-government. The 1974 budget moves us firmly toward that goal.[75]

The organizational changes of the Nixon presidency assumed that the problems of choice and the problems of management could not be divorced from one another.[76] It was a tacit rejection of some of the important elements of the Progressive era that had become legitimized in the new definition of liberalism that grew out of the New Deal. It was a denial of the benevolence of the administrative state; more importantly, it denied the scientific opinion upon which the legitimacy of bureaucratic rule rested—that it was indeed nonpartisan or technical, and that its authority rested upon its neutrality.

Richard Rose suggested that Nixon's presidency "was distinctive in that the means chosen to his political end were administrative, rather than legislative or based upon appeals through the mass media." [77] The strategy of the administrative presidency required that Nixon, "unlike his modern predecessors, did not seek to make his mark through the legislative route for the achievement of domestic policy objectives."[78] Rather, he sought to decrease the power of the national government and the national legislature by managing the bureaucracy and making policy by reorganization, budget impoundment and reduction, personnel shifts, and regulation writing.[79] Such an attempt was necessarily fraught with political danger. It marked the first time since the New Deal that the increase in the power of the president did not simultaneously involve as a byproduct any authorization by, or increase in, the power of the legislature. In fact, the movement of power away from the bureaucracy and the national government involved a reversal from the earlier days. As Price has noted,

One of the truly great ironies of the Nixon era is that the President portrayed, in his disgrace, as a power-mad fiend whose removal was necessary to the preservation of America's liberties, spent most of his presidency trying to get rid of power. Though portrayed as the architect of the Imperial Presidency, it was he who tried to reverse

[75]*Historic Documents*, p.183.
[76]Cf. Richard Rose, *Managing Presidential Objectives* (New York: Free Press, 1976), pp. 51–53.
[77]Ibid.
[78]Nathan, *Administrative Presidency*, p. 73.
[79]Ibid., pp. 73–75.

four decades of increasing centralization of authority. . . . Many of his struggles with the Congress were over precisely that—pitting congressional determination to expand federal powers against Nixon's determination to reduce federal powers.[80]

In attempting to reorganize the bureaucracy, the president was acting alone, apart from his party in the legislature and nearly every organized group that had a stake in centralization, including the national press and other national elites.

> Nixon's presidency was embattled over a set of basic philosophical divisions about the states, the communities, and the people themselves. This was a dispute over the extent and division of political power in a free society. . . . But one of the most basic battles of all was a war for supremacy between the old elite—which dominated the media, the academic world, the tastemakers and the trendsetters—and the new forces, that sprang essentially from the nation's heartland, and that found their political focus in Nixon himself. This was a fight over values, and the way those values would be determined, and by whom. On both sides, it came to been seen as a struggle for survival. It was this battle, more than the others, that stoked the fires which eventually consumed the Nixon presidency.[81]

It was clear that Congress as a body would not attempt to dismantle what it had assembled, nor would it allow greater executive control that involved a diminution of its own authority.[82] And it must not be forgotten that the minority party membership in the legislature also benefited from its access to the bureaucracy.[83]

THE POLITICS OF CONFRONTATION

Nixon's decision in his second term to begin seriously the process of decentralization led to a politics of confrontation. In attacking the interests that benefited from centralized administration, he also attacked the legitimacy of the opinions that sustained them. The two dominant opinions, one based on a view of equality which, in the hands of the new class, denied the element of majority consent; the other, derivative of the pluralist nature of American politics required the consent of every significant group in society. Both looked to the bureaucracy as the means of satisfying its demands. The new class looked to the bureaucracy as the apparatus to ensure the redistribution of economic wealth;

---

[80]Price, *With Nixon,* p. 194.

[81]Ibid., pp. 117–118.

[82]In this struggle, as James Sundquist observed, Nixon "chose the issues when he set out to liquidate through administrative action in defiance of the Democratic Congress, not only much of what the New Frontier and the Great Society had created, but even programs that had their origin in the New Deal itself. And it was for the activists to defend, and to counterattack. Conservative senators and representatives who might share the President's disdain for the programs their party colleagues have enacted still spring to the defense of the Congress' right to determine when and if those programs are to be dismantled." *American Party System,* p. 580.

[83]Cf. William A. Rusher, *The Making of the New Majority Party* (New York: Sheed & Ward, Inc., 1975), p. xxii.

the more orthodox view considered the bureaucracy as the web of the pluralist system. These two views were not incompatible. As Allen Schick has noted:

> Pluralism, always a presence in American politics, came to be regarded as its democratic linchpin in the mid-twentieth century. With the blossoming of . . . "interest group liberalism," the use of government power to provide benefits to powerful interests, the great bureaucracies of the federal government functioned as dispensaries of the "who gets what" of American politics. . . . Interest groups were a political link between a Congress that authorized and a bureaucracy that delivered benefits. Rather than viewing one another as adversaries, these two power centers forged a political symbiosis that enabled the interest group state to flourish.[84]

However, after the 1960s it was not merely the powerful who benefited from this relationship of Congress and the bureaucracy. Rather, Congress "which has always been a surrogate for the powerful . . . has since the advent of social welfare programs been an ombudsman for the powerless."[85] With the organization of the historically weak claimants (blacks, the handicapped, women, and certain ethnic minorities), access to the bureaucracy and positions of power in the federal government provided organized minorities greater power in national administration than could be obtained in state or local governments. A centralized bureaucracy, allied with Congress and isolated from presidential leadership and majority opinion, offered a satisfactory vehicle to achieve their goal of greater centralized planning and economic redistribution. In confronting Congress and the bureaucracy, Nixon ignored the rules of consensus politics and appeared to deny the pluralistic basis of American society.[86]

Moreover, Nixon had attempted to confront Congress in areas in which it was least equipped to defend itself. As Ralph K. Huitt observed:

[84]"Congress and the Details of Administration," *Public Administration Review,* 36 (September/October 1976), p. 518.

[85]Arthur S. Miller, "Congress: A Great Beached Whale," *The Progressive,* 41 (February 1977), p. 22.

[86]Jon Wiener has suggested that Nixon's attack on the Democratic Party was "a violation of the rules of pluralistic politics—that party competition, by mutual agreement remains within clearly defined limits; that no one seeks the annihilation of his opponents. The winners are . . . willing to compromise, they do not use their power to retaliate against those who opposed them. . . . What was the crime for which Nixon was forced out of office? . . . He treated liberals as if they were radicals." "Tocqueville, Marx, Weber, Nixon: Watergate in Theory," *Dissent,* 213 (Spring 1976), pp. 171, 177. The defenders of the bureaucracy were also defending a pluralist society. As Seidman noted, "organizational structure is one way of expressing national commitment, influencing program direction and ordering priorities. Executive branch structure is in fact a microcosm of American society. Inevitably it reflects the values, conflicts and competing forces to be found in a pluralistic society." *Politics, Position and Power,* p. 14. Woll and Jones even insisted that the bureaucracy is crucial to the proper functioning of the constitutional system. It "puts important limits on the power of the President because it has independent sources of political power. . . . The pluralistic and independent bureaucracy, although often inefficient and yielding to special-interest group pressure, helps to preserve the balance of powers among the branches of government that is necessary for the preservation of our system of constitutional democracy." Peter Woll and Rochell Jones, "Bureaucratic Defense in Depth," in Ronald E. Pynn, ed., *Watergate and the American Political Process* (New York: Praeger Publishers, 1975), pp. 217, 224.

Historically the principal checks Congress had had on the President came from maintaining control of the negatives—that is, the President asks for what he wants, and congressional power comes from the liberty to decide how much of it to let him have. But Nixon did not seem to want anything from Congress. . . . Many members of Congress wanted more than he did. Trying to oppose Nixon on domestic programs was, some Congressmen put it, like pushing a string. There was no resistance. Instead, Nixon tried to run things without Congress. Impounding funds, deferring the spending of them, shifting money from one purpose to another—these gave control of what really mattered, the allocation of government resources.[87]

This management system to gain control of the bureaucracy included personnel shifts to gain better control of the departments by bypassing the Cabinet; reorganization; regulation writing; and impoundment or reduction of funds, which resulted in the enervation of whole programs within the bureaucracy. Nathan suggested "the budget strategy for 1973–1974 represented such a strong use of fiscal powers as to effectively constitute a new type of executive power. . . . Few more direct ways could be imagined to take on the bureaucracy."[88]

Similarly, Nixon sought to reorganize whole activities out of existence. In early 1973, he attempted to abolish completely the Office of Economic Opportunity. In addition, the special offices in the White House for Consumer Affairs and Science and Technology "were devolved to new agency homes and eliminated as Executive Office units." Reorganization, however, "was not limited to the Executive Office. . . . The establishment of the super secretaries constituted an important use of reorganization as a tool enabling the President's men to get a firmer hold over the machinery of domestic government."[89] Nixon also attempted to use regulation-writing as a means of attaining policy goals. This authority was to be used in conjunction with the federal budget for fiscal 1974.

> In the field of social services new rules were issued early in 1973 that restricted the way in which funds to aid the poor through social services could be expended. . . . The new rules . . . required that these funds only be used for people with defined and specific conditions of need, and then only under a system of detailed accounting for the services provided. Here the aim was to reduce the options available to social-welfare professionals, long subject to Administration criticism and strongly entrenched in the welfare bureaucracy of HEW. On the other hand, in the manpower field, the regulation power was to be used not to introduce government controls, but to reduce them. . . . The aim was to decentralize by implementing the Administration plan for manpower special revenue sharing through administrative action in the form of changed regulations under existing statutory authority.[90]

[87]"White House Channels to the Hill," in Harvey C. Mansfield, Sr., ed., *Congress Against the President* (New York: Praeger Publishers, 1975), p. 76.
[88]Nathan, *Administrative Presidency*, p. 74.
[89]Ibid., p. 74.
[90]Ibid., p. 75.

The presidential impoundment of appropriated funds, however, created the most difficult problem for Congress. Other presidents had impounded funds. But, unlike the others, under Nixon "impoundment had become not an instrument of economy but of policy. If Nixon could establish the idea of policy impoundment at presidential pleasure, he would divest Congress of this 'most effectual weapon' [power of the purse] and significantly alter the theory of the Constitution."[91] In politicizing the use of impoundment authority, Nixon prompted one commentator to suggest: "the history of impoundment goes back to Jefferson, but Nixon's distinctive contribution was to refuse to spend money voted by Congress for projects of which he personally disapproved."[92] In so doing, he was able to thwart the intentions of Congress.

Through such strategy Nixon had confronted Congress in areas in which it was the most vulnerable. He achieved executive reorganization without the necessity of constitutional authorization, and then he began reordering national priorities through control of the budget.[93] Certainly Nixon was himself vulnerable in his confrontation of Congress as the means of gaining control of the bureaucracy. He had to rely solely upon his electoral mandate as the legitimacy for taking such action. Yet in his campaign he struck his most responsive chord with an attack on Washington and its bureaucracy. If the majority had become distrustful of government for its failure to respond to the majority's demands, executive power was still most vulnerable as the most visible symbol of governing. Thus the president was most susceptible to the charges of the abuse of power because the strength of his victory rested on the assumption that power would be returned from Washington back to the localities and the people. He was put in the awkward position of centralizing authority in his personal staff in order to divest administrative control from the bureaucracy. Leonard Garment, then a member of Nixon's legal staff, observed that "the central paradox of the Nixon administration was that in order to reduce *federal* power, it was first

[91]Arthur M. Schlesinger, *The Imperial President,* pp. 239–240.

[92]Hart, "Presidential Power Revisited," p. 59.

[93]John Hart has suggested that "Nixon achieved the desired effect by creating the new system of responsibility and control within the White House irrespective of Congressional action. The power outcome of this action was considerable. The President had concentrated responsibility within a small group of close aides in the White House, downgraded the heads of departments and was in a position to organize policy around broad, over-arching areas which were not matched by the Congressional committee system. The President achieved this end by exploiting a power vacuum, acting within a framework that was unaffected by the usual checks and balances of American politics. If there was any source of power behind this action it was just the fact that Nixon claimed he had the power to act, daring the other branches of government to stop him. . . . There was no one to influence, persuade or bargain with and, moreover, the President had specifically rejected these techniques after the initial failure of his attempt to use the legislative route. He had confronted Congress on this issue instead of working within a pattern of consensus politics." "Presidential Power Revisited," p. 58. If Hart is correct, it is no wonder that observers, like Woll and Arthur S. Miller, concluded that "the principal check on the Presidency, . . . is the permanent Federal government, not Congress." Miller, *Congress,* p. 25.

necessary to increase *presidential* power."[94] "In order to return 'power to the people,' " William Safire colorfully argued at the time, "Nixon first has to wrench it out of the hands of satraps that had controlled it for generations, and they naturally charged him with seeking all their power for himself."[95]

That the bureaucracy and those committed to administrative centralization would fight back with all the vigor they could muster was to be expected. That they could ally themselves with other centers of authority threatened with the loss of power was crucial to their success. The Congress and the bureaucracy needed a national focus in the attempt to delegitimize the actions of the president as being contrary to the public interest; such a focus could be provided by the national media.[96] The media, not unsympathetic to the concentration of power in Washington, provided the national focus of attention, and Congress and the bureaucracy used the media to great advantage in this encounter.[97] Watergate, to be sure, tended to obscure (to the public, at least) the collision course Nixon had embarked upon in early 1973; but given the "revolutionary" nature of that course,[98] the equivalent of a Watergate was an absolute necessity for the defenders of the New Deal order.

Theodore White has written that "the Watergate affair is inexplicable in terms of older forms of corruption in American history where men broke laws for private gain or privilege." Moreover, White suggested, "the men involved were involved at a moment, in 1972, when history was moving their way. They

---

[94]Garment, quoted in A. James Reichley, *Conservatives in An Age of Change: The Nixon and Ford Administrations* (Washington, D.C.: Brookings Institution, 1985), p. 259.

[95]*Before the Fall* (New York: Belmont Tower Books, 1975), p. 231.

[96]Elie Flatto has suggested, "In the two years prior to Nixon's resignation an impeachment process has in fact been going on in which television played a key descriptive as well as determinative role, as the traditional political legalistic concept of an impeachment of yesteryear no longer proved relevant. . . . The phenomenon of Nixon's resignation would not have been possible without the continuous . . . televised disclosures of the Watergate scandal, particularly . . . without [those] of Senator Ervin's Committee." "The Impeachment of Richard Nixon," *Contemporary Review,* 226 (March 1975), p. 146.

[97]Seth Cropsey has noted that "many newspapermen are called investigative reporters, but their investigations generally consist in printing leaks handed to them by one group of bureaucrats . . . bureaucrats whom the White House has threatened, slighted, outmaneuvered, or disposed, did their best to get even. CIA director Richard Helms, who could have asked the FBI chieftains to stop its Watergate investigation, did not. FBI chieftains, galled by Gray's appointment, leaked information about the White House-Watergate connection. IRS bureaucrats repaid the White House for swallowing up their agents and power by spilling Nixon's damning tax returns into print. The really ominous message . . . whatever one might think of Nixon, is that the bureaucracy was almost bound to win. Compared even to Richard Nixon, their unrestrained growth and increasingly independent power . . . would seem to pose by far the greater threat to our system of government." "Of Drugs and Bureaucrats," *Commentary,* 64 (November 1977), pp. 78, 80.

[98]Samuell Lubell suggests that "Nixon transformed the presidency, organizing it for political overkill and upsetting the constitutional balance with Congress and the electorate. George McGovern and his youthful aides may have fancied themselves as the carriers of radical and sweeping change. The real political revolutionary was Richard Nixon." *The Future While It Happened* (New York: W. W. Norton & Co., 1973), p. 31.

were trying to speed it by any means, fair or foul. By so doing, perhaps, they wrecked their own victory. And that, as history may record, compounds their personal felonies with national tragedy."[99] Whether Nixon's men were moving with or against history is as difficult to understand as Watergate itself. Whatever its reasons, Watergate ended the attempts to decentralize administrative power. With the resignation of several top White House aides, the press was advised, without fanfare, "that the President was reinstituting a 'direct line of communication with the Cabinet' and discontinuing the experiment with counselors."[100] The attempt to reorganize and manage the bureaucracy was over. After Nixon's resignation, President Ford's transition advisors, headed by Rogers C. B. Morton, "were highly critical of the OMB role and recommended that steps be taken to prevent OMB from boring holes 'below the waterline' in the Departments."[101] In his first address to Congress, Ford pledged an administration that would seek "unity in diversity" and restore an open presidency. American pluralism and the constitutional order were apparently saved from the revolutionary presidency of Richard Nixon.

Nixon was considered an "aberration" and wholly inconsistent with the American political tradition because he ignored the ordinary means of political life in his desire to attain his own ends. He looked at the other ruling elements of the political order (not only Democrats) as though they were enemies of the regime.

> He did indeed contemplate, as he said in his 1971 State of the Union Message, a New American Revolution. . . . But the essence of this revolution was not . . . power to the people—the essence was power to the presidency. . . . It may be that he was the first President in American history to conclude that separation of power had so frustrated government on behalf of the majority that the constitutional system had become finally intolerable—and to move boldly to change the system.[102]

How did Nixon seek to change the system? Arthur Schlesinger suggested he sought to do so by subversion of the principle of the separation of powers.[103] In the election of 1972 Nixon attempted to alter the constitutional system by appealing to the majority to ratify his view of the office as a plebiscite.[104] It was

---

[99]*The Making of the President—1972* (New York: Atheneum, 1973), p. 367.

[100]Seidman, *Politics, Position and Power*, p. 118.

[101]Ibid.

[102]Schlesinger, *Imperial Presidency*, p. 252.

[103]Schlesinger insisted that Nixon's theory of government "was a central attack on the role of Congress in the American polity." Ibid., p. 240.

[104]The attitude of the liberals toward the majority had apparently changed. As James Burnham had noted, "Liberalism tends toward a plebiscitary interpretation of democracy. Government ought to reflect the will of the democratic majority as immediately . . . and accurately as possible. Liberals thus distrust those political institutions and processes that mediate, deflect, distort or otherwise interfere with the direct expression of the popular will." *Suicide of the West* (New York: John Day Co., 1964), p. 78.

the electoral victory itself and Nixon's belief that his election by the majority constituted a mandate that led to a crisis.[105] As Schlesinger noted:

> The expansion and abuse of presidential power constituted the underlying issue, the issue that . . . Watergate raised to the surface, dramatized, and made politically accessible. Watergate was the by-product of a larger revolutionary purpose. At the same time, it was the fatal mistake that provided and legitimized resistance to the revolutionary Presidency.[106]

Was the essence of the Nixon revolution "power to the presidency" as Schlesinger maintained? Or had Nixon attempted to extend the authority of the contemporary majority by imposing limitations upon the power of the permanent government? If the latter, he failed to legitimize that attempt with reference to the principle that provided the moral authority upon which majority rule rests. That it had become increasingly difficult to do so could be seen in the extent to which an appeal to the principle of equality had become more difficult. The new class and orthodox liberal opinion was unequivocally committed to equality, but the basis of that commitment had been compromised by the radical equalitarianism of the new class, not to mention orthodox "social science."[107] The new class view of equality (which rested at bottom on compassion) was animated by the desire to achieve social justice and, as such, it was practically indistinguishable from the necessity to create the classless society. A new legitimacy, therefore, had come to reside in the bureaucracy as the primary means to ensure the equitable redistribution of wealth. Consequently, the bureaucracy was supported by the "class interests" of the social scientists who had a stake in the neutrality of the administrative state, and the new class which had an interest in a greater role for government as the engine of compassion. If the new

---

[105]Schlesinger argued that "the plebiscitary conception . . . dominated the 1972 election. Nixon cut loose from his party, ran his campaign through the Committee to Reelect the President, . . . concentrated on collecting the largest possible majority for himself. Once he had gained that majority, his associates propagated the mystique of the "mandate." The mandate, it was alleged, justified the President in doing anything that he believed the interests of the nation required him to do. Since the Democrats won Congress by a considerable majority they thought that they had a mandate too— one to carry out the Democratic platform. But the White House defined the presidential mandate as definitive and overriding. . . . The mandate became the source of wider power than any president had ever claimed before. Whether a conscious or unconscious revolutionary, Nixon was carrying the imperial Presidency toward its ultimate form in the plebiscitary Presidency—with the President accountable only once every four years." *Imperial Presidency*, pp. 254–255.

[106]Ibid.

[107]As Harry Jaffa has suggested, "the radical subjectivity of the social sciences with respect to what it calls values has crept into the law, and into the opinion upon which the law rested. . . . This created a situation in which the feeling of equality is identical to equality itself. . . . The feeling of inequality had become a well-nigh irresistible principle of ultimate appeal. The utopianism and the intolerance of the new politics—the success of which would surely spell out the end of constitutional democracy—was rooted in the social scientism of the academy," Jaffa, *Crisis of the House Divided*, preface.

class wanted to humanize the bureaucracy and make it representative,[108] the administrators wanted to keep it the center of the pluralist system.

The intellectual opinion was nearly unanimous in its view that Nixon's actions resulted from the desire to aggrandize presidential (hence personal) power. According to the Panel of the National Academy of Public Administration, Nixon's motive in attempting to politicize the bureaucracy "seems to have been Presidential power, its enlargement, its exploitation, and its continuation."[109] The power was to be used "to impose upon the government the ideological views of the President."[110] In failing to recognize the neutrality of the bureaucracy, the president was deprived of the "technical competence of the experts in the executive branch." As a result, "the emergence of a powerful White House staff . . . had seriously diminished the responsibilities of the career, professional staff of OMB and its capacity to provide the kind of objective and expert counsel to the President, which characterized earlier operations."[111]

Unlike the Commission on Administrative Management, which sought to legitimize Roosevelt's centralization based on the scientific principles of management,[112] the Nixon decentralization was regarded by intellectuals as a threat to the Constitutional system itself. In its report to Senator Ervin's Committee, the Panel suggested that had Watergate not intervened, the American constitutional order may have been transformed into "Max Weber's ideal type of monarchy ruled from the top through a strictly disciplined hierarchy system" with elections or impeachment as the only means of holding a president accountable. It seems somewhat paradoxical that the Panel would consider Nixon's antibureaucratic efforts as Weberian. Along with Woodrow Wilson, Weber had provided a rationale for the necessity of maintaining the separation of politics and administration. He had insisted that "in a modern state the actual ruler is necessarily and unavoidably the bureaucracy."[113] As a result, in a bureaucracy, administration replaced politics.[114] Weber argued for the superiority of the bureaucracy as a result of its greater rationality. Peter Berger has observed:

Modernity may be defined as a complex of social patterns based on the application of thoroughly rational methods to the solution of human problems. Max Weber . . . has called "rationalization the prime moving force of the recent era in world his-

[108]Cf. Eugene P. Dvorin and Robert H. Simmons, *From Amoral to Humane Bureaucracy* (San Francisco: Canfield Press, 1972); also Arthur D. Larson, "Representative Bureaucracy and Administrative Responsibility: A Reassessment," *Midwest Review of Public Administration,* 7 (April 1973), pp. 79–89.

[109]*Watergate: Implications,* p. 7.

[110]National Academy of Public Administration, *Implications,* p. 7.

[111]Ibid., p. 42.

[112]Gulick had noted "organization requires . . . a system of authority that requires a single directing executive authority." "Science, Values," pp. 6–7.

[113]Max Weber, *Economy and Society* (New York: Bedminster Press, 1968), p. 1393.

[114]Cf. Ralph P. Hummel, *The Bureaucratic Experience* (New York: St. Martin's Press, 1977), pp. 165–192.

tory." Its pervasive spirit marks all the new social constructions of this period, especially the major ones—the bureaucratic state, and the system of industrial production. Each of these represents a revolutionary "rationalization" in its particular sphere of influence. Each has brought forth types of men—administrators, engineers—who share an ethos of empathetic rationality.[115]

Nearly every discipline in the social sciences had come to regard rationality from this Weberian perspective.

The discipline of Public Administration itself had been born as a result of the distinction between politics and administration. It had lent its support to the aggrandizement of executive power and had sought

> to undermine the checks and balances that have existed in the American system.
> . . . The profession has devoted 40 years to aggrandizing presidential power. It has consistently sought . . . to strengthen the President at the expense of all other elements that make up the governmental system. . . . Every writer was for a strong presidency. Absolutely nobody was for a weak one.[116]

The support of the presidency—like the support of the majority he was to lead—was an indispensable feature of the Progressive era and the abandonment of both signaled the end of the era.

It was clear, however, that administrators—as well as new class liberals—had an interest in the maintenance of a centralized administration. "That which does not increase the activities of government does not serve the interest of this new class any more than that which did increase the activities served the interests of the old one."[117] In the wake of the breakup of the old liberalism, the importance of the private, and particularly of property, had given way to an importance of the public and the establishment of services rendered in the bureaucracy.[118] But the new class interest, despite its pretention, was as self-serving as any.

> The most persuasive explanation is that a class interest is served here, the post-industrial surplus of functionaries who, in the manner of industrialists who earlier turned to advertising, induce demand for their own product. . . . It may even have precipitated a structural change in the demands that may be made of society. It is the largest accession yet to the armamentarium of those whose interest or inclination tends toward increasing the social activities of the state.[119]

[115]"Ideologies, Myths, Moralities," in Irving Kristol and Paul Weaver, eds., *The Americans: 1976* (Lexington, Mass: Lexington Books, 1976), p. 341.

[116]James L. Sundquist, "Reflections on Watergate: Lessons for Public Administration," *Public Administration Review,* 34 (September/October 1974), p. 453.

[117]Daniel P. Moynihan, "Social Policy: From Utilitarian Ethic to Therapeutic Ethic," in Kristol and Weaver, eds., *The Americans: 1976,* p. 46.

[118]Moynihan speculated, "that in a post-industrial society the importance of property recedes and that of a government advances." If the old class "mastery was based on control of property," he maintained, "the more recent seems to be based on control of government." Ibid., p. 43.

[119]Ibid., p. 44.

The exploitation of the principle of equality for what has been called a "class interest" resulted in a crisis in American politics, as well as an intellectual crisis that produced a division in nearly every discipline in the social sciences. That division concerned the posture that the social sciences should adopt toward the problems of society at large. How should they relate to the centers of political power in the society? The creation of the "new economics," the "new political science," or the "new public administration" within those disciplines urged an abandonment of the neutrality that had characterized social sciences in the past. They insisted that the social sciences could not retain a value-free posture; rather, they must adopt and adapt themselves to the requirements of the new equality.[120]

The 1972 Democratic presidential nominee and the Democratic national convention offered a platform that conformed in many respects to the demands of the new class and the new view of equality.[121] The election itself was reflective of the ambiguities that adhered in the American society; it also offered a preview of the institutional struggle that would occur in subsequent years. For in the 1972 election Nixon spoke of the need for a "new Majority," and McGovern was nearly always concerned with morality and "decency" in government. Thus the perennial American problem was again articulated, perhaps more clearly than before, if by opposing sides: the necessity of the creation of a decent majority. If Nixon had nearly all the votes on his side, McGovern insisted to the end that he was in the right.[122] And here of course, was the problem. Nixon had the majority, but he lacked legitimacy which, however, did not become apparent for a few more years. Why did Nixon fail to gain legiti-

---

[120]Victor Thompson noted that "the new public administration" and the "new political science" urge the frank adoption of an egalitarian value system. Our teaching and research should be aimed at helping the poor and the powerless. . . . The basic value, therefore, is the equalization of economic and political power . . . the basic objectives of administration should be to solve the problems of poverty and racial or ethnic prejudice. The role of administration is to be somewhat subversive, promoting these goals regardless of congressional or presidential mandates or the wishes of the "organized interests." This viewpoint represents a most amazing effort to establish a new claimant in the place of the . . . public. . . . Public administrators . . . should use their resources to advance the interests of their special clients." *Without Sympathy or Enthusiasm: The Problem of Administrative Compassion* (University, Ala.: University of Alabama Press, 1975), pp. 65-66.

[121]In the election, on the one hand, was a significant and powerful minority armed with the rhetoric of equality who wanted to use the power of government in the progressive manner in which presidents from Theodore Roosevelt to Wilson, from FDR to JFK had done—in the interest of the people. On the other hand, it looked as though the majority of the people sought a restraint upon that power. And a president who represented such a majority was no longer the instrument of progress. As Theodore White noted, "We live . . . at the end of a generation, when the ideas of hope and grandeur that moved the decades of the 1930s and 1940s, having achieved their triumphs, imprisoned new thinking. Those ideas increased the power of the state beyond the experience of any previous generation. . . . The majority wished to pursue those ideas no further now." *The Making of the President—1972* (New York: Atheneum, 1973), p. 371.

[122]This was the title of his campaign manager's account of the election. Cf. Gary Hart, *Right From the Start* (New York: Quadrangle Books, 1973).

macy with his overwhelming electoral victory? It was not, as has subsequently been argued, the result of a fraud perpetuated upon the electorate.[123] The results of the 1972 election were as genuine as any in American history. What had become questionable by this time in its legitimacy was the majority itself, or the opinions that animated the majority. As Samuell Lubell noted just after the election, "Above all, what the Nixon Majority needs today is effective resistance."[124]

The criticisms of the constitutional system from the time of Woodrow Wilson onward rested on the assumption that the factionalism of government worked to obstruct majority rule and prevent adequate representation of the national interests. The implicit criticism of the imperial presidency was that the president has succeeded too well in counteracting the factional and centrifugal forces in American government The president had come to embody popular opinion and the majority will so well as to run roughshod over the particular interests represented in Congress. Some began to question whether there were important interests, besides the national interests, that ought to be represented. "The President tends to emphasize the national consideration and the interests of a great diversity of people more often then Congress does," Grant McConnell observed in a timely work on the presidency. "But national interests, the interests that are most widely shared, should not always be preferred to particular interests. It is firmly in the American tradition to protect minorities."[125]

Charles Hardin echoed this complaint, that the bond between the president and the people had led to presidential solipsism and to extensive perversion in government.[126] It had become apparent that the principle of equality—compatible with consent and majority rule—had been replaced in respectability (among intellectuals) by a new class view in which social justice had become the paramount objective. As McConnell noted, "The obligation of the president in the largest terms is to mobilize power and direct it toward the ends of social justice and national security."[127] The defense of the bureaucracy had become the last line of defense of the "intellectual opinion" that had equated executive leadership with the necessity to ensure social justice. The abandonment of the majority was reflected by a change in political alignment; "the crucial dividing line of partisan alignment was no longer income but education."[128] Arthur Sch-

---

[123]White noted, "the view of the 1972 election as fraud is comforting to many . . . who have been unable to accept the proportions of the 1972 vote. Watergate has . . . restored their faith in the American people. The people had been . . . tricked. . . . [They] could be rehabilitated. . . . Had they known the truth, they would have turned Nixon out." White, *Making of the President—1972*, p. 367.

[124]Lubell, *The Future While It Happened* (New York: W. W. Norton & Co., 1973), p. 16.

[125]*The Modern Presidency* (New York: St. Martin's Press, 1976), p. 42.

[126]*Presidential Power and Accountability* (Chicago: University of Chicago Press, 1974), pp. 10–12.

[127]McConnell, *The Modern Presidency*, p. 110.

[128]Arthur M. Schlesinger, Jr., *Crisis of Confidence: Ideas, Power and Violence in America* (Boston: Little, Brown & Co., 1969), p. 188.

lesinger argued, "It is the less educated, low-income whites who tend to be the most emotional and primitive champions of conservatism. . . . The affluent and better educated, on the other hand, tend to care more about *rationality, reform, and progress.*"[129] The abandonment of the white working class was another striking sign of the drift of new liberalism away from the majority.[130] "Majority will, the historic foundation of democracy, cannot, then, be counted on to inaugurate the regime of equality that is desired by intellectuals."[131] It may also have become apparent to the intellectuals that the president, too, could no longer be counted upon to do so.

In an essay written after Watergate, Robert S. Hirshfield explored the dynamism in the relationship that exists between the president and the majority, and the danger posed by such a relationship. "Constitutional flexibility . . . has made the President both the most dynamic and the most dangerous of our political institutions."[132] He is dynamic because he must respond and attempt to lead a national majority. "There is no substitute for the President," Hirshfield noted, "as the sole representative of the national interest, as the focus of our political system, as the major initiator of change in our society."[133] Consequently, by the end of the Nixon administration, it had become clear that the presidency posed a threat to further progress. The president, like the majority he hopes to lead, may desire change in a direction that is not compatible with the ends of progressive liberalism. The question that had arisen by this time was one of determining change that was compatible with the ends of social progress and equal justice and change that was not. As a result, the collision of the intellectuals and the majority resulted from a difference of opinion concerning the ends of government, and the legitimacy of power in the attainment of those ends.

The mid-1960s witnessed a disjunction between democratic means and ends that grew out of the failure to understand the principle of equality as other than ideology or prejudice. Consequently, the legitimacy of the majority was questionable because of its lack of attachment to what were perceived to be democratic values (social and economic justice). The new class, on the other hand, was willing to forego democratic means (majority rules) to attain those ends. It may have marked the first time that the "authoritative" opinion, which

---

[129]Ibid.

[130]Everett Carl Ladd, Jr., has suggested that the split in the Democratic Party as a result of the influence of the new class has made it difficult for the Democrats to win the presidency. "New Class Liberals wield considerable influence within such major and expanding institutions as government bureaucracy, the press, the academy. . . . They can influence the choice of a presidential nominee . . . but the candidate's appeal to the nation as a whole is thereby compromised." "The Democrats Have Their Own Two-Party System," *Fortune,* 96 (October 1977), p. 216.

[131]Robert Nisbet, "The Pursuit of Equality," *The Public Interest,* 35 (Spring 1974), p. 103.

[132]"The Scope and Limits of the Presidential Power," in P. C. Dolce and George Skau, eds., *Power and the Presidency* (New York: Charles Scribner's Sons, 1976), p. 293.

[133]Ibid., p. 303.

sought in the name of equality to limit the power of the people, had the capacity to do so. It also marked a dangerous disjunction between equality and its organizing principle—majority rule. For the first time the newly "enlightened" opinion was willing to forego consent as the indispensable element of a legitimate government.

THE POST-IMPERIAL PRESIDENCY

In the wake of Watergate the public discourse and the scholarly literature on the presidency stressed a common theme: the president must be made accountable.[134] But for the first time since the Progressive era, in the view of many intellectuals, the president was not seen to be accountable to the majority. Rather, the president was to be restrained within the rigid bounds of the constitutional system.[135] This was an interesting turnabout for those who once attacked the Constitution for its antidemocratic tendencies. Their attitude in regard to the presidency was revelatory of their attitude toward the majority. When majority will was considered to be most reflective of the democratic elements of the society—as that which encouraged governmental activity designed to promote social welfare—the presidency was the focus of the attention to provide such leadership.

> Liberals, as partisans of democracy and social reform, have always objected to those elements of the Constitution which were designed to "refine" the will of the people and to make it difficult to undertake ambitious social programs. . . . The Constitution . . . could be made to promote liberal values . . . if the powers and dignity of the Presidency were enhanced.[136]

Thus the progressive view traditionally supported a broadening of the sphere of government activity. It preferred the national majority over local majorities. It was committed to a free press as part of its attachment to "national public opinion as against the forces of tradition and localism."[137] By the same token, its opposition was precisely a consequence of the view that the states were representative of local prejudice, and that Congress, which represented the special interests of the localities, was less favorably receptive to the progressive elements in American society. As Paul Weaver observed:

> the Presidency . . . was uniquely equipped to authorize and give legitimacy to political and social programs which are of urgent importance but which can be

---

[134]Cf. Theodore C. Sorenson, *Watchmen in the Night: Presidential Accountability after Watergate* (Cambridge: MIT Press, 1975); Elliot Richardson, *The Creative Balance* (New York: Holt, Rinehart & Winston, 1976).

[135]Arthur M. Schlesinger, Jr., insisted that "we should have a strong Presidency within the Constitution. . . . He must operate . . . within an equally strong and effective system of accountability." "The Imperial Presidency" in Dolce and Skau, eds., *Power and the Presidency*, pp. 269–270.

[136]Paul Weaver, "Liberals and the Presidency," *Commentary*, 60 (October 1975), p. 47.

[137]Cf. Ibid.

counted on to meet opposition or be hamstrung if left to the inherently obstructiona-list procedures of the national legislature.[138]

In the new view, the president must be restrained and held accountable by both formal and informal means. The formal modes of accountability, Arthur Schlesinger indicated, "are the written restraints on Presidential power in the Constitution, the Presidential accountability to law, to Congress, to the courts." The informal modes "are accountability to one's colleagues in the Cabinet and the executive branch, to one's political party, to the media of opinion, to public opinion in general."[139] The presidency had become imperial, in Schlesinger's view, because of recent incumbents' attempts to isolate the office from the rest of the political system. Imperial presidents had closed themselves off from the bureaucracy and the executive establishment, they cultivated hostility toward bureaucracy in the electorate, and sought to undermine the moral consensus that brought about its creation. For Schlesinger, a president like FDR could not have acted in an imperial manner. He noted

> FDR respected the system of accountability. He held Cabinet meetings twice a week. He held press conferences twice a week. . . . He was very accessible to members of Congress. . . . In other words, he did not run a closed Presidency. I think the peculiar characteristics of the imperial presidency is that it is a closed Presidency. It rejects the system of accountability.[140]

The rhetorical attack on the presidency, and the defense of the separation of powers, indicated the abandonment of the view made respectable in the Progressive era that the Constitution was undemocratic precisely because it prevented the majority from ruling. Majority rule was no longer the essence of democracy, precisely because the majority—and middle-class morality reflective of it—had become an obstacle to progressive liberalism. The abandonment of the presidency was an implicit attack on what had come to be considered, under Nixon, the unchecked power of the majority. There was small irony in the fact that a conservative, Willmoore Kendall, had not long ago defended Congress as an institution because of its conservatism. Now, for the first time, the liberal defense of Congress was based on the perception that it was a more progressive institution than the presidency.

The defenders of the presidency, in this period, denied that the office was imperial. Indeed, they argued that the presidency was characterized by weak-

---

[138]Ibid.

[139]"The Imperial Presidency," in Dolce and Skau, eds., *Power and the Presidency, op. cit.* p. 270.

[140]Ibid., p. 271. The acceptance of Schlesinger's view would be to deny the possibility of another Roosevelt. If Roosevelt accepted the forms of accountability, it was only when they did not interfere with the substance of his demands. He was willing to act with Congress and the Cabinet; he was also willing to act without them. He was not accountable to the laws simply, but to the spirit of the laws and the people. The recreation of a moral vision occurred in a time when the law had begun to lose its legitimacy—that legitimacy could not be restored by an appeal to the laws or the formal and informal modes of accountability.

ness. Consequently, the presidency had become too weak to sustain the system of checks and balances within the Constitution. As the office became weaker, presidents were forced to confront the Congress and the political system with claims of absolute discretionary power. Robert G. Dixon noted:

> In 1974 the first presidential resignation culminated an especially agitated period of congressional-executive relations. The battleground included impoundment of funds, war power, the Agnew agony, . . . veto power, . . . the scope of authority in respect to executive agreements and executive orders. . . . Underlying these passing events are enduring problems of separation of powers. The history of legislative-executive relationship has been marked by a steady pressure from Congress to adopt measures and procedures conceptually closer to a regime of shared powers than to the separation the framers envisaged. The executive has lately responded with theories of absolute discretion.[141]

The powers of the presidency derive not so much from formal or Constitutional grants of authority, but from the ability of the president to lead public opinion as reflective of the majority, and thereby influence other officials. In the period after the Progressive era, and particularly in the New Deal, the national party, with the cooperation of other national elites and the national press, was instrumental in the creation and the maintenance of a national executive-centered coalition. It functioned well when leading elements in the system agreed upon common goals and acted in concert. When the country has been led, Samuel Huntington observed, it has been a result of

> the president acting with the support and cooperation of key individuals and groups in the Executive Office, the federal bureaucracy, Congress, and the more important businesses, banks, law firms, foundations, and media, which constitute the private sector's Establishment.[142]

If the president was indispensable in the creation of such a liberal establishment by providing direction and purpose, then once the constitutional system had become democratized, the president was not nearly so important to its successful operation. In time, the presidency came to be viewed as the greatest danger to its continuation.

The delegitimization of the presidency was necessary to inhibit its potential to create a climate in which the antipathy toward the growing power of the administrative state could be exploited. It was also compatible with the interests of the new class and the new egalitarians who, having gained access to the public treasury, were willing now to exploit those institutions that were compatible with its purposes. Whereas progressives had once praised the unity of the executive, they were now content to speak of the diversity of the nation. Con-

---

[141]"Congress, Shared Administration, and Executive Privilege," in Mansfield, Sr., *Congress Against the President,* p. 125.

[142]Huntington, *The Democratic Distemper,* p. 24.

gress, therefore, was regarded as the branch that was truly representative of the people, the most democratic branch. For a short time, even the constitutional separation of powers was thought to be vindicated by Congress's actions during Watergate. That action had gone a long way in preserving liberty and democratic government against the imperial designs of the presidency.

One may be permitted to wonder, however, if a constitutional balance was restored. If power appeared to have shifted to the legislature in the short run, the long-term problem resulted from the presidents' inability to derive moral authority from the majority, apart from election. In such circumstances, it becomes difficult to defend the office against the ordinary power of the legislature.[143] Consequently, success in office would depend upon the president's ability to bargain with other elites within the political system. For the first time since the Progressive era, the president could not depend upon the moral and political authority derived as spokesman of the majority, to enable him to act in the public interest as a counterweight to legislative parochialism. Indeed, the notion of a public interest itself had become so obscured when elite opinion abandoned the presidency and the legitimacy of the majority, that the president could only with great difficulty claim to speak for a public, or a national, interest.

Elite conceptions of the public interest were gradually replaced by an ideology that denied any common interests, but increasingly recognized the demands of group or class (economic, ethnic, racial). The apparatus—the bureaucracy—was already in place as the mechanism through which the equitable distribution of the benefits of society could occur. Although the separation of powers had been defended briefly as an effective guard against the abuse of power, thereby protecting constitutionalism, before long it was again attacked for its propensity to deadlock the operation of government, thereby preventing the efficient administration of programs intended to ensure an equitable distribution of wealth and power.

The presidency had come to be viewed as an obstacle to progressive reform. The progressive branch of government was one that could defend and oversee the administrative bureaucracy to prevent regressive shifts. By the end of the Nixon presidency, Congress had come to be viewed as the institution most hospitable to the maintenance of a humane bureaucracy.[144] Accordingly,

---

[143]As Montesquieu noted, "Were the executive power not to have a right of restraining the encroachments of the legislative body, the latter would become despotic; for it might arrogate to itself what authority it pleased, it would soon destroy all other powers." *Spirit of the Laws*, p. 157.

[144]Interestingly, defenders of the legislature at first opposed bureaucratization. James M. Beck, in an early work on the bureaucracy, points to the reason for such opposition. "Bureaucracy, as an invidious term, primarily refers in a democratic government to the aggrandizement of the Executive at the expense of the Legislative branch of the government. . . . In the broader sense, it refers to the irrepressible war between the individual and the State, and involves the question as to the just limits . . . of the State over the property and life of the individual." *Our Wonderland of Bureaucracy* (New York: The Macmillan Co., 1932), p. x.

elite and enlightened opinion shifted to its defense. But the political legitimacy of the administrative state had not come about. The majority, and any candidate who could win the presidency, appeared hostile to its consolidation. Hence, it is difficult to gauge the consequences of a fully bureaucratized order on the American constitutional system because it has not occurred. Perhaps it cannot occur within the structure of the Constitution. Nonetheless, the federal government has become sufficiently centralized administratively to alter the incentives of the institutions of government, making it difficult for the separation of powers to operate as was intended. The separation of powers was intended to protect political rule—the chief end of which is liberty. Bureaucratic rule is indifferent, if not hostile, to the maintenance of the conditions of freedom. In any event, the modern liberal regime is dramatically transformed by the attempted consolidation of the administrative state.

Chapter 5

Congress, the Presidency, and the Politics of the Administrative State

I am of the opinion that, in the democratic ages which are opening upon us, individual independence and local liberties will ever be the products of art; that centralization will be the natural government.

—Tocqueville, *Democracy in America*

The Nixon administration forced a reappraisal of the institution of the presidency by intellectuals, politicians, and academics alike. For several generations the presidency had been perceived to be the most progressive institution of American government. Nixon had shown that an activist presidency could be used in the service of the forces of reaction. The abandonment of the presidency led many to place their hopes on Congress or, increasingly, on the Courts. The success of the Great Society had transformed the interests and attitudes of significant national elites toward the legislature; it was no longer the parochial defender of local interests. The increased expenditures and the administrative centralization that greatly increased the power and stability of the majority party in the legislature (incumbents are virtually reassured reelection) had resulted in a situation in which the nurture and the maintenance of the executive establishment was as important to the Congress as its creation had been to Democratic presidents since the Progressive era. It was not surprising, then, that "people who used to celebrate the Constitution as a flexible and 'living' document now speak of it in legalistic tones reminiscent of John Calhoun."[1] Nor was it surprising that the presidency and the majority were to be restrained within the bounds of a rigid interpretation of the Constitution. The emphasis was on a literal interpretation of the doctrine of the separation of powers.[2] A newly legitimized legislature, which could conserve the values of progressive liberalism, was the best defense of a now-powerful minority.

The new respectability of Congress as an institution was quickly apparent in the academic literature in the post-Watergate period. The legislature came to be celebrated as the most representative institution of government.[3]

> The pro-legislative reformers . . . [intend] to make legislative participation in policy formation meaningful, and to allow Congress to assert its own priorities, even over executive opposition, without resort to excessive centralization. Their ideas, including those implemented in the 1971–75 period, lead to even more diffusion of authority and to intensified bargaining as the dominant means of conflict resolutions.[4]

Those reforms of Congress in the early 1970s created a dispersion of power within Congress that was unprecedented in American history. As a result, "congressional decision making (as an autonomous process) . . . depend[ed] on an institutionalized system of subcommittee government."[5]

The diversity of the legislature in the society at large tended to obscure responsibility and accountability, and the growing democratization within each House tended to weaken centralized leadership. It gave various committee chairmen the opportunity to develop close relationships with the bureaucracy in its jurisdiction.[6] Such dispersal of authority suited the maintenance of a far-

---

[1]Paul Weaver, "Liberals and the Presidency," *Commentary*, 60 (October 1975), p. 48.

[2]Thomas Cronin noted, "It would seem best to revivify existing checks and balances, encourage the development of a vigorous loyal opposition. . . . Separation of powers can be restored by existing constitutional and political means. The key is to make sure that every president is a part of the larger political system. Congress and the parties can and must see that this is done." *The State of the Presidency* (Boston: Little, Brown & Co., 1975), p. 315.

[3]Richard Fenno expressed the new view quite clearly. "Congress, not the president, best represents the diversity of views that exists in this country. Congress, not the president, is most closely in touch with the people who live beyond the nation's capital. Our recent experience with two presidents . . . helps remind us that Congress remains the most representative institution." "Strengthening a Congressional Strength," in Lawrence C. Dodd and Bruce I. Oppenheimer, eds., *Congress Reconsidered* (New York: Praeger Publishers, 1977), p. 262.

[4]Leroy N. Rieselbach, *Congressional Reform in the Seventies* (Morristown, N.J.: General Learning Press, 1977), p. 76.

[5]Lawrence Dodd, "Congress and the Quest for Power," in Dodd and Oppenheimer, eds., *Congress Reconsidered*, p. 301.

[6]Lawrence Dodd suggested that "committee government . . . undermines the ability of Congress to perform the one function for which committee government would seem most suited— aggressive oversight of administration." This is so because "the individuals on the committees that

flung bureaucracy—the core of interest group pluralism.[7] As Harvey Mansfield, Sr., observed,

> The Democratic Study Group, the Congressional Black Caucus, the Women's Caucus, the District of Columbia regional caucus . . . have embodied efforts to consolidate strength for the advancement of positive, if perhaps parochial goals."

These are, he suggests, "claimants, not governors, the logical end of their multiplication is the Polish veto."[8]

The trend in congressional reform was toward increased participation and democratization, as well as decentralization.[9] But decentralization of the institution could only become possible after administrative centralization had already occurred. Despite decentralizing reform, there was one area in which Congress required centralized authority—public finance. The legislative necessity of budget control was indicative of the extent to which the interests of Congress as a body—regardless of party—had diverged from those of the president.[10] Congress sought to make its own accommodations with the bureaucracy, which of course required control of spending totals. In an era of increased decentralization and dispersal of power within Congress, budget reform was a significant exception. Except in the one area of fiscal policy, there remained no regular institutional structure in either House to deal effectively with matters that cut across the jurisdiction of two or more committees. With its power dispersed,

---

pass legislation will be the very people least likely to investigate policy implementation. They will be committed to the program . . . and will not want to take actions that might lead to a destruction of the program." Rather, they tend to "leave the agency largely to its own devices and rely on informal contacts and special personal arrangements. . . . Members . . . are unwilling to resolve this problem by creating permanent and powerful oversight committees because such committees . . . would threaten the authority of legislative committees to control and direct policy in their allotted policy area. Committee government thus allows a failure of executive oversight." Ibid., pp. 280–281.

[7]Harvey C. Mansfield, Sr., noted, " The dispersion of authority has resulted in greater equality among members of the Congress, with the proliferation of the subcommittees nearly every member can become a chairman or ranking minority member." "The Dispersion of Authority in Congress," in Mansfield, *Congress Against the President* (New York: Praeger Publishing, 1975), p. 8.

[8]Ibid., p. 19.

[9]The reforms were certainly not without self-interested motives. It was conducive to reelection. Richard Fenno noted, "when members of Congress think institutionally . . . they think in terms of a structure that will be most congenial to the pursuit of their individual concern—for reelection, for influence or policy. . . . The committee system, the epitome of fragmentation and decentralization is the proper starting point for judging the performance of Congress. . . . Both chambers . . . chafe against centralizing mechanisms. "If as Ralph Nader says, Congress is 'The Broken Branch,' "How Come We Love Our Congressmen So Much?" in Norman J. Ornstein, ed., *Congress in Change* (New York: Praeger Publishers, 1975), pp. 281–282.

[10]Senator Muskie noted that the budget reform "is not a bookkeeping tool. It is a policy instrument that gives us new control over the direction America takes." *Congressional Digest*, 55 (March 1976), p. 75.

Congress was organized to deal with narrow problems but not with broad ones. Its structure still impelled it to think parochially.[11]

The delegitimization of the majority had resulted in a new legitimacy of diversity, and the organized interests represented by the legislature. "Defenders of Congress argue that the national interest is, in the last analysis, the sum of the local interests."[12] Budget reform was an attempt on the part of Congress to ensure that the parts would not be sacrificed to the whole. Increasingly, it came to be believed that the whole was only the sum of the parts.

THE POLITICS OF BUDGET REFORM

The battleground in executive–legislative relations, which had become increasingly hostile by 1973, revolved around the necessity to control the federal budget. From the president's perspective, it was the key to the management of the executive branch and the eventual decentralization of government. From a congressional standpoint, budget control would provide the means of maintaining the programs established by the partisan consensus of the New Deal and Great Society. Moreover, public spending had become a primary means of ensuring reelection. Bureaucratic patronage meant as much to the sustenance of an administrative state as party patronage had in a liberal regime.

The federal budget and public expenditure had become the key to the differences in purpose and constituency that divided, and alienated, the political branches of government.[13] In the 1974 budget, Nixon

> attempted to drastically revise the scope and role of the federal government in society. The central instruments for deadlocking progressive bills were no longer

---

[11]James Sundquist, "Congress and the President: Enemies or Partners?" in Henry Owen and Charles L. Schultze, eds., *Setting National Priorities, the Next Ten Years* (Washington, D.C.: Brookings Institution, 1976), p. 613.

[12]Ibid., p. 600.

[13]The presidential majority was animated by the desire to control the increase of power in the federal bureaucracy as well as slow government spending. But as Rieselbach noted, "something quite the opposite was beginning to become evident in Congress. As the 1970s began, the big cities enjoyed reasonable representation and growing seniority power within Congress. As political competition in the South spread and produced real challenges in former one-party districts, a growing proportion of the safe, stable, one-party districts that remained were located in the central cities, where democratic voters frequently constitute overwhelming majorities. Given the continuing decline in central city population and the ten-year time lag before a new reapportionment, the relatively liberal central-city constituencies were destined to have increasing overrepresentation in the House as the 1970s advanced." Consequently, "the democratizing and liberalizing trends of the early 1970s happened to converge in the 94th Congress. . . . Liberals [had] secured command of most of the levers of authority." *Congressional Reform*, pp. 7, 59 (see Footnote 4).

the House Rules and Appropriations committees, but the Presidential budget and impoundment process, and the veto.[14]

The Congressional Budget and Impoundment Control Act of 1974 was the congressional response to the first serious attempt to control the federal bureaucracy.

The new congressional budget system attempted to reduce the long dominance of the White House over the budget and bring Congress into fiscal policy-making. It "forces Congress for the first time, to assert an explicit fiscal policy."[15] John Kenneth Galbraith indicated the importance of the budget to fiscal policy and the reason why presidents could no longer be trusted to control it. "In modern times," he noted,

> the national budget has become a decisive factor in economic performance. It extensively determines whether demand will expand, prices rise, unemployment increase and—in consequence of government borrowing and the resulting deposit creation—whether the supply of money will expand. . . . The balancing factor in economic management will have to be the national budget.[16]

If monetary policy is "unavailable for regulating aggregate demand in the economy, only fiscal policy remains," Galbraith argued. "The solution . . . is to separate the budget of the national government from the fiscal policy."[17] With the budget act, Congress "launched an historic effort to strengthen its capacity to exert its . . . authority over revenues, expenditures and the general economic condition of the nation."[18]

The Budget Control Act was passed by substantial majorities in both the House and the Senate, "but the driving force for reform was an unholy alliance of fiscal conservatives and social welfare oriented liberals."[19] From the congressional perspective there were many motives for acceptance of budget legislation, not the least of which was the opinion that the budget was a technical

---

[14]Orfield, *Congressional Power*, p. 298. Orfield notes also that the so-called undemocratic devices in Congress have taken on a new life in the hands of the liberals. "Many of the tools of Congressional resistance" have "been employed in defense of important social goals" (p. 63). An example was the filibuster in 1972—which prevented enactment of Nixon's anti-busing legislation (p. 62).

[15]James Sundquist, "Congress and the President" in H. Owens and C. Schultze, eds., *Setting National Priorities*, pp. 596–597.

[16]Galbraith, *Money: Whence It Came, Where It Went* (Boston: Houghton-Mifflin, 1975), p. 303.

[17]Ibid., p. 307.

[18]C. William Fisher, "The New Congressional Budget Establishment," *National Tax Journal*, 29 (March 1976), p. 9.

[19]Lance Leloup, *Budgetary Politics* (Brunswick, Ohio: King's Court Press, 1977), p. 134. To say this act passed with a substantial majority is an understatement; its passage reflected virtual unanimity. In the House only six votes were cast against it; none in the Senate. Like the Budget and Accounting Act of 1921—which passed overwhelmingly—and also reflected a similar alliance between conservatives and liberals—the legitimacy of prevailing attitudes concerning the presidency

device—a neutral mechanism of management control.[20] The liberals wanted to retain spending priorities and to prevent presidential control; the conservatives merely wanted to balance the budget. The Act purported to offer a means of relating expenditures and revenue so that the choices could be made clear to everyone.[21] One observer noted:

> The Budget Act charges Congress to do what has never been done before; to fit isolated, unrelated fiscal decisions into a logical coherent process, treating the federal budget as a rational whole. It allows Congress to act with fiscal responsibility and to set its own budgetary priorities and prerogatives.[22]

Most importantly, however, budget legislation reflected Congress' belief that it "needed budget reform to help check the power of the presidency and to help regain their own constitutional power of the purse."[23] The "resurgence of Congress" is the result of the resounding demonstration that the constitutional system itself must be insulated from the perils of an overweening Presidency—most of all perhaps—when the incumbent enjoys great popularity."[24]

Consequently, after budget reform, as former OMB Director James Lynn remarked, "the buck stops at Congress' door." In the past, he noted, "Congress could get the credit for spending that benefits all sorts of interest groups—while knowing perfectly well that the President would impound the money."[25] Nixon had spoiled that sport by his "policy impoundments," which meant he

---

was reflected in the voting. The period after World War I reflected optimism and hope in the progress of the science of management—and the moral superiority of the president—purified of the politics of self-interest, which resulted in a tide which could not be resisted. Similarly, in 1974, an act that all agreed was among the most important in executive–legislative relations in a half-century passed almost without partisanship. This time the presidency had fallen in esteem and the budget act was seen to be a necessary means to weaken the "imperial" presidency.

[20]Harrison Fox and Susan Webb Hammond suggest that "one of the most important recent congressional reform measures [Budget Act] was marked up by groups of staff and given final approval by the members." *Congressional Staffs: The Invisible Force in American Lawmaking* (New York: Free Press, 1977), p. 1.

[21]Long before the imperial presidency, Nelson Polsby had noted "budget-making is often admired on the presidential side because of what is regarded as excellent presidential coordination of budget policy, at the same time, the alleged fragmentation of the congressional appropriations process is . . . criticized. In fact, the contrasts between the ways in which Congress and the President handle the budgetary policy are not as compelling as the similarities. . . . Neither Congress nor the President consider all programs in relation to all other programs. . . . Disagreements . . . reflect . . . differing preferences about what sorts of public policy are desirable." *Congress and the Presidency* (Englewood Cliffs: Prentice-Hall, 1964), p. 97.

[22]James A. Thurber, "Congressional Budget Reform and New Demands for Policy Analysis," *Policy Analysis*, 2 (Spring 1976), p. 197.

[23]Ibid., p. 201.

[24]Alton Frye further noted, "it has become one of the highest missions of legislative politics to steer bureaucratic politics, . . . to induce program and policy formulations responsive to [Congressional] preferences." *A Responsible Congress: The Politics of National Security* (New York: McGraw-Hill, 1975), pp. 221, 225.

[25]Cited in Juan Cameron, "The Noble Experiment in Congressional Budget Discipline," *Fortune*, 93 (May 1976), p. 210.

substituted his judgment for that of Congress without regard merely for efficient management or economy. In confronting Congress in this matter he sought to force Congress to cut spending.

> Members of Congress who vote for spending proposals find themselves unhappy with the resulting totals or the tax rates related to them. It appears undesirable either to turn down spending bids or to raise taxes to accommodate totals. The president accuses Congress of wanting the credit for spending but not the blame for taxing. Impoundment is his challenging response: either take the onus for raising taxes or allow me to make my limits stick by refusing to spend beyond them.[26]

Before Congress settled the matter with the Impoundment provision of the Budget Act, Wildavsky had wondered whether impoundment represented "a temporary abuse of executive power or functional adaptation to a system in which congressmen prefer to take the credit for spending but wish to blame the president for taxing."[27] In passing the Budget and Impoundment Control Act, Congress sought to sidestep the president.[28] Thus as an unidentified high-ranking OMB official claimed that the Budget Act with Title X (the procedure that limited the president's ability to impound funds) is "encouraging executive branch agencies to develop their own direct power relationship with appropriations subcommittees in Congress, at the expense of presidential control." This trend, he added, "could lead to the creation of bureaucratic fiefdoms, answering more to Congress than to the President. What we are talking about here is Congressional government—and chaos." In the long run, he observed, the balance between the executive branch may be substantially altered by "virtually destroying presidential control over federal spending."[29] In the wake of the battle over control of public spending, Congress had emerged greatly strengthened.

> The Nixonian aggressions against that legislature had been repulsed, the offending President himself had actually been driven from office, and Congress had set up barriers through legislation that would prevent new "usurpations." Not only had the pre-Nixon status quo been restored, but also the pre-Johnson and in some respects even the pre-Franklin Roosevelt and pre-Theodore Roosevelt relations be-

---

[26]Aaron Wildavsky, *Budgeting, A Comparative Theory of Budgetary Processes* (Boston: Little, Brown & Co., 1975), p. 393.

[27]Ibid., pp. 30–31.

[28]Members of Congress were willing to deal directly with the agencies of the executive branch, whose interests in the maintenance of administrative centralization were as compelling as those of Congress itself.

[29]"As long as you can get to the right people in Congress," he noted, "you really don't have to pay attention to the President. . . . You know that even though the President may send up a budget that you don't like, the President has little control if you can persuade Congress to give you more money." Donald Smith, "Impoundment Act: A Time for Testing," *Congressional Quarterly Guide* (Washington, D.C.: Congressional Quarterly, Inc., 1976), p. 57, 59.

tween the branches. In fact, in some matters Congress was on firmer ground than any it had ever occupied before.[30]

EXECUTIVE–LEGISLATIVE RELATIONS IN BUDGET CONTROL: A NEW DEAL

On January 21, 1976, President Ford's Budget Message revealed a new reality in legislative–executive relations. He sought to tailor the budget to the requirements of a majority, compatible with the needs of private individuals. The budget "helps to define the boundaries between responsibilities that we assign to governments and those that remain in the hands of private institutions and individual citizens."[31] Consequently, Ford requested a cut in the rate of federal spending; he proposed "permanent income tax reductions so that individuals and business [could] spend and invest these dollars instead of having the federal Government collect and spend them."[32] Ford assumed what every president since Warren G. Harding had taken for granted—that "the budget reflects the President's sense of priorities. It reflects his best judgment of how we must choose among competing interests. And it reveals his philosophy of how the public and private spheres should be related."[33] But this was no longer the case and had not been the case for at least a year.[34] As Brock Adams (D-Wash.) of the House Budget Committee noted, "Perhaps the most important aspect of the final budget resolution of fiscal year 1977 is the fact that it contains the budget of Congress and not that of the President."[35] When President Ford

> proposed a budget for fiscal 1976 with a $52 billion deficit—resulting from $350 billion of expenditures and about $298 billion of revenues. . . . What happened? In fact, the Congress ignored that budget. It increased expenditures over and above the President's recommendations; under the new budget procedures that it had just adopted, the Congress for the first time in history went on record explicitly voting for a budget deficit larger than the President recommended—almost $25 billion larger.[36]

More important, perhaps, "appropriations in particular categories differed markedly from the Executive proposals. . . . Cuts were inflicted on defense and

---

[30]James Sundquist, "Congress and the President," p. 596.

[31]*The Budget of the United States Government, Fiscal Year, 1977* (Washington, D.C.: Government Printing Office, 1976), p. M3.

[32]Ibid., p. M4.

[33]Ibid., p. M3.

[34]The Budget and Impoundment Control Act of 1974 (Public Law 93–344) went into effect in 1976.

[35]Judy Gardner, "Budget Conferees Approve 413.1 Billion Dollar Ceiling on Fiscal 1977 Spending," *Congressional Quarterly Weekly Report*, 34 (September, 1976), p. 2789.

[36]Charles Schultze and James T. Lynn, *The Federal Budget: What Are the Nation's Priorities* (Washington, D.C.: American Enterprise Institute, 1976), p. 54.

foreign aid outlays; more was allocated for education and social welfare programs."[37]

In seeking to control budget totals, Congress was expanding its control of public spending to limit executive discretion in the areas that mattered. It had already attained important control of the spending priorities by expanding the uncontrollable portion of the budget through legislative means.[38] As President Ford had stated in his budget for fiscal 1975:

> Although the federal budget has grown in size, a more ominous change in the character of the budget has occurred. In recent years the growing predominance of "mandatory" over "discretionary" expenditures has resulted in changing legislative-executive relations concerning the setting of national priorities. In 1967, 59% of total federal spending was virtually uncontrollable due to existing laws. . . . Since then, repeated increases in uncontrollable programs have been enacted into law. . . . In 1975, about 74% of the budget will be virtually uncontrollable.[39]

In setting mandatory expenditures, Congress allowed presidential discretion only in areas in which it was indifferent to the maintenance of the current level of spending, or in which no significant interest or constituency was involved. In viewing the budget for fiscal year 1977, "approximately 65% of the controllable expenditures in the entire federal government [were] in the area of national defense."[40] If a president wanted to exercise economy in government, he was almost forced to cut back in the area of national defense. In fiscal year 1976, $63.8 billion of the Department of Defense budget of $92.8 billion was controllable, in contrast to $20 billion of Health, Education and Welfare's budget of $127.7 billion.[41]

The election of Jimmy Carter to the White House in 1976 did not result in improving relations between the branches. Politics did not return to normal with the election of a Democrat, with large majorities in both Houses of Congress. Unlike Nixon and Ford, President Carter was not faced with a Congress dominated by the opposition party. Yet Carter was unable to provide leadership for his party in the legislature. The interests of the two branches had diverged significantly. "Until the presidential election of 1976, Democratic presidential nominees since the New Deal have supported . . . the maintenance of the administrative branch and even the expansion of the bureaucracy to meet pressing public problems.[42] But Jimmy Carter had promised major reforms of the bu-

---

[37]Leroy Reiselbach, *Congressional Reform*, p. 54 (see Footnote 4).

[38]Controllable, or discretionary, expenditures are those that can be increased or decreased without changing substantive law.

[39]*The Budget, Fiscal Year, 1975*, pp. 38–39.

[40]Ibid., p. 34.

[41]Ibid.

[42]Peter Woll, *American Bureaucracy* (New York: W. W. Norton, 1977), p. 218.

reaucracy, not to mention a balanced budget.[43] Moreover, Carter had summed up his first State of the Union address by suggesting that:

> Government cannot solve our problems. It cannot set our goals. It cannot define our vision. Government cannot eliminate poverty, or provide a bountiful economy, or reduce inflation, or save our cities, or cure illiteracy, or provide energy.[44]

Carter's conduct in office did not follow the traditional Democratic pattern. It has been argued that he betrayed the constituency that elected him. Michael Harrington insisted that "Jimmy Carter's victory last November, it is widely and rightly said, was achieved by a New Deal-type coalition of workers, minorities and the liberal middle class, and the South." But, as Harrington noted: "It is not so widely recognized, however, that this coalition has brought to power an administration opposed to the principles of the New Deal itself."[45] It is debatable whether Carter owed his election to a New Deal-type constituency. It is more likely that the national majority had become increasingly suspicious of the power of the bureaucracy which, though not created during the New Deal, was largely a product of a similar coalition in the Great Society.[46] Whether Carter abandoned the constituency that elected him or represented a new majority, it was clear that he was a different kind of Democrat. Kevin Phillips has suggested that "Jimmy Carter, the only Democratic President to interrupt the long Republican hegemony after 1968, was accused . . . of an 'eccentric effort to carry the Democratic Party back to Grover Cleveland.' Despite his support for substantial new Federal regulation, Carter clearly deviated from his party's larger post-New Deal norm. He built foundations that would become conservative architecture under Reagan: economic deregulation, capital-gains tax reduction, and the tight-money policies of the Federal Reserve."[47]

The difficulties of the Carter Administration were not simply the failure of presidential leadership.[48] Carter's presidency made it clear that a Democratic president with majorities in both Houses of Congress could not reconcile the demands of the national majority with those of the legislative majority of his

[43]Ford had promised to balance the budget in 1979, Carter in 1981. Cf. *The 1978 Budget in Transition from Ford to Carter to Congress* (Washington, D.C.: American Enterprise Institute, 1976), pp. 137–144.

[44]Carter, quoted in Clayton Fritchey. Fritchey observed that "no other Democratic president in this century has ever taken that line. It contradicts everything the party has stood for since the time of Woodrow Wilson." *Los Angeles Times*, 29 January 1978, Pt. IV, p. 5.

[45]Harrington, "A Status Quo Economy," *Harpers*, 255 (September 1977), p. 34.

[46]The Volcker Commission Report subsequently criticized President Carter, as well as Reagan, for "running campaigns that not only strongly criticized Washington but also attacked the people who work for the government." National Commission on the Public Service, *Leadership for America: Rebuilding the Public Service* (Lexington, Mass.: D.C. Heath, 1989), p. 63.

[47]Phillips, "The Politics of Rich and Poor: Wealth and the American Electorate in the Reagan Aftermath," *The New York Times Magazine*, June 17, 1990, pp. 26–28.

[48]For a view of the Carter presidency as an example of failed leadership, see Barbara Kellerman, *The Political Presidency: Practice of Leadership* (New York: Oxford University Press, 1984), esp. pp. 185–219.

own party in Congress. The party leaders and the members of Congress continued to represent a political consensus created during the Great Society. It had become solidified in the structure of the bureaucracy itself. Furthermore, the institution of Congress had changed to reflect the necessity of running an administrative state. The leadership did not simply control the members, nor were the goals of party or the institution paramount. Each member made his own accommodation with the bureaucracy, and operated as individual policy-entrepreneurs. Carter noted subsequently "that there was no party loyalty or discipline when a complicated or controversial issue was at stake—none. Each legislator had to be wooed and won individually. It was every member for himself, and the devil take the hindmost!"[49] It was nearly impossible for Carter to lead, because the underlying consensus that animated the national majority politically and philosophically was opposed to that which animated the majority party in the legislature. To the extent that Carter tried to satisfy the constituency—the national majority—that he needed for reelection, he came into conflict with the leadership and the members of his own party.

President Carter's dilemma was apparent in the fluctuation in public approval of his performance, which indicated the difficulty of attempting to satisfy the conflicting demands of the national majority and the Democratic leadership. A *New York Times* poll showed

> public support of the President has broadened in the first 100 days of his Administration because many Americans . . . believe he has turned out to be more conservative than they expected. . . . Even more significant was the public's clear impression that Mr. Carter, by stressing his desire to balance the Federal budget and taking action that disappointed organized labor and liberal Democrats, had moderated his image.[50]

The support that Carter gained from the public at large by his perceived attempt to balance the budget was offset by the criticism of his own party in the Congress. *New York Times* reporter Martin Tolchin noted that

> a deepening division, both political and philosophic, between President Carter and Democratic leaders in Congress emerged today at a second White House meeting on legislative priorities. The dispute involves the President's assertion yesterday that his top priority was a balanced budget by 1981, a position regarded as political heresy by Democrats in Congress who stress the need for social welfare programs.[51]

Perhaps the clearest indication of the "political and philosophical" differences that had split the Democratic Party and prevented support of Carter in

---

[49]Jimmy Carter, *Keeping Faith: Memoirs of a President* (New York: Bantam Books, 1982), p. 80.

[50]James M. Naughton, "Support for Carter Widens," *New York Times,* 29 April 1977, p. 1.

[51]"Democrats Criticize Carter on Priorities—Congress Leaders Stress Need for Social Welfare Programs," *New York Times,* 4 May 1977, p. 1.

Congress was reflected in the statements of the 1972 Democratic presidential nominee, Senator George McGovern:

> Carter has placed one goal above all others—balancing the federal budget by 1981.
> . . . But the Carter formula for a balanced budget would weigh most heavily on the
> 10 million unemployed, and underemployed Americans, on the minorities trapped
> in decaying central cities, and on the majority of Americans who need health insur-
> ance, decent housing, and effective transportation. . . . Federal spending for social
> needs is not the root of recent inflation.[52]

Partisanship (or self-interest) was no longer sufficient to ensure support of the presidency; rather, ideological differences had become paramount. As McGovern suggested, "dissenters in the House and Senate cloakrooms would like to be loyal to a Democratic President. But there is also the higher obliga-tion of the Congress to the dispossessed, the unemployed, the victims of social and economic injustice."[53] Perhaps, as Garry Wills suggested, the Carter ad-ministration marked the end of the liberal presidency.[54]

By the end of the Carter administration, it had become clear that the crisis of authority in government and the presidency had become acute. In 1980, Richard Neustadt speculated about the viability of the presidency. "Watching President Carter in early 1979 sparked the question, is the Presidency possi-ble?"[55] Bureaucratization produced a difference of interest between Congress and the presidency that must be distinguished from the traditional rivalry be-tween the branches, which was the result of the separation of powers. With a solid majority in both houses of Congress, Carter could not persuade members of Congress, nor the leadership, that his policies deserved support. Neither party, nor concerns for the national interest, could overcome the typical mem-bers' concern that local interests could best be served from Washington. Indeed the Speaker of the House, Tip O'Neill, was fond of saying that all politics was local. But the power and the money was now in the hands of the national government.

---

[52]"Memo to the White House," *Harpers,* 225 (October 1977), p. 33.

[53]Ibid., p. 35. The Democratic Party itself was split in its commitment to equality; unlike some of the members of Congress, the president could not be oblivious to the requirement of consent. He could not ignore the majority. Tocqueville noted that the defense of the adminis-trative state rests on one single thing. "The foremost or indeed the sole condition required in order to succeed in centralizing the supreme power in a democratic community is to love equality or to get men to believe you love it. Thus the science of despotism, which was once so complex, has been simplified and reduced, as it were, to a single principle." *Democracy in America,* pp. 319–320.

[54]Garry Wills, "Carter and the End of Liberalism," *New York Review of Books,* 24 (May 12, 1977), p. 16.

[55]Richard Neustadt, *Presidential Power: The Politics of Leadership from FDR to Carter,* 3rd ed. (New York: John Wiley, 1980), p. 208.

THE ADMINISTRATIVE PRESIDENCY
AND THE ADMINISTRATIVE STATE

The election of Ronald Reagan to the presidency in 1980 exemplified both the strength and the weakness of the presidential office in the period after the consolidation of the administrative state. Reagan showed that the president could still be a leader, but only in a limited number of areas, and not in ways that threatened the foundations of the administrative state. Moreover, it had become increasingly difficult to transform American politics fundamentally from the presidential office in accord with the majority will.

Reagan continued the recent trend of running for the presidency by attacking Washington. He raised anti-bureaucratic rhetoric to the level of high campaign art.[56] But Reagan did not try to dismantle the bureaucracy; he wanted to limit its expansion and bring it under the political control of a contemporary majority. He echoed the rhetoric of every president since Nixon:

> In this present crisis, government is not the solution to our problem; government is the problem. From time to time we've been tempted to believe that society has become too complex to be managed by self-rule, that government by an elite group is superior to government for, by, and of the people. Well, if no one among us is capable of governing himself, then who among us has the capacity to govern someone else? All of us together—in and out of government—must bear the burden.[57]

Reagan attempted to control the bureaucracy through the use of budgets and tax cuts. Although the cuts themselves did not reduce spending drastically, they were an indication that spending "would no longer be allowed to grow faster than the economy." The tax cuts represented important changes in tax policy, "an implicit recognition that steeply progressive tax rates were no longer sustainable and tended to stifle the economy in a peacetime, increasingly small-unit society."[58] Franklin Roosevelt, the architect of the modern presidency, thought government needed to play a new role in the economic life of the nation. Reagan, an admirer of FDR, had come to see government as a force that stifled economic growth. Roosevelt "had been one of the creators of America's big-unit society. He mistrusted unregulated markets and gravitated naturally to solutions which created new big governmental units like NRA, AAA, TVA. . . . He was comfortable working with the leaders of big business and big labor. . . . Roosevelt adapted government to demands already put on it by society." In a similar fashion, "Reagan's budget and tax cuts can be seen as an attempt to

[56]Reagan, once a New Deal Democrat, had long sought to limit the expansion of government power. He attained national prominence during the Goldwater campaign in 1964, delivering a televised speech on behalf of Goldwater that "consisted of a single idea, universal in application: centrally administered government weakens a free people's character." Milkis and Nelson, *The American Presidency* (Washington, D.C.: Congressional Quarterly Press, 1990), p. 334.

[57]"Inaugural Address," January 20, 1981, quoted in Ibid., pp. 334–335.

[58]Michael Barone, *Our Country: The Shaping of America from Roosevelt to Reagan* (New York: The Free Press, 1990), p. 615.

adapt government to the small-unit economy and society which had been quietly developing for decades."[59] Reagan, like FDR, was only adapting American government to accommodate the new conditions of economic life. Moreover, as Richard Neustadt has noted, "Reagan was convinced . . . that Roosevelt's New Deal had been not completed but perverted by the Great Society of LBJ (expanded in its regulatory features and its welfare measures under Nixon)."[60] Reagan hoped to use the presidency to reclaim American government and adapt economic policy to serve the interests of a contemporary majority, in keeping with an older tradition of American politics.

The smoothness of the Reagan presidency in his first term, and the first two years of his second term, and the persistence of his personal popularity, appeared to convince many observers that the presidency was fundamentally sound. Reagan was the first president since Eisenhower to complete two full terms in office. Recent critics of the presidency, from Johnson to Carter, had blamed the incumbents for their failure to provide sound, effective, or decisive leadership. Reagan appeared able to provide good leadership. The "awesome responsibility" of the office seemed to pose little difficulty for him. His style of management, which included delegating ample authority to subordinates, and his winning personality, enabled him to manage the presidency with considerable success. The old refrain, the "office is too big for one man" was not heard throughout most of Reagan's presidency.[61] Yet, events in his second term, including the elections of 1986 in which the Democrats regained control of the Senate, showed that the Reagan presidency was vulnerable to the new forces and conditions of American politics that had emerged with administrative centralization. Reagan, unlike FDR, could not fundamentally alter American politics.

Reagan was the first president to successfully accommodate the office to the requirements of an administrative state.[62] He did so by using the administrative discretion of the office, which had become necessary for the continued operation of the administrative state.[63] Richard Nathan has suggested that "the

[59]Ibid., pp. 615–616.
[60]*Presidential Power and the Modern Presidents: The Politics of Leadership from Roosevelt to Reagan* (New York: The Free Press, 1990), p. 277.
[61]See Jeffrey Tulis, *The Rhetorical Presidency* (Princeton, N.J.: Princeton University Press, 1987).
[62]Joel D. Aberbach has suggested that "when Ronald Reagan came to the presidency, . . . a change-oriented incumbent who had the will now had means beyond those available to Nixon to influence the executive branch. Further, Reagan had the example of Nixon's experience to learn from—the techniques used and the pitfalls." "The President and the Executive Branch," in Colin Campbell and Bert A. Rockman, eds., *The Bush Presidency: First Appraisals* (Chatham, N.J.: Chatham House Publishers, 1991), p. 227.
[63]Reagan attempted, as Nixon had, to concentrate power in the White House. Fred Greenstein has noted that "Nixon and Reagan had the courage to act on what once were the convictions of liberals, taking it for granted that the president should use whatever power he can muster, including power to administer programs, to shape policy." "Nine Presidents in Search of a Modern Presidency," in Fred I. Greenstein *Leadership in the Modern Presidency* (Cambridge, MA: Harvard University Press, 1988), p. 345.

essence of the Reagan approach to management is the appointment of loyal and determined policy officials. This, of course, is not a new idea; the difference is that the Reagan administration has in substantial measure carried it out."[64] Reagan used an administrative strategy to control the executive branch that was much like Nixon's in his second term. He took "advantage of opportunities to transfer and remove career officials in domestic agencies felt to be unsympathetic to the administration's objectives." The Reagan administration appointees "used reductions in force (RIFs) to push senior civil servants they did not trust into routine positions, and they used the power to appoint noncareer Senior Executive Service (SES) officials aggressively."[65] Reagan's strategy did not involve attempts to lead Congress; moreover, he confronted Congress directly only in a few areas of importance. His success in limiting discretionary domestic spending and inhibiting new revenue sources as a result of tax policies allowed him to "put domestic agencies on the defensive and turned the agenda of American politics into one focused on deficit reduction, rather than program development and improvement." As Aberbach noted, "the question preoccupying the bureaucracy and congressional leaders throughout most of Reagan's eight years in office, especially in nondefense areas, was the question Reagan wanted on the agenda: "What ought we *not* do?"[66] Nonetheless, "Reagan never did transform Washington completely. Rather, he strengthened the Republican beachhead in the federal government, solidifying his party's recent dominance of the presidency and providing better opportunities for conservatives in the Washington community." In the process, however, "his two terms witnessed a revitalization of the struggle between the executive and the legislature; indeed, his programs laid the foundation for more fundamental conflicts between the branches."[67]

Richard Fenno has suggested that "the politics of budget making was the central preoccupation of the Reagan presidency."[68] Although Reagan had attempted to lower federal expenditures as well as tax rates in his first term, his success was limited to a modest reduction in income tax rates.[69] He succeeded in reordering priorities, however, by increasing real amounts of spending for

[64]Nathan, *The Administrative Presidency* (New York: John Wiley & Sons, 1983), p. 74.

[65]Joel F. Aberbach, "The President and the Executive Branch," in Campbell and Rockman, eds., *The Bush Presidency*, p. 228.

[66]Ibid., p. 229.

[67]Milkis and Nelson, *The American Presidency*, p. 346.

[68]Fenno, *The Emergence of a Senate Leader: Pete Domenici and the Reagan Budget* (Washington, D.C.: Congressional Quarterly Press, 1991), p. ix.

[69]By the end of Reagan's first term, his economic policy, often called Reaganomics, though not uncontroversial, had ceased to be a contentious issue. Those measures such as the tax reform bill were made possible because the underlying terms of economic debate had been transformed by the success of Reagan's policy, and its perceived public ratification in the election of 1984. Even the Democrats in Congress, led by the House Ways and Means Committee chairman Dan Rostenkowski, pushed for a lowering of tax rates. The result was a significant reform of the tax laws. See Joseph J. Minarik, *Making America's Budget Policy: From the 1980s to the 1990s* (Armonk, N.Y.: M. E. Sharpe, Inc., 1990).

defense, and decreasing rates of increase in social spending. The federal budget nonetheless grew significantly in every year of the Reagan presidency. His desire to halt the growth in the size of government, relative to the size of the private sector, failed. When Reagan took office in 1980, the size of the federal budget, as a percentage of the gross national product (GNP), stood at about 22.5%. At the end of his first term, nearly 24% of the GNP was consumed in the public sector. By the time Reagan left office, spending in the public sector stood at 22.4%, just about where it had been when Reagan took office.[70] However, the growth of federal expenditures was not financed by higher taxes, despite the fact that there had been a significant tax increase in 1982; this tended to blunt the effect of the large tax cuts of the previous year. The inability to cut expenditures, coupled with the effects of the recession, and the necessary increase of entitlements, led to a massive rise in the size of the federal deficit. Even the vigorous growth of the economy in the last years of Reagan's first term could not offset the increase in expenditures. Reagan's huge electoral victory in 1984 and the continuing improvement in the economy made tax increases politically difficult. Although nearly everyone seemed to favor a balanced budget, no one could succeed in cutting the size of government. Consequently, the deficits grew.

There was, however, constant and considerable worry in Washington over the inability to control the federal deficit and the growing national debt, which led to the passage of The Balanced Budget and Emergency Deficit Control Act in December of 1985. This act, authored by Senators Gramm, Rudman, and Hollings, resulted in substantial changes in the congressional budget process, which mandated fixed deficit targets, and required the Comptroller General— the head of the General Accounting Office (GAO)—to determine automatic spending cuts (sequestration), if Congress and the President disagreed on specific budget cuts.

Consequently, the federal budget continued to be a main focus of attention in Reagan's second term, particularly in light of the Supreme Court's ruling in July of 1986. In the case of *Bowsher v. Synar,* the Court invalidated a significant aspect of the Balanced Budget and Emergency Deficit Control Act of 1985. Although Congress had all the necessary constitutional authority to make spending cuts, it had become politically impossible to make such cuts. However, Congress did not want the president's priorities to prevail in public spending. Hence, it was not the president or the Director of the Office of Management and Budget, nor anyone else in the executive branch, who was to oversee the automatic spending cuts provided by the Gramm-Rudman-Hollings Act. Although the law mandated the formula for the cuts, the actual implementation of the cuts was to be made by the Comptroller General. It was the sequestration

---

[70]Richard Rose, *The Postmodern President: George Bush Meets the World* (Chatham, N.J.: Chatham House Publishers, 1991), p. 250.

provision of the act, which delegated executive authority to the head of the GAO, an agency the Court viewed as an arm of Congress, that led to the invalidation of such a delegation of authority.[71]

The constant battles over spending cuts and tax increases that characterized the first years of the Reagan administration had become mere skirmishes or had taken on the character of guerrilla warfare within the bureaucracy by the beginning of his second term. But the ongoing source of confrontation between Reagan and the Democrats in Congress involved priorities laid down in Reagan's proposed budgets, and his insistence that the budget must remain within the deficit limitations imposed by the Gramm-Rudman-Hollings Act. The administration's fiscal 1988 budget called for a deficit of $107.8 billion, with outlays of $1.024 trillion and revenues of $916.6 billion. The centerpiece of the budget was a $42.4 billion deficit reduction program. The budget was considered dead on arrival when presented on Capitol Hill. Although Reagan proposed the lowest defense increase of his administration, he called for large cuts in other areas: a $5.5 billion cut in education, a 28% cut in housing and urban programs, and a 41% cut in agriculture outlays over a three-year period. The Democrats rejected most of the deficit-cutting ideas. The chairmen of the budget committees, Representative William Gray III and Senator Lawton Chiles, argued that the deficit targets could not be met without such gimmicks as the use of overly optimistic economic predictions and spending estimates. The Democrats agreed that Congress should concentrate on a package of spending cuts and revenue increases that would reduce the projected deficit to $130 billion. They insisted that meeting the Gramm-Rudman-Hollings target would trigger a recession. In an attempt to cope with the deficit, Speaker Jim Wright met with Democratic members of the House budget committee to begin building support for a tax increase as part of the fiscal 1988 budget package. Reagan's inability to prevent Democratic domination of budget priorities showed that in ordinary circumstances, the demands of the bureaucracy and their constituencies must be met.[72]

Public confidence in the Reagan administration was high throughout most of his presidency; but public opinion is known to be influenced by what the

[71]Gramm-Rudman-Hollings never accomplished its objective. As Anthony King and Giles Alston have observed, "whenever it looked even remotely likely that the provisions of Gramm-Rudman-Hollings would have to be invoked, the president and Congress made sure that they would not be. The president and Congress 'cooked the books.' . . ." "Good Government and the Politics of High Exposure," in Campbell and Rockman, eds., *The Bush Presidency*, p. 253 (see Footnote 68).

[72]Reagan tried to bolster support for his agenda in his State of the Union message on January 27, 1987. Facing a Democratic controlled Congress for the first time, Reagan refused to compromise on his priorities. He insisted on pressing forward with SDI, opposing Soviet expansionism, and he renewed his support for aid to the Contras in Nicaragua. Many Democrats, expecting a more conciliatory tone, complained bitterly that Reagan was excessively partisan. In an attempt to show that he was still a force to be reckoned with, Reagan vetoed his first piece of legislation in the 100th Congress. He refused to sign the Clean Water Act, which he argued was pure pork-barrel legislation, which would bust the budget. Congress easily overrode his veto.

public perceives to be events of political importance. Such perceptions are often manipulated by other elite groups in the political and social system, especially those in the institutions of government, the press, and the bureaucracy. These groups, who are rivals of the president, become a significant force if their spokesmen can gain the focus of attention in the media. Public policy making, too, is now primarily a function of interested elite groups and concerned issue networks throughout the society. Although other powerful elite groups were dissatisfied with the Reagan presidency, Reagan's skill in appealing to the electorate, and his ability to compromise at crucial times, defused any united opposition. Nonetheless, there was a profound uneasiness with the direction in which Reagan had moved the political spectrum; the political center was now decidedly to the right. This was especially true in regard to economic issues and social spending, as well as the conduct of foreign policy. House Democrats, in particular, had long been resentful of Reagan's reordering of priorities in regard to social spending vis-à-vis defense spending, his militant anti-Communist rhetoric, not to mention his attempt to defend against nuclear war by the Strategic Defense Initiative rather than by negotiated nuclear disarmament. Moreover, his willingness to violate SALT II, his unwillingness to impose sanctions on South Africa, and his policy of opposition to the Sandinista government in Nicaragua were bitterly contested. There was also considerable discomfort with Reagan's policy in the area of civil rights.[73]

The Reagan administration has been called "the most administratively ambitious since the advent of the modern presidency."[74] Moreover, "the administrative presidency was a mechanism to ensure responsiveness to a political agenda that Reagan, and certainly his followers, hoped would outlast his own tenure in office."[75] But an administrative strategy could not replace the necessity of creating a new consensus in American politics; such a consensus would require a realignment of the electorate. The 1986 election proved to be critical in terms of the long-term consequences of the Reagan agenda. It was confirmation of the fact that Reagan had not altered the political landscape of America. He was not able to bring about a political realignment. In the 1986 election, the

---

[73]Democrats in the Senate opposed a number of Reagan nominees to the federal judiciary, including Judge Robert Bork's nomination to the Supreme Court, insisting that they were not fully committed to vigorous enforcement of civil rights. The Justice Department was also criticized for its opposition to affirmative action quotas and timetables. Furthermore, Attorney-General Edwin Meese angered many, including several sitting Justices of the Supreme Court, by initiating a public debate concerning the proper standard for judicial interpretation. Meese insisted that judges ought to be guided by the "original intention" of the Founding Fathers, or the express language of the Constitution. In effect, Meese had argued once again for a "strict construction" of the Constitution in judicial interpretation. This controversy was reflective of a profound debate that has occurred in American politics in the last two decades. The heart of the debate concerned nothing less than the meaning of equality itself.

[74]Milkis and Nelson, *The American Presidency*, p. 342.

[75]Bert A. Rockman, "The Style and Organization of the Reagan Presidency," in Charles O. Jones, ed., *The Reagan Legacy* (Chatham, N.J.: Chatham House, 1988), p. 11.

Republicans were vulnerable in the Senate because 22 of the 34 incumbents were Republican. The Republicans lost a total of eight Senate seats and five House seats, while gaining eight governorships. The statistics indicate that given past performance, the electorate was not particularly harsh on the Republican Party. The results were significant, nonetheless, as the Democrats regained control of the Senate. The dream of an emerging Republican majority appeared to be just that. What was more important for practical and political purposes was that in Reagan's last two years he was faced with a united Congress in opposition.

The election itself was symptomatic of numerous contradictory tendencies in the political system and the electorate that have prevented the kind of electoral realignment that the Republican Party had been seeking. Although Reagan was a very popular president who sought to make the election a referendum on his presidency, the administration was unable to make a coherent or principled appeal on national issues. The Republic Party lacked a compelling, unified campaign theme. In his many campaign stops for Republican Senate candidates, Reagan sought to convince the electorate to cast one last vote "for the Gipper."

The Democrats, however, were careful not to take on the president directly, hence the election lacked clarity as regards issues of national significance. As one observer noted: "it is no surprise, that Democratic congressmen and senators campaigned as if there were 'no great national issues'; doing so has served them well. But they have found strange bedfellows in Republican politicians, who approach recent elections like inter-conference football games—not as serious partisan contests."[76] If the campaign was noteworthy for lack of focus on partisan issues of national importance, it was characterized by so-called negative campaign advertising on television.

In terms of consequences, perhaps the most important thing about the 1986 election was that the Democrats recaptured control of the Senate. Even so, most of the new Democrats in the Senate won on the strength of their understanding of local issues; in some cases they were better campaigners. It is widely believed that many of the Republican candidates for the Senate, including a number of the incumbents of the class of 1980, were weak and ineffective campaigners, particularly when deprived of national partisan issues. The Republican Party had spent too much money on this election, and they were overly dependent on professional campaigners and television time. The hard campaign work of meeting and animating the voters was neglected.[77]

---

[76]Walter Dean Burnham, "Elections Dash GOP Dreams of Realignment," *The Wall Street Journal,* November 26, 1986, p. 20.

[77]Once again, the so-called gender gap appeared to play an important role in the election. It appears that the Republicans would have hung on to Senate seats in Georgia, North Carolina, North Dakota, and Nevada, and were likely to win seats in Colorado, Louisiana, and possibly California if the women's vote had not deviated significantly from that of men. Indeed, "women gave Democrats 5 to 10 percentage points more of their votes than men did in Tuesday's election for the Senate.

The popular interpretations of the elections pointed to the significance of the Democrats' recapture of the Senate. Although, undoubtedly important, the election followed a common pattern of postwar trends. When viewed in historical perspective, the Republicans did not fare badly. Indeed, they lost only six seats in the House and gained a number of governorships. But the Republican Party and the administration had failed to get the public stamp of approval for a broad and deep realignment that had characterized critical elections in the past. Walter Dean Burnham has made clear what such a realignment entails. Electoral realignments in the past had

> pivoted around collective national issues and ideological differences that penetrated unusually deeply into the citizenry. Crucial electoral minorities stopped doing what they had been doing, began doing something else, and then kept on doing it for years or decades to come. These changes in behavior were channeled through political parties, then the sole organizers of the electoral market. This produced change in the identity of the majority and minority parties. Moreover, such change was usually manifest not just at the presidential top, but at most or all significant levels of election in our complicated constitutional scheme. Republican or Democratic 'eras' following realignment were marked as a rule by the national majority party's control of the White House, both houses of Congress and most important state governments.[78]

The Reagan Republicans had won the presidency in two decisive elections, won and lost the Senate, and never came close to winning the House, let alone the state legislative bodies. As a result, the Reagan administration was vulnerable to those political forces that opposed his attempt to prolong his policies beyond his presidency.[79]

Although Reagan's public policies involved a significant break with the past, public policymaking realignment is not the same as political realignment of the electorate. Burnham observed:

> Practically no one doubts that there has been a major realignment in public policy since 1980. But policy is the domain of activist elites. Historically, major realignments of policy have usually followed realignments within the public at large.

In U.S. House races, women gave Democrats 6 percent more of their votes than men did." John Dillon, "GOP Stumbles Over the Gender Gap," *The Christian Science Monitor*, November 7, 1986, p. 1.

[78]Burnham, "Elections Dash GOP Dreams," p. 20.

[79]When the election results had become clear, retiring Speaker of the House, Democrat Thomas P. (Tip) O'Neill, declared that "if there ever was a Reagan revolution, it's over." Walter Dean Burnham also noted: "as 1986 recedes into history, the Reagan era is much closer to its end than to its beginning." Perhaps Burnham, too, meant to suggest that the Reagan revolution was no longer a force to be reckoned with. In other words, it had become questionable whether Reagan's impact on American politics would extend much beyond his term of office. Burnham, "Elections Dash GOP Dreams," p. 20.

Today, this relationship is practically dissolved. Electoral realignment has not happened. The 1984 election was a forceful demonstration of this fact.

He insists, therefore, that the 1986 elections "give the idea of electoral realignment in our time a virtual coup de grace."[80] Party is certainly of great importance, "but its hold over the electorate has drastically eroded, and with accelerating pace, over the past generation." The consequence of this "is that policy realignment operates in an electoral vacuum." These policy realignments, which are the product of political activism by elite groups, without popular participation or legitimation, have occurred in the 1960s and the 1980s. The "Great Society" and the so-called "Reagan Revolution" are examples of such policy realignments. But it appears that there was little active involvement by the general public, and little mass demand for such policies. One can point to the tax reform legislation as an example of policy realignment. It seemed clear, Burnham noted, that "the politics of the 1986 tax reform act, an insiders' production from beginning to end, is a near-perfect example of major change quite unrelated to any mass demand for or involvement in its making." This disjunction between policy-active elites and the mass electorate concerning influence in politics has always existed. But the "near-dissolution of the partisan linkages between the two realms makes the relationship between rulers and ruled more problematic than it has been since the early days of the republic."[81] With the decline of parties and the reluctance of incumbent Congressmen to run partisan campaigns, the people remain a decisive force only in presidential elections. Public policy issues in our time seem to lack the broad and deep public support that results from a critical or realigning election, in which partisan issues are legitimized by public vote.

Governing "in accordance with the principles of democracy in a mass, heterogeneous society, requires a foundation of active consent by the governed. And the political party is conceived as supplying that systematized communication of governors and governed which is productive of such consent."[82] If the parties no longer provide the means by which policy is legitimized in the electorate through partisan involvement of the people in the electoral process, what has taken the place of parties? What has replaced the partisan campaign, with its emphasis on controversial issues of great importance or even principles of a high order? In short, how does a democratic people give its consent to the policies of its leaders without an organizational equivalent of the party? Burnham suggests that the "electoral market today is largely organized by the media and by individual candidates, together with their apparatus of professional 'hired guns' in the polling and political advertising trades. In a media

---

[80]Ibid., "Elections Dash GOP Dreams," p. 20.
[81]Burnham, ibid.
[82]Harry V. Jaffa, "The Nature and Origin of the American Party System," in Jaffa, *Equality and Liberty* (New York: Oxford University Press, 1965), pp. 4–5.

age, the relevance of party as a channel for voting decisions has disappeared among a very large fraction of those adult citizens who still bother to vote at all under these conditions." The result, of course, is that many citizens no longer take the time to vote. Well over 100 million Americans who could have voted did not do so in 1986. If the South is excluded, "turnout in 1986 fell to the lowest levels in more than 150 years." Even "if the South is included, the 1986 participation rate of about 38% was still the third lowest of all time; only in 1926 and 1942 was it lower."[83] Burnham has concluded that abstention of eligible voters from the polls is the largest American mass movement of modern times.

The decline of partisanship has been nowhere more evident than in the races for the House of Representatives. The continued electoral success of incumbents in the House is a much researched phenomenon. Numerous political scientists have shown the extent to which bureaucratic patronage has taken the place of party patronage in the contemporary Congress. Members of Congress are increasingly able, largely as a result of the establishment of a bureaucratic and regulatory apparatus, to make nonpartisan appeals—i.e., as ombudsman—to electorally decisive minorities in their districts who can virtually assure their reelection. With numerous perquisites at their disposal, and campaign finance limits placed upon their opponents, congressmen rarely run partisan campaigns.[84] Of course, such campaigns are expensive, because they often rely on technological innovation and professional management. Not only are incumbents in a strong position to raise money, but "challengers find themselves at a serious disadvantage in the competition for campaign funds." It is therefore difficult for a minority party to mount an effective campaign strategy against the "interacting strategies of individual members of the majority party." The reason is that "members pursue reelection as individuals, emphasizing personal characteristics and service to the district, carefully avoiding responsibility for the collective performance of Congress or their party." Consequently, it is difficult to "assign blame because members of the majority are so practiced at disassociating themselves from the collective effects of their individual activities."[85] So clear is the advantage of incumbency that the former chairman of the Democratic National Committee, Michael Kirwin, remarked that "no congress-

---

[83]Burnham, "Elections Dash GOP Dreams," p. 20.

[84]Gary Jacobson has observed the effect of incumbency on party discipline: "contemporary electoral conditions are scarcely conducive to effective action by political parties. Candidates have learned to get by without much assistance from party organizations, relying instead on campaign management professionals, the mass media, and their own personal followings." The effect, he says, is that "elections at different levels have become increasingly separated from one another, reducing the shared partisan fate." Consequently, "politicians operate as individual political entrepreneurs, pursuing personal careers in a political environment where parties are a dwindling presence." "Congressional Campaign Finance and the Revival of the Republican Party," in Dennis Hale, ed., *The United States Congress* (Boston: Boston College, Thomas P. O'Neill Symposium on Congress, 1982), pp. 313–314.

[85]Ibid., p. 316.

man who gets elected and minds his business should ever get beaten. Everything is there for him to use if he'll only keep his nose to the grindstone and use what is offered." The elections throughout the 1980s proved how difficult it is to defeat incumbent members of the House. In 1986, 1988, and 1990, approximately 98% of incumbents running for election were reelected.

The public financing of presidential elections has led to an increase of private spending in congressional elections. The primary beneficiary of private spending has been incumbent members of Congress, whose power and influence over particular areas of national policy has made such spending extremely profitable. It has also become clear that members of both parties have benefited from a centralized bureaucracy and regulatory apparatus that is responsive to congressional intervention. Congress as a body has an interest in preventing effective political or presidential control of the executive branch establishment. Campaign finance reform legislation has also heightened the tension between the president and Congress and has made it more difficult to reconcile the demands of the interests and constituencies that elect each of the respective branches. Perhaps we have reached the point where "the rules of campaign finance seem to encourage a situation in which Presidents and members of Congress come to office with systematically different interest-group electoral bases. Legislative–executive relations might be improved . . . if the branches' electoral bases were made more similar." But campaign finance reform has done precisely the opposite: it has exacerbated those differences. Moreover, it has "helped reinforce the nationalization of interest-group politics that followed the expansion of the federal government's role."[86]

The ongoing regulation of the special interests becomes the essence of liberal democratic politics and presupposes the existence of a centralized administration. It has transformed the principal function of Congress from one of legislation on behalf of a general or national interest to detailed administration and regulation of particular interests. Furthermore, members of Congress seek to avoid partisanship in the ordinary sense, ignoring parties and principle while emphasizing service. It seems clear that "party conflict has increasingly given way to activity that enhances the ability of incumbents of both parties to retain office." If the partisan divisions have been obscured, it is perhaps true that "in a good many ways the interesting division in congressional politics is not between Democrats and Republicans but between politicians in and out of office."[87]

Reagan's failure to achieve a new consensus through a critical realignment is not merely a failure of the Republican Party. It may be indicative of a pro-

---

[86]Michael D. Malbin, ed., *Money and Politics in the United States* (New Jersey: Chatham House Publishers, 1984), pp. 255–256.

[87]David Mayhew, quoted in Gary Jacobson, *Money in Congressional Elections* (New Haven: Yale University, Press, 1980), p. 6.

found problem that threatens to undermine the stability of our democratic institutions. As Burnham has written:

> One of the basic questions for the 1990s is whether politicians can find some way to provide stable and coherent government under such conditions. Another, equally serious, is the future of democracy in America. Historically, parties have organized our complex government and, in the process, have given the whole enterprise legitimacy among the public. There is no substitute for them.[88]

The Iran-Contra affair was the event that showed that the Reagan administration was not immune to the pattern of politics that had developed in recent administrations. According to this pattern, the crucial division in American politics is no longer the partisan distinction between the parties, but rather the institutional division between the executive and the legislative branches and the interests and constituencies that support them. Reagan's perceived success in dealing with Congress on a very limited range of issues may have obscured the extent to which the presidential office has been weakened beyond the ability to perform the tasks assigned to it under the Constitution. In institutional terms, Iran-Contra marked a fundamental shift in power between the branches that returned politics to normal in Washington. Former Defense Secretary James. R. Schlesinger observed at the time that we are witnessing a massive shift of power from the president to Congress. Even in the conduct of foreign policy, and especially covert operations, the power of the executive branch was challenged by powerful staffs in Congress. The Reagan administration was nearly consumed in domestic rivalry, not necessarily between the parties, but between the political branches of government. Perhaps Hugh Heclo was right when he observed a decade earlier that "it has become too difficult in Washington to gain political control of the bureaucracy through the right means—openly exercising political leadership—and too easy by the wrong means—quietly manipulating procedures behind the scenes."[89]

Although Ronald Reagan presided over the most successful administration since the advent of the administrative state,[90] he was unable to transform American politics in a manner consistent with the will of the majority in two large electoral victories. Moreover, Reagan did not attempt to transform the broad landscape of American politics. He succeeded in substituting his will for that of the majority party in the legislature on a very narrow range of issues, not a small feat in recent times. But he could not bring about a new electoral realignment in which his party could gain control of both houses of Congress. The

---

[88]Burnham, "Elections Dash GOP Dreams," p. 20.

[89]Heclo, *A Government of Strangers* (Washington, D.C.: Brookings Institution, 1977), p. 264.

[90]Although George Bush's presidency has been quite successful, achieving the highest public approval rating of any president since polling began, he has not attempted to use the office to effect a transformation of American politics. On the contrary, he has attempted to consolidate the changes made by Reagan. As Richard Rose has noted, "President Bush's conception of the Presidency is that of a guardian." *The Postmodern President*, p. 308.

growth of the administrative state had made it more difficult to dislodge incumbent members of Congress. Not only had bureaucratic patronage replaced party patronage, but the administrative role of individual legislators had largely replaced their legislative functions. In the process, members of Congress succeeded in disassociating themselves from partisan roles on questions of importance to the nation. In addition, the typical member was able to separate his personal fate from that of the institution of Congress, as well as party. The growth of the executive establishment has not necessarily enhanced the power of executives, let alone of the president. Indeed, an astute observer has noted that "the chief constitutional basis of our politics, the separation of powers, is under severe pressure from the institutions and practices of the administrative state. Paradoxically, the principle beneficiary of the growth of the executive bureaucracy has been Congress, not the president, who sees his responsibilities (as head of the executive branch) continually enlarged but his power steadily diminished."[91]

THE NEW CONGRESS: KEYSTONE OF THE ADMINISTRATIVE STATE

In every presidential election since 1972, the successful candidate ran for office by attacking the bureaucratic establishment in Washington. Since 1968 it has become clear that a president's ability to govern in the national interest is undermined by administrative centralization. Consequently, every recent president has sought to control the bureaucracy in order to decentralize administratively, with a view to governance in accord with general principles or a public interest. On the other hand, Congress has benefited from and has become the defender of a centralized administration. In practice, this has often required obstructing the president's ability to govern in accord with the mandate of a majority. It has prevented unified presidential control of the bureaucracy. Furthermore, Congress has inhibited its own capacity to govern in accord with a general or national interest, by deemphasizing its legislative or law-making and its deliberative functions while at the same time strengthening its administrative oversight capability. Hence, Congress reorganized itself in such a way as to disperse power broadly among its members in committee or subcommittee, with a view to allowing individual members the ability to intervene routinely in the execution phase of the governing process. As a result, some of the most important political battles between the president and Congress revolve around the question of which branch will control the bureaucracy, and in whose interest. In these circumstances, it has become almost as difficult to distinguish the executive and legislative function of the respective political branches as it has

[91]Charles Kesler, "Separation of Powers and the Administrative State," in Gordon S. Jones and John Marini, eds., *The Imperial Congress: Crisis in the Separation of Powers* (New York: Pharos Books, 1989), p. 23.

been to discern the difference between the public and private sphere in the postbureaucratic society.

In the public mind, Congress as an institution is expected primarily to deliberate and legislate or make general laws in the national interest. Secondly, it is to represent and serve the particular or private interests and constituencies of the localities that make up the nation. As a body or an institution, Congress is judged on its ability to make good public law in the national interest. On the other hand, individual members of Congress are more often judged on the basis of their ability to provide the kinds of goods and services that can satisfy the private interests of organized groups or electorally decisive minorities within a district. The problem posed by this dilemma is that it is not possible to make good general laws in the public interest and at the same time provide the particular necessities sought by private interests. At the national level, it is not possible to govern in the public interest and administer at the same time. Nonetheless, this problem was solved in a satisfactory way for individual members, but not for the institution of Congress, by the creation of a bureaucracy whose public mandate was so large and its purposes so broad that the impact of its rules and regulations touched upon nearly every interest and detail of life in society. By delegating authority to the bureaucracy, Congress could avoid being held responsible for the obtrusive regulations foisted upon society. The bureaucracy could be blamed for its meddlesome rules rather than blaming Congress for failing to provide proper guidelines in its delegation of authority, assuming national legislation was necessary in the first place.

There is little doubt that the growth of the administrative state or a centralized bureaucracy has contributed to the difficulty of reconciling the conflicting demands and interests of members of Congress with those of the institution of Congress itself. What is good for the member is not necessarily good for the body as a whole, let alone the nation. However, any attempt to explain this apparent paradox must take into account the inherent tension that exists within a large or diverse liberal republic between the public and private spheres, or the state and society. This tension provides a basis for the distinction between local and national interests, or the private as opposed to the public good. In the past, the private and parochial interests of citizens were most often administered at the local and state level, or in society, in the economic marketplace. At that level, it was possible to resolve, in a satisfactory manner, the differences implicit in the distinction between the public and private, the general and particular, or the governing as opposed to the administrative elements of a regime. The nation was characteristically governed on the basis of general principles; it was both governed and administered at the state and local level.

The secret to successful reconciliation of the differences involved in the public and private spheres lay in the decentralized character of the American regime. Prior to bureaucratization, Congress as an institution was held to the standard of governing in the national or general interest. After centralization, individual congressmen were judged by their ability to satisfy the private interests of their constituents. Administrative centralization thus undermined a crucial ingredient of liberal democracy, what Tocqueville called "local institutions" or "provincial liberties." The devitalization of local institutions, which made the distinction between the general and particular politically unintelligible, also made it practically impossible to achieve a reasonable reconciliation of those respective interests. As Tocqueville noted, "when the central administration claims completely to replace the free concurrence of those primarily concerned, it is deceiving itself, or trying to deceive you." This is so, he suggests, because, "a central power, however enlightened and wise one imagines it to be, can never alone see to all the details of the life of a great nation. It cannot do so because such a task exceeds human strength. When it attempts unaided to create and operate so much complicated machinery, it must be satisfied with very imperfect results or exhaust itself in futile efforts."[92]

The Founding generation recognized the inherent difficulty in distinguishing the governing and administrative function, and the necessity of careful delineation of the administrative sphere. In *Federalist* 72, Alexander Hamilton observed that

> . . . the administration of government, in its largest sense, comprehends all the operations of the body politic, whether legislative, executive, or judiciary; but in its most usual and perhaps precise signification, it is limited to executive details, and falls peculiarly within the province of the executive department.

What are those particular things that "constitute what seems to be most properly understood by the administration of government" and therefore should fall under the province of the "chief magistrate," according to Hamilton? They are

> the actual conduct of foreign negotiations, the preparatory plans of finance, the application and disbursement of the public money in conformity to the general appropriations of the legislature, the arrangement of the army and navy, the direction of the operations of war.

In Hamilton's view these are all details of administration and are executive in nature. Moreover, these

> distinctly administrative actions of our national government cannot be ordered by law (if for no other reason than that they require secrecy). More importantly, administration of the law itself cannot be ordered by law: the executive must be left free to decide which laws to enforce, and even, sometimes, whether to enforce the law at all; no law can change this necessity.[93]

---

[92] J. P. Mayer, ed., *Democracy in America* (Garden City: Doubleday Anchor Books, 1969), p. 91.

[93] See John A. Wettergreen, "Constitutional Problems of American Bureaucracy, in I.N.S.V. Chadha." Paper presented at the annual meeting of the American Political Science Association, New Orleans, Louisiana, 1985, p. 13.

Until recently, the American regime was centrally governed but administratively decentralized. In the period between 1965 and 1975, Congress created a bureaucracy capable of administering the details of American life centrally. Many Congressmen objected to the fact that the political function of Congress as a body was changed by its increased preoccupation with the administrative process. Representative Gillis Long (D-La.) complained: "We (Congress) were turning ours from an institution that was supposed to be a broad policymaking institution with respect to the problems of the country and its relationship to the world, into merely a city council that overlooks the running of the store everyday."[94] Such objections were ineffectual and short-lived. Subsequently, Congress came to prefer administration and regulation to legislation. The growth in size and the centralization of the administrative and regulatory bureaucracy only serve to confirm this fundamental change. In the period between 1970 and 1974,

> . . . not only did the number of commercial regulatory agencies increase from fifty to seventy-two, but also thirty-five of those fifty established agencies were substantially reformed. For the first time, agencies with 'economy-wide' (in fact, 'society-wide') purview and vast administrative discretion were established.[95]

Indeed, since 1975, the characteristic activity of the central government has become the regulation or the administration of the details of the social, political, and economic life of the nation. Such a development could not but strengthen organized interests and their ties with the legislature at the price of executive control of the details of administration. Even the courts have developed an important role in administrative decision-making and execution. Perhaps the most important consequence of the growth of the regulatory state is the increasing involvement of the courts in administrative decision-making and execution.

> . . . substantially less than 10 percent of the federal budget is spent on domestic programs performed directly by federal employees and the lion's share of federal programs are administered by independent third parties through grants, contracts, and transfer payments. Such arrangements not only invite litigation, but since disputes among parties in these relationships cannot be resolved authoritatively within the executive branch, they virtually command a litigation strategy by third parties. . . . In addition, Congress has added commands of its own in the form of direct requirements for public participation in the judicial review of administrative decision making and appropriations for attorneys' fee awards. Once judges accepted the appropriateness of their courts as sites for the resolution of such disputes, they became significant, sometimes the most significant actors in the administrative process.[96]

---

[94]Ibid., p. 31.
[95]Wettergreen, "Constitutional Problems of American Bureaucracy, p. 5.
[96]Harold Seidman and Robert Gilmour, *Politics, Position, and Power* (New York: Oxford University Press, 1986), pp. 136–137.

The expansion of federal governmental power in this period was not merely accomplished through creation of public agencies, but through proliferation of government-sponsored enterprises that were privately controlled, the so-called twilight zone bodies. The links between the public and private sector were forged and maintained through the growth of state budgets and increased control over economic and social relations. Nonetheless, public growth could not be calculated simply by looking at the size of state budgets. Public authority consisted of more than public expenditures or tax subsidies, or even increased regulatory power. Government could and did provide loan guarantees and other means by which certain public or even private enterprises were provided the opportunity to obligate the Treasury. In response to the passage of the Congressional Budget and Impoundment Control Act of 1974, these so-called "off-budget" expenditures could be excluded from the official budget process and the necessity of annual appropriations. Such expenditures are not harmful merely because they have increased the scope and power of the central government, or because they may constitute less efficient use of economic resources. They obscure responsibility and distort important distinctions in liberal governments. As Seidman and Gilmour have observed:

> . . . labeling as "private" what is in reality "public" for cosmetic reasons or to obtain fictitious budget reductions can contribute to loss of faith in our democratic institutions. . . . Distinctions between what is public and what is private are becoming increasingly blurred, but we cannot abandon these distinctions altogether without fundamental alterations in our constitutional system. The maintenance of this distinction has been considered essential both to protect private rights from intrusion by the government and to prevent usurpation of government power.[97]

Administrative centralization did not strengthen the governing capacity of the national institutions; on the contrary, it weakened them. As government's role was expanded and its functions increased, it became bigger and more intrusive, but not stronger and more decisive. Rather, as Walter Lippmann pointed out long ago, "to be big is not necessarily to be strong." Indeed, Lippmann insisted that the growth of modern or bureaucratic government threatened "the devitalization of the executive power." The ensuing "disorder," he suggested, "results from a functional derangement in the relationship between the executive power on the one hand, the representative assemblies and the mass electorates on the other hand." Lippmann contended that "democratic

---

[97]Ibid., p. 313. The importance of these changes in the standard of political life, which occurred as a result of blurring the distinction between the public and private sphere, and government and regulation, has also made it more difficult to uphold the legitimacy of government. As John Wettergreen has noted: "'government' is the adjustment of private interests to the public good and 'regulation' is the adjustment of private interests to each other. A shift of the government's activities from governance to regulation implies a shift of the political standard from the public interest to private interests." Unlike the political branches of government, regulatory agencies are explicitly prevented from attempting to deliberate in a comprehensive manner concerning the public good. "Constitutional Problems of American Bureaucracy," p. 5.

states are susceptible to this derangement because congenitally the executive
. . . is weaker than the elected representatives. . . . And the normal tendency
of elections is to reduce elected officers to the role of agents or organized
pluralities." Such governments, he maintained, are, "to be sure, big governments, in their personnel, in the range and variety of their projects, the ubiqui-
tousness of their interventions." But they are not strong governments. "They
are, in fact, swollen rather than strong, being too weak to resist the pressure of
special interests and of the departmental bureaucracies."[98] Hence, when modern
democratic governments are bureaucratized, they are faced with the apparent
paradox of being less able to govern the more they try to administer the details
of life in society. Centralized administration almost requires decentralization of
government.

Administrative centralization, moreover, has exacerbated the tension between the executive and the legislature in a way that subsequently worked to
undermine the separation of powers. The difference of interest between the
president and Congress, which bureaucratization has produced, must be distinguished from the traditional rivalry between the branches, which is the consequence of separation of powers. The presidency, the only truly national elective
office, is ultimately antagonistic to central administration; Congress, especially
the House, is naturally sympathetic because of its closer ties to narrower interests. When administration is centralized, "it does not naturally fall under the
authority of any one branch. . . . Instead, it becomes a bone of contention
among them." Moreover, Congress gets "the better of the division because of
its superior attention to localized interests (and its superior part in delibera-
tions)." Before centralization, "congressmen surveiled the president, to protect
non-national interests from the untoward effects of national executions. The
ultimate protection was to refuse to make laws touching these interests on the
ground that they were not national interests."[99]

In the same manner, "the President surveiled Congress with an eye to the
national (or, at least, trans-sectional) interest, if only because his political interest required a broader coalition." Hence,

> before the choice to centralize was made, separation of powers was an important
> prop for decentralized administration, in which congressmen had an interest (even
> during the New Deal), and for centralized governance, in which the President had a
> special interest. In sum, the whole central government had a common interest in
> deliberating the national interest, and in distinguishing it from narrower interests.

Administrative centralization makes it far less necessary for Congress to subordinate private and parochial interests to a national interest. Rather, Congress in
the period during and after the Great Society "brought all the partial interests to

---

[98]*The Public Philosophy* (New York: Mentor Books, 1955), p. 44.
[99]Wettergreen, "Constitutional Problems of American Bureaucracy," p. 44.

the center, where they do almost nothing but try to compromise national execution and legislation." Consequently, "decrees, i.e., bureaucratically promulgated regulation, have replaced public laws as the typical expression of public authority."[100]

In the aftermath of administrative centralization, the president still has a political interest in central governance, but the Congress has lost its interest in decentralized administration. The constitutional separation of powers

> did not deadlock national governance on national issues, but encouraged it by making the cooperation of the two branches necessary. However, administration does not require that cooperation. So today, the branches stand divided against themselves, one wishing to govern and the other to administer. . . . [Hence,] the conflict between the two branches is no longer the result of differing opinions of the national interest.[101]

Once administration was centralized, no legislative body could legislate, in a general manner, all the details of the life of a great nation. Congress had to delegate authority to administrative bodies. Of course, it could continue to play a significant role in the administrative process, or void an exercise of delegated authority through the use of a legislative veto. But Congress has a number of ways of ensuring that the bureaucracy is responsive to its members. Perhaps the most important formal power is its statutory authority to create departments and agencies as well as determine their size, not to mention the ability to control their budgets. Ripley and Franklin have pointed to several means by which Congress keeps the bureaucracy responsive to its will. "In the technical sense, only statutes have the force of law. However, Congress has also made its will felt in programmatic terms through language contained in committee reports. And the executive branch often treats this language as binding." Also, "Congress may require that parts of the bureaucracy make certain information available to it through reporting requirements in statutes." Perhaps most important is control of authorizations and appropriations, which require numerous formal and informal contacts between administrators and congressmen. Consequently, "Congress inevitably is the focus of attention from bureaucrats requesting and defending their agencies' budgets, and budget decisions are an important congressional technique for influencing programmatic performance in the executive branch."[102] It is not surprising that career civil servants are often more attentive to the wishes of relevant members of Congress than to their elected or appointed superiors in the executive branch.

The implicit premise of legislative delegation and the necessity of administrative oversight is the belief that administrative bodies, scientifically neutral

---

[100]Ibid., pp. 44–45.
[101]Ibid., p. 45.
[102]Randall B. Ripley and Grace A. Franklin, *Congress, the Bureaucracy, and Public Policy* (Chicago: The Dorsey Press, 1987), pp. 78–79.

and technically rational, can best carry out the will of the people. The political reason of the people, or the deliberation of the partisan representative legislative bodies, is ineffective in fulfilling the people's intention. Furthermore, administrative bodies benefit from the technical rationality of the social sciences. The scientific method is superior to the political process as the means of serving the will of the people. As Harvey Mansfield, Jr., has commented:

> The trick, then, is to leave the people their will and take away their reason; then social science can bring *its* reason to serve *their* will, showing them how to get more of what they want. The value neutrality of social science is the best or only means by which government can bring value to the people.[103]

It is no wonder that legislative bodies have become increasingly apprehensive concerning the necessity of public deliberation and the efficacy of political reason as the means by which modern problems can be solved. Thus, within the legislatures public deliberation and law making has given way to delegation of authority to those administrative bodies capable of utilizing the expertise of those trained in the scientific method, or the technical rationality of the now-authoritative social sciences, in solving the problems of modern society.

In the flurry of legislative activity that occurred in the middle 1960s, Congress erected a centralized administrative apparatus whose task was to solve, in a technically rational way—using the methods of science and social science—the social and political problems of industrial or postindustrial society. However, if Harry McPherson, a top Johnson aide, is to be believed, the animating force behind the Great Society was not the desire to legislate reasonable public policy. Rather it had its origins in the malaise of the intellectuals and the leadership class. It was essentially driven by the private passions of troubled elite groups whose guilt could be alleviated by a creative public effort on behalf of the poor and middle classes.[104]

Such an effort required the wholesale utilization of the expertise of the modern university. Rational deliberation of the public interest, which was not beyond the ken of an ordinary legislator, was replaced by a bureaucratic rationality designed to solve in a minute way all the problems of a technological society. As James Ceaser has written, "it is undeniable that social scientists

---

[103] "The Constitution and Modern Social Science," *The Center Magazine*, vol. 19, September/October, 1986, p. 52.

[104] McPherson noted that "a new philosophy of government had emerged since New Deal days. In essence it held that our problems were more of the spirit than of the flesh. People were suffering from a sense of alienation from one another, of anomie, of powerlessness. This affected the well-to-do as much as it did the poor . . . all were in need of community, beauty, and purpose, all were guilty because so many others were deprived while they, rich beyond their ancestors' dreams, were depressed. What would change all this was a creative public effort; for the middle class, new parks, conservation, aid to the arts; for the poor, jobs, training, Head Start, decent housing, medical care, civil rights; for both, and for bridging the gap between them, VISTA, the Teacher Corps, the community action agencies, mass transportation, model cities." *A Political Education* (Boston: Atlantic Monthly Press, 1972), pp. 301–302.

helped supply the ideas that underlay many of the Great Society programs. It was, in fact, the heyday for social science, as the 'new professionals' within the government who had been trained in the social sciences stepped in to help devise the new programs, borrowing freely from current theories floating around academia. The era of the policymaking state had arrived."[105]

With the arrival of the policymaking state, the kind of detailed information necessary to run it was not at the disposal of the typical legislator.[106] The knowledge of the expert became the most valuable commodity of such a government. Furthermore, as Theodore Lowi noted, such "government is almost impossible to limit. Liberalism tends to universalize the scope and responsibility of government, and science then makes the liberal argument almost unassailable." This explains "why legislation has grown broader and broader in scope, has become more and more abstract in definition, and is more and more universal in its applicability." Lowi concluded that

> the liberal approach to government has made government a magnet and has rendered representatives powerless to say no or to establish priorities among theories and needs. If a theory points to consequences, there is an obligation to act upon it. In fact, during the last two or three decades, the legislative process has not even required that legislators be knowledgeable about what to do or how to do it. It simply accepts the theory ('whereas . . .') and indicates that there is an injury and a likely cause ('here's the problem . . .'); then it delegates to an administrative agency the responsibility for doing something about it ('go deal with it . . .').[107]

Administrative centralization allowed members of Congress to take credit for providing those subsidies or services, including regulatory relief, that benefited particular constituents.

Congress maintains a federal bureaucracy deliberately organized to make it perme-

---

[105]"The Theory of Governance of the Reagan Administration," in Salmon and Lund, eds., *The Reagan Presidency and the Governing of America* (Washington: Urban Institute Press, 1984), p. 70.

[106]Lest one conclude that members of Congress merely wanted to oversee the executive administration, rather than have the capacity to formulate policy, it is clear the reforms of the 1970s were of a different kind. As Michael Malbin has noted, "every time congressional staffs have increased, the publicly stated justification has been the same: Congress needs its own sources of information if it is to remain independent of the executive branch and of private interest groups. Over the years, this justification became almost ritualized, even as the staffs became steadily more partisan and less purely informational. But in 1970 it took an interesting turn. Although the Legislative Reorganization Act of 1970 spurred a new spurt in growth, it also required the Congressional Research Service and the General Accounting Office to move beyond their traditional functions, reference and audit, to a new function: *providing Congress with policy analysis.* The 1972 act creating the new Office of Technology Assessment, and the Budget Impoundment and Control Act of 1974 creating the Congressional Budget Office, gave those two new agencies similar mandates." "Congress, Policy Analysis, and Natural Gas Deregulation: A Parable about Fig Leaves," in Robert A. Goldwin, ed., *Bureaucrats, Policy Analysts, Statesmen: Who Leads?* (Washington, D.C.: American Enterprise Institute, 1980), p. 62.

[107]Theodore Lowi, "Ronald Reagan—Revolutionary," in Salmon and Lund, eds., *The Reagan Presidency and the Governing of America,* p. 51.

able to congressional intervention—not only to the chamber as a whole, but to subgroups and even individuals. So long as an agency cooperates when members make specific requests, it is unlikely to suffer long-term losses no matter how poor its performance.

Moreover, Congress disguises its responsibility in the delegation of authority. Morris Fiorina asks,

> Why take political chances by setting detailed regulations sure to antagonize some political actor or another? Why not require an agency to do the dirty work and then step in to redress the grievances that result from its activities? . . . Let the agency take the blame and the member of Congress the credit. In the end everybody benefits. Members successfully wage their campaigns for reelection. And while popularly vilified, bureaucrats get their rewards in the committee rooms of Congress.[108]

Whereas individual members of Congress have benefited from this arrangement with the bureaucracy, the institution of Congress has had greater difficulty in performing its primary function as a body, which is general lawmaking in the public interest. "The particularistic elements in our society will always triumph over the general interest as long as they are nourished and supported by committees and subcommittees that share their limited concerns."[109]

In a bureaucratic state, it is not much of an exaggeration to say that the typical activity of a member of Congress is the superintendence of the details of administration. Power has been decentralized and dispersed among numerous subcommittee chairs. At the same time, personal and committee staff has grown tremendously. Party and leadership authority has only been centralized when it has been necessary to prevent presidential use of power that could undermine congressional domination of the bureaucracy. In such areas as fiscal policy formation or budget control, not to mention impoundment of funds, presidents of either party could no longer be trusted. Nonetheless, majority control of the House continued to be of great importance to the Democratic Party. That party created the bureaucracy and learned to benefit from its existence. If deprived of majority status, the Democrats would lose the ability to organize and control the House and determine its ends. If the members' connection with the bureaucracy was severed, incumbency would be far less important, making electoral success much more precarious. Congress, therefore, has organized itself in such a way as to allow individual members the ability to control, on a day-to-day basis, the various areas of public policy legally assigned to the federal bureaucracy. As individual entrepreneurs defending particular and organized interests, members of Congress have become very adept at advancing those interests while at the

---

[108]Fiorina, "Congressional Control of the Bureaucracy: A Mismatch of Incentives and Capabilities," in Dodd and Oppenheimer, eds., *Congress Reconsidered*, p. 343.

[109]Seidman and Gilmour, *Politics, Position, and Power*, p. 340.

same time obscuring responsibility for the growth of the administrative state. Their skill is reflected in the stunning rate of incumbent electoral success.

The detailed control of the ongoing activity of the centralized bureaucracy is the means by which Congress has transformed itself into something rivaling an executive. In many areas of public policy, including foreign policy, members of Congress can thwart or substitute their will for that of the executive. And within the legislature as an institution, the Democratic Party in the House serves as permanent minority government in opposition to the constitutionally elected representative of the majority, the president. Moreover, the complexity and obscurity of that relationship allows members of Congress to avoid accountability and responsibility for their actions. It is for this reason that the House of Representatives, the body once thought to be closest to the people and most reflective of its opinions and interests, is the least responsive to the will of the contemporary majority.

In 1965, in a celebrated essay entitled "Congressional Responses to the Twentieth Century," Samuel P. Huntington commented upon the relative weakness of the legislature. He asserted "today's 'aggressive spirit' is clearly the executive branch." The loss of power by Congress, Huntington suggested,

> can be measured by the extent to which congressional assertion coincides with congressional obstruction. This paradox has been at the root of the "problem" of Congress since the early days of the New Deal. Vis-à-vis the Executive, Congress is an autonomous, legislative body. But apparently Congress can defend its autonomy only by refusing to legislate, and it can legislate only by surrendering its autonomy. . . . Congress can assert its power or it can pass laws; but it cannot do both.[110]

Huntington traced the root of the decline in Congressional power to the insulation and parochialism of the body.

> Perhaps the single most important trend in congressional evolution during the twentieth century has been the growing insulation of Congress from other social groups and political institutions. In 1900 no gap existed between congressmen and other leaders of American society and politics.

Within a half-century, he noted, "the institutional evolution of Congress . . . had produced a marked gap between congressional leaders and the bureaucratically oriented leadership of the executive branch and of the Establishment."[111] In 1965, Huntington could still write:

> The country at large has become urban, suburban, and metropolitan. Its economic, social, educational, and technological activities are increasingly performed by huge national bureaucratic organizations. But on Capitol Hill, the nineteenth-century

---

[110]In David Truman, ed., *The Congress and America's Future* (Englewood Cliffs, N.J.: Prentice-Hall, 1965), p. 6.
[111]Ibid., p. 8.

ethos of the small town, the independent farmer, and the small businessman is still entrenched behind the institutional defenses which developed in this century to insulate Congress from the new America.[112]

Congress had lost its power, Huntington maintained, because it had become defective as a representative body. He asked,

How can national institutions be represented in a locally elected legislature? In the absence of any easy answer to this question, the administration has tended to emerge as the natural point of access to the government for these national organizations and the place where their interests and viewpoints are brought into the policy-making process. . . . The American system of government is moving toward a three-way system of representation. Particular territorial interests are represented in Congress; particular functional interests are represented in the administration; and the national interest is represented territorially and functionally in the Presidency.[113]

Huntington pointed to a remedy for the problem that confronted Congress in 1965. "Congress is in a legislative dilemma because opinion conceives of it as a legislature," he noted. "Representative assemblies have not always been legislatures. They had their origins in medieval times as courts and as councils. An assembly need not legislate to exist and to be important." Huntington suggested the Congress abandon its legislative function.

Legislation has become much too complex politically to be effectively handled by a representative assembly. The primary work of legislation must be done, and increasingly is being done, by the three "houses" of the executive branch: the bureaucracy, the administration, and the President.[114]

If the legislative function of Congress had become obsolete, what role should it play? "Far more important than the preservation of Congress as a legislative institution," Huntington asserted, "is the preservation of Congress as an autonomous institution. When the performance of one function becomes 'dysfunctional' to the workings of an institution, the sensible course is to abandon it for other functions."[115] Huntington insisted "that the legislative function has declined in importance, while the growth of the federal bureaucracy has made the administrative overseeing function of Congress more important." The advice Huntington offered to the legislature was to abandon its constitutional role. Consequently, he suggested that members of Congress ought "to focus upon functions of constituent service and bureaucratic control which insulation and dispersion do enable it to play in the national government."[116]

Within ten years of Huntington's description of Congress as an endangered

[112]Ibid., p. 16.
[113]Ibid., p. 17.
[114]Ibid., p. 29.
[115]Ibid.
[116]Ibid., p. 31.

institution, on the heels of Richard Nixon's resignation, there seemed to be little doubt that Congress was once again "the aggressive spirit" in American government. With the centralization of administration that occurred in the wake of the Great Society, representation of territorial interests was no longer necessary—federalism had been transformed. "One of the truly significant changes . . . is that state and local governments—counties, cities, regional governments and the like—have taken on virtually all the patterns of behavior which, in the past, we associated with clientele interest groups."[117] Congress quickly realized it could benefit local constituencies better by regulating the functional interests of society from the center. Its success in regaining power was dependent upon the growth in scope and authority of the administrative apparatus, and the ability of members to direct on a regular—if informal—basis, the details of administration.

In a bureaucratic society, Lowi is no doubt correct when he notes that "administration" is "politics in its most serious form."[118] The task of ruling the bureaucracy required the creation of a congressional bureaucracy and the capability of an institutional intelligence. Many of the battles between the executive branch and the legislative branch revolved around the question of who had greater access to information and knowledge of the internal working of the bureaucracy. By the end of the 1970s Congress had more than 30,000 employees working directly for its members and committees. Moreover, its influence had become dependent upon its ability to function like an executive. As James Sundquist has observed:

> . . . as members become managers of professional staffs, the chambers disintegrate as "deliberative bodies" in the traditional sense of legislators engaged in direct interchange of views leading to a group decision. . . . With each passing year, the House and Senate appear less as collective institutions and more as collections of institutions—individual member-staff groups organized as offices and subcommittees.[119]

Furthermore, "the growth of a congressional bureaucracy and institutionalization of committees and subcommittees have deepened the moats dividing the fiefdoms and accentuated the innate disposition of the Congress to concentrate on administrative details rather than basic issues of public policy."[120]

The congressional bureaucracy, created to oversee the executive branch administration of the details of the political, economic, and social life of the

---

[117]Allen Schick, *"Discussion,"* in William S. Livingston, Lawrence C. Dodd, and Richard L. Schott, eds., *The Presidency and the Congress* (Austin: LBJ School of Public Affairs, 1979), p. 158.

[118]"The State in Politics: The Relation Between Policy and Administration," in Roger Noll, ed., *Regulatory Policy and the Social Sciences* (Berkeley: University of California Press, 1985), p. 67.

[119]Sundquist, *The Decline and Resurgence of Congress* (Washington: The Brookings Institution, 1981), p. 411.

[120]Seidman and Gilmour, *Politics, Position, and Power,* p. 40.

nation, allows members the ongoing means to monitor and intervene in the affairs of the executive branch. It is a simple fact of life that every group or interest that comes to Washington (and few interests can afford to stay away from Washington) must soon reckon with the power of Congress and individual Congressmen as the true bosses of the centralized bureaucracy. One could no longer say, as Huntington did in 1965, that Congress is a parochial body, insulated and isolated from the real sources of power in American society. By 1975, Congress had become, in Morris Fiorina's phrase, the "keystone" of the "Washington Establishment."[121]

In the widespread delegation of authority to departments and agencies of the federal government, Congress has often exempted itself from the rules that govern the rest of society. Such exclusions prompted Senator Leahy of Vermont to accuse Congress of acting as though "what is good and fair for the country is not necessarily good and fair for Congress."[122] General laws in the public interest have given way to specific rules regulating specific interests. As the ultimate holder of the delegated authority, Congress, not unreasonably, exempted itself from the effect of such laws or regulations that impinge upon its power or sovereignty. One observer noted:

> Congressmen have exempted themselves and their employees from the provisions of the Fair Labor Standards Act of 1938, the Civil Rights Act of 1964, the Equal Employment Opportunity Act of 1972, and the Social Security Act. The operations of their offices are exempt from the Occupational Safety Act (which created OSHA), and they do not have to answer requests under the Freedom of Information Act and the Privacy Act.[123]

However reasonable it may be in terms of accomplishing its work for the Congress to avoid various provisions of the law or regulations that fall upon its fellow citizens, such precedent is far removed from the spirit of lawmaking and constitutionalism that animated the framers of our government. When Madison in *Federalist* 57 argued the various circumstances that would prevent the House of Representatives from taking oppressive measures, he noted that

> they can make no law which will not have its full operation on themselves and their friends, as well as on the great mass of the society. This has always been deemed one of the strongest bonds by which human policy can connect the rulers and the people together. It creates between them that communion of interests and sympathy of sentiments, of which few governments have furnished examples; but without which every government degenerates into tyranny.

In answer to the question: "What is to restrain the House of Representatives

---

[121]See Fiorina, *Congress: Keystone of the Washington Establishment* (New Haven, Conn.: Yale University Press, 1977).

[122]Cited in J. McIver Weatherford, *Tribes on the Hill* (South Hadley, Mass.: Bergin & Garvey Publishers, Inc., 1985), p. 49.

[123]Ibid.

from making legal discrimination in favor of themselves and a particular class of society?", Madison replied: "The genius of the whole system; the nature of just and constitutional laws; and above all, the vigilant and manly spirit which actuates the people of America—a spirit which nourishes freedom, and in return is nourished by it." Madison warned further that "if this spirit shall ever be so far debased as to tolerate a law not obligatory on the legislature, as well as on the people, the people will be prepared to tolerate any thing but liberty."[124]

There has been considerable debate in recent years concerning the state of our governing institutions. At different times we have been alerted to the danger of the "imperial presidency" or an "imperial judiciary." However dangerous either of those may be to the preservation of constitutional government or individual liberty, a healthy, strong, and constitutional legislature can legally prevent abuse from the other branches by invoking its constitutional authority. There has been little outcry, whether popular or among elite groups, concerning the danger or likelihood of an "imperial legislature." Perhaps this is merely tacit recognition of the fact that Madison was right when he noted that legislative authority must necessarily predominate in republican governments. Furthermore, it might seem unnecessary to worry about legislative tyranny in a country with free and periodic elections. Nonetheless, Madison was fearful of legislative corruption as perhaps being symptomatic of the corruption of the people themselves.[125] There is no specific power or constitutional device that could prevent the abuse of legislative authority. Rather, it was, as Madison noted, the "genius of the whole system," including "the nature of just and constitutional laws," that would prevent legislative tyranny. Above all, he insisted, it is "the vigilant and manly spirit which actuates the people of America," which would be the best check on legislative abuse of power.

It is not easy to determine the spirit that animates contemporary American society: however, the animating force within the institutions of government indicates a profound indifference to the genius of constitutional government. Moreover it is doubtful that the Founders ever thought that the leaders of the people would be less solicitous of constitutional forms than the people themselves. Yet they were surely aware that legislative bodies are as susceptible to corrupting influences as any other institution of government. The corruption of the legislature is more subtle and difficult to observe than executive or judicial

---

[124]*Federalist,* No. 57.

[125]Madison divided governments according to their animating spirit, and noted the characteristics of corruption. "A government operating by corrupt influence; substituting the motive of private interest in place of public duty; converting its pecuniary dispensations into bounties to favorites, or bribes to opponents; accommodating its measures to the avidity of a part of the nation instead of the benefit of the whole: in a word, enlisting an army of interested partisans, whose tongues, whose pens, whose intrigues, and whose active combinations, by supplying the terror of the sword, may support a real domination of the few under an apparent liberty of the many. Such a government, wherever to be found, is an impostor." Spirit of Governments," in the *National Gazette,* February 18, 1792.

corruption. Legislative corruption would not necessarily become apparent through outwardly tyrannical acts of the legislative body, such as the passing of unjust laws. It is more likely that such corruption would be reflective of legislative indifference to the constitutional order as a whole. It may be indicative of insufficient spirit or lack of character on the part of the legislators, and their unwillingness to do those things that are necessary to preserve free and reasonable government. Consequently, it could mean that the members of the legislature would perpetuate themselves and their interests by acting in a manner contrary to the role prescribed to the legislative body by the Constitution, and the principles of liberal democratic theory.

In the view of the Founders, the greatest threat to political liberty was posed by legislatures becoming the vehicle of tyrannical majorities. The dangers that majority factionalism posed to stability and the protection of private rights in a small democracy is analogous to a similar danger in an extended republic. If the members of the legislature, and the dominant interests in government, i.e., the bureaucracy, become no more than a faction on behalf of the interests of government or bureaucratic rule, deliberation and representation of a public interest or a common good would be unnecessary, not to say impossible. Government itself would no longer be the interest that transcends factionalism, it would *be* a faction. And, like "the will in the community independent of the majority—that is, of the society itself," which Madison spoke of in *Federalist* 51, it "may as well espouse the unjust views of the major, as the rightful interests of the minor party, and may possibly be turned against both parties." In short, such a will is unrestrained, and the government is no longer constitutional. Because of its overriding power and its unique connection to the people themselves, the danger of legislative corruption has long been recognized as the gravest danger to free government. In *Federalist* 71, Hamilton expressed with perfect clarity the Constitutional problems posed by legislative usurpation of power. He noted:

> . . . to what purpose separate the executive, or the judiciary, from the legislative, if both the executive and the judiciary are so constituted as to be at the absolute devotion of the legislative? Such a separation must be merely nominal and incapable of producing the ends for which it was established. It is one thing to be subordinate to the laws, and another to be dependent on the legislative body. The first comports with, the last violates, the fundamental principles of good government; and whatever may be the forms of the Constitution, unites all power in the same hands.

Some years before the American Constitution was written, the celebrated theorist of democracy, Montesquieu, pointed to the conditions under which liberty and democratic governments were likely to be destroyed. Like Hamilton and the Framers of the Constitution, he insisted that good government would require a viable separation of the powers of government. In addition, like the

Framers, he insisted that this principle of democratic constitutionalism would most likely be undermined through the corruption of the legislature. Montesquieu observed that: "as all human things have an end, the state we are speaking of will lose its liberty, will perish. . . . It will perish when the legislative power shall be more corrupt than the executive."[126]

---

[126]*The Spirit of the Laws*, pp. 161–162.

Chapter 6

The Administrative State
and the Crisis
of Constitutional Government

It is getting harder to *run* a constitution than to frame one.
                        Woodrow Wilson, *The Study of Administration*

A peculiar kind of administrative state, distinctively American, was consolidated within the constitutional order during the past several decades. It did not violate in any way the letter of the Constitution. Nonetheless, it has had a profound impact upon perceptions of the legitimacy of government at the national level. Since 1968, every candidate who has succeeded in winning the presidency has been perceived to be anti-Washington, or more anti-bureaucratic, than his opponent. A leading political scientist has suggested that "during the 1970s as confidence in government plummeted, we reached a remarkable consensus on our central political problem—a bureaucracy that had become too powerful and independent."[1] Indeed, a decade after Ronald Reagan proclaimed that "government is the problem," an astute political analyst could still insist that "big

---

[1]William T. Gormley, Jr., *Taming the Bureaucracy* (Princeton: Princeton University Press, 1989), p. 232.

government, not race, is now the essential partisan issue in American politics."[2]
The administrative state has yet to gain legitimacy. The centralized bureaucracy
rests uneasily within the structure of American constitutionalism.[3] As Peri
Arnold has noted:

> American government became bureaucratic while still conforming to the arrange-
> ments of a pre-bureaucratic regime. The accommodation between the administra-
> tive state and the traditional regime is one of the grand themes that must be pursued
> as we search for an understanding of American political development.[4]

Bureaucratic government has remained a contentious issue in American politics
and has lacked legitimacy because it rests upon a theory of government that is
outside the American political tradition. Bureaucratic centralization has produced a disjunction between the theoretical and practical dimension of politics,
between the principles that legitimize action, and the practice of the institutions
of government. In terms of legitimacy, the American tradition is one of limited
government. In practice, American constitutionalism has attempted to maintain
limited government by separating the powers of government and distinguishing
between the public and private spheres. In principle, there is no limitation upon
the power of government in the administrative state. The proponents of the
administrative state have viewed separation of powers as an antiquated relic
guaranteed to ensure deadlock. In their view, the fundamental distinction in
politics is not between the powers of government, nor is the distinction between
the public and private sphere fundamental to society. Rather, the crucial distinction is that between the political institutions and parties that authorize and legitimize action, and the administrative apparatus that rationalizes it and puts it into
practice. However, Progressive theories that looked to the administrative state
as a means of overcoming limitations imposed by the Constitution have never
succeeded in undermining attachment to the principles of constitutionalism in
America. Consequently, the Constitution has remained the source of legitimacy
and the standard by which to measure authority in the American regime. The
American administrative state has to be judged, therefore, not on the basis of
political theories that presuppose the legitimacy of the state. Nor can it be
assumed that administrative centralization is the inevitable consequence of the
necessity to adapt to changes in society brought about by industrialization and
urbanization or progress in science and technology. The American administrative state was put in place *after* the major transformations of society had oc-

---

[2]William Schneider, "Key Civil Rights Issue is 'How Far'?" *National Journal* (March 30,
1991), p. 774.

[3]Some scholars have tried to reconcile bureaucracy and constitutionalism. One such scholar,
John Rohr, has written a book whose purpose "is to legitimate the administrative state in terms of
constitutional principle." *To Run a Constitution: The Legitimacy of the Administrative State* (Lawrence: University Press of Kansas, 1986), p. ix.

[4]Peri E. Arnold, *Making the Managerial Presidency* (Princeton, New Jersey: Princeton University Press, 1986), p. xi.

curred. It was the result of conscious political choice. Consequently, the American administrative state must be judged by its impact upon the practical politics of the constitutional system. How does it affect the conditions of prebureaucratic rule: of limited government, separation of powers, and American federalism? To the extent the administrative state is a problem in American politics, it is the result of the manner in which the institutions of government and the constituencies allied to them have adapted to the presence of a centralized bureaucracy.

The decisive fact of American politics in the past decades is the consolidation of the administrative state. The growth of the administrative state has resulted in a transformation of the institutions of American government and the interests and constituencies allied to them. Nowhere has this transformation been of greater importance than in the changes that have occurred within the institutions of government, particularly within the first branch, the central political branch of government, the legislature.[5] These changes in Congress reflect acceptance of the view, first stated authoritatively in America by Woodrow Wilson, that the real source of power in the modern state lies in the administrative realm, or in the ability to control the bureaucracy. Wilson's view rests on a theory of the state that is based on an acceptance of fundamental principles of German thought. Those principles are wholly at odds with the natural rights' tradition of the American Founding Fathers.

The constitutional order was founded on the assumption that the two functions, that of legislation and administration, corresponded to the functions of the two political branches within the national government. In addition, the Founders presupposed an autonomy that allowed a viable operation of politics and administration at the state and local level, not merely at the national level. Hence, the political order was one of centralized government and administration of the general affairs of the nation, and decentralized government and administration of state, local, and primarily private matters. The politics/administration dichotomy, on the other hand, effectively obliterates this distinction. The *will* of the majority, embodied in the nation alone—and not the states and localities—is the source of all legitimacy. The states and localities become a focus of administrative activity, but genuine political autonomy, or power, is lacking.[6]

In Wilson's view, the realm of politics is concerned with executive articulation of the national will and legislative embodiment of that will. Politics or government is the domain of will embodied in law, and administration is the

---

[5]As Michael Malbin has suggested, "to a large extent, the growing governmental agenda has been responsible for many of Congress's institutional changes." "Factions and Incentives" p. 106 (see Footnote 7).

[6]Tocqueville was among the first to observe that in such circumstances citizens would cease to involve themselves in politics without real power to address their local concerns. They would become increasingly preoccupied with private life.

nonpolitical implementation of that will. More precisely, politics is the attempt to embody the will of a majority as articulated in public law; administration is the rational means by which to implement that will. The Progressive view denied any limitation, upon the power of the state, precisely because it is the embodiment of the will of the people.[7] However, liberal democracy—or constitutional government—is premised on the notion that passion or will is in conflict with reason and moderation. Faction can never be removed from politics. The constitutional order is an attempt to institutionalize the rule of law or reason, not of legislative or majority will, as fundamental to good government. Thus, certain areas have been declared out of bounds for any state activity. In a constitutional regime, the government is a guarantor of rights and not the positive embodiment of any will, even that of an unreasonable majority.

In principle, therefore, the centralized administrative state intended the erosion of the foundations of constitutionalism, or limited government. Nor was such a consequence unforeseen. As Tocqueville observed long ago, "so true is it that socialism and centralization thrive on the same soil; they stand to each other as the cultivated to the wild species of a fruit."[8] Indeed, the leading thinkers of the Progressive era had great difficulty in distinguishing socialism—or centralization—from democracy. However, a distinction between democracy and constitutional government was taken for granted by Progressive leaders. Woodrow Wilson, for example, in his *Essay on Socialism*, could find no principled difference between democracy—as understood by the Progressives—and socialism. Rather, he insisted that both democracy and socialism differed from the government established by the Constitution. In elucidating that difference, Wilson observed that socialism

> proposes that all ideas of a limitation of public authority be put out of view, and that the State consider itself bound to stop only at what is unwise or futile in its universal superintendence alike of individual and of public interests. The thesis of the state socialist is, that no line can be drawn between private and public affairs which the State may not cross at will.[9]

In elaborating the difference, Wilson suggested,

> the germinal conceptions of democracy are as free from all thought of limitation of the public authority as are the corresponding conceptions of socialism; the individual rights which the democracy of our own century has actually observed, were suggested to it by a political philosophy radically individualistic, but not necessarily democratic. Democracy is bound by no principle of its own nature to say itself nay

---

[7] As Woodrow Wilson had noted, the state could no longer constitute a threat to the liberties of the individual. Rather, "the modern idea is this: the state no longer absorbs the individual, it only serves him." *The State* (Boston: D.C. Heath & Company, 1898), p. 48.

[8] *The Old Regime and the French Revolution* (Garden City: Doubleday, 1955), p. 164.

[9] Arthur F. Link, ed., *Papers of Woodrow Wilson* (Princeton: Princeton University Press, 1968), vol. 6, p. 561.

as to the exercise of any power. Here, then, lies the point. The difference between democracy and socialism is not an essential difference, but only a practical difference—a difference of *organization* and *policy,* not a difference of primary motive [Wilson's emphasis].[10]

Hence constitutional government, as limited government, in Wilson's view, is incompatible with the Progressive theory of democracy.

THEORETICAL CHARACTER OF THE ADMINISTRATIVE STATE

The administrative state, particularly as it was conceived in the Progressive era and developed politically, evolved out of a philosophical tradition that presupposed the idea of the state as the rational embodiment of the will of the people. In the *Philosophy of Right,* a theoretical justification of this view, Hegel insisted that his work, "containing as it does the science of the state, is to be nothing other than the endeavor to apprehend and portray the state as something inherently rational."[11] The tradition of German thought as it evolved after Hegel is hostile, therefore, to the limited character of constitutionalism, with its emphasis on limited government and the protection of natural rights, and the belief in the inherent rationality, not of states, but of individuals.

The German view, which gives theoretical legitimacy to the growth of the power of the state, reflected a desire to embody the will of the people through the vehicle of the state, with an enlightened and rational bureaucracy. As Hegel observed, "the state, as the spirit of a people, is both the law permeating all relationships within the state and also at the same time the manners and consciousness of its citizens."[12] Therefore Hegel cautions against confusing the state with civil society. Liberal societies, or constitutional government of the kind created by the Framers, had not evolved to the higher plateau of the state. "If the state is confused with civil society," Hegel noted, "and if its specific end is laid down as the security and protection of property and personal freedom, then the interest of the individuals as such becomes the ultimate end of their association, and it follows that membership of the state is something optional."[13] Hegel denies that such can be the case. The individual cannot attain the full and complete life of a citizen in a civil society that has not evolved into a state. "Since the state is spirit objectified, it is only as one of its members that the individual himself has objectivity, genuine individuality, and an ethical life."[14]

---

[10]*Ibid.,* p. 561–62.
[11]Hegel, *Philosophy of Right.* Translated by T. M. Knox (London: Oxford University Press, 1972), p. 11.
[12]Ibid., section 274.
[13]Ibid., section 258.
[14]Ibid.

This view of the state and the bureaucracy, articulated by Hegel and other German theorists who became teachers of the leaders of the Progressive movement, presupposed the possibility of reconciling the distinction between the public and the private sphere, not to mention the alleviation of the tension between the particular will and the general will, the state and society. In short, it presupposed a resolution of the problem posed by modern liberalism, first presented but left unsolved by Rousseau. That problem required nothing less than the necessity of turning individuals, or the bourgeoisie, into citizens, or communal beings. In other words, the bureaucratic state presupposes the end of limited government or liberal constitutionalism. It is not accidental that the Progressives were hostile to the American Constitution.

In addition, it is reason as opposed to will that is a presupposition of the rule of law and a capacity to deliberate; the faculty of reason was undermined by the presumption of the inherent rationality of the state, not to mention modern social science methodology. The state, and modern social science, purported to have the capacity to institutionalize rationality in the service of will through utilization of a universal class, the bureaucracy. This view of the state, stripped of some of its German and philosophical trappings, underlay much of Progressive thought in America in the 1880s and after. The modern state, now *nation*, was considered the rational embodiment of the will of the people; it was thought to be a living and evolving organism. Unlike a rigid and static constitution, which sought to limit power, the idea of the nation presupposes a dynamic and positive use of power to embody the will of the majority. Such power, once thought to be a danger to the liberties of the people, could be used for beneficent purposes in the interest of the people themselves. Consequently, government need not be limited, because it could not be a danger to the people. This is so because the rights of individuals are no longer in conflict with those of the community or the people themselves. The tension between the demands of the individual and the community, the minority and majority, between the private and public, or society and government, which formed the basis of modern liberal constitutionaism, was said to be resolved in the rationally constructed state. In Hegel's view, and in that of the historicists who followed that view, reason and will were no longer in conflict. Similarly, the Progressives believed that scientific rationality could become the means of carrying out the will of the people.

Paradoxically, this was to be accomplished by utilizing that class of persons who are devoid of a personal passion for power. Their very disinterestedness would ensure the kind of rationality necessary to carry out the will of the state. This universal class, the bureaucracy, is, in Hegel's words, "the crucial link between the particularism of civil society and the universality of the state." As Hegel noted:

the universal class has for its task the universal interests of the community. It must therefore be relieved from direct labor to supply its needs, either by having private means or by receiving an allowance from the state which claims its industry, with the result that private interest finds its satisfaction in the work for the universal.[15]

This class of civil servants "is at the apex of the social pyramid." Sholomo Avineri has indicated the reason for the supremacy of a bureaucratic elite: "It is the only class of society, whose objective is *knowledge* itself, not nature, artefact or abstraction, as is the case with all other classes."[16] Lorenz Stein, an early German Hegelian theorist of public administration who greatly influenced Woodrow Wilson, pointed to the characteristics of this class of bureaucrats immune from human passion: "[They] have the capacity to care deeply for the welfare of the whole and to subordinate to it any special interest. These men are therefore predestined to state service, to service on behalf of the idea of the state."[17]

The American Founders held no such view of the state. The notion that the antinomy between state and society, individual and community, and reason and will, could be resolved was mere "utopian speculation" for both Federalists and Anti-Federalists alike. The state could not be rational, will could not replace reason, nor could history replace nature. For the Founders, reason was the means by which the "self-evident truths" were made intelligible. Nature gave man the capacity to reason, which in turn informed him of his natural rights as a human being. The role of government was the protection of those natural rights of individual moral beings. Consequently, a common good was ascertainable because of a common denominator, which was, or had always been, reason. Indeed, Edward S. Corwin could still say in 1929 that liberalism's "most fundamental assumption" is the notion "that man is primarily a rational creature, and that his acts are governed by rational considerations." It is this assumption upon which "the doctrine that the people should rule rests."[18]

However, with the growing influence of progressive thought and an increased governmental agenda, there was new concern with specialization and an infatuation with science. One progressive leader, E. L. Godkin, suggested that "the next great political revolution in the Western world" will give "scientific expression to the popular will, or, in other words . . . place men's relations in society where they never yet have been placed, under the control of trained

[15]Ibid., section 205.
[16]Shlomo Avineri, *Hegel's Theory of the Modern State* (London: Cambridge University Press, 1972), p. 108.
[17]Quoted in Robert D. Miewald, "The Origins of Wilson's Thought," in Jack Rabin and James S. Bowman, eds., *Politics and Administration: Woodrow Wilson and American Public Administration* (New York: Marcel Dekker, 1984), p. 20.
[18]Quoted in David M. Ricci, *The Tragedy of Political Science: Politics, Scholarship, and Democracy* (New Haven: Yale University Press, 1984), p. 78.

human reason." William Nelson has observed that "this new scientific spirit permeated every discipline related to the art of government."[19]

The scientific study of politics, not to mention those of economics, society, and law, did much to undermine not only the belief in the practical utility of reason, but also those "self-evident truths" that are the product of that reason. The disciplines of political science, as well as those of economics, sociology, and law, were born at the end of a century in which history had replaced nature in political philosophy, and will had replaced reason, all in the service of progress. As Corwin has observed:

> the extension of certain implications of evolutionary thought challenges some of the more fundamental elements of classical American political thought. The corner- stone of the latter at its inception was the notion of a natural law of final moral and political values which were the discovery of reason. The natural law of experimen- talism, on the other hand, is the natural law of the sciences, which exists indepen- dent of and indifferent to moral values. So there are no final truths, and reason as such is left without any reason for being.[20]

Although will embodied in the idea of the state replaced reason, on the assump- tion that passion or will could be rational, it was hardly an unmediated popular will. On the contrary, the various disciplines in the social sciences must provide the method and the expertise to solve the problems of modern society. Nonethe- less, those public bureaucracies designed to serve the will of the people became the source of the greatest public skepticism toward government. It is not acci- dental that every successful presidential candidate since 1968 has run for na- tional office by running against the Washington establishment.

POLITICAL CHARACTER OF THE ADMINISTRATIVE STATE

There is little doubt that the growth of a centralized bureaucracy has trans- formed politics in America. It has contributed to the difficulty of reconciling the conflicting demands and interests of members of Congress with those of the institution of Congress itself. What is good for the member is not necessarily good for the body as a whole, let alone the nation. However, any attempt to explain this apparent paradox must take into account the inherent tension that exists within a large or diverse liberal republic, between the public and private spheres, or the state and society. This tension provides a basis for the distinction between local and national interests, or the private as opposed to the public

---

[19]William Nelson has noted that "reformers in the last third of the nineteenth century turned to science to accomplish their reconstructive task." Nelson points to some of the leading thinkers of the day, including E. L. Godkin. Nelson, *The Roots of American Bureaucracy, 1830–1900* (Cam- bridge: Harvard University Press, 1982), p. 82.

[20]Edward S. Corwin, "The Impact of the Idea of Evolution on the American Political and Constitutional Tradition," in Richard Loss, ed., *Corwin on the Constitution,* vol. 1, (Ithaca: Cornell University Press, 1981), pp. 192–193.

good. In the past, the private and parochial interests of citizens were most often administered at the local and state level, or in society, in the economic marketplace. At that level, it was possible to resolve in a satisfactory manner the differences implicit in the distinction between the public and private, the general and particular, or the governing as opposed to the administrative elements of a regime. In the past, the nation was characteristically governed on the basis of general principles; it was both governed and administered at the state and local level.

The secret to successful reconciliation of the differences involved in the public and private spheres lay in the decentralized character of the American regime. Prior to bureaucratization, Congress as an institution was held to the standard of governing in the national or general interest. After centralization, individual congressmen were judged by their ability to satisfy the private interests of their constituents. Political centralization thus undermined a crucial ingredient of liberal democracy, what Tocqueville called "local institutions" or "provincial liberties." It also blurred the distinction, crucial to liberal societies, between the public and private, or the state and society. The devitalization of local institutions, which made the distinction between the general and particular politically unintelligible, also made it practically impossible to achieve a reasonable reconciliation of those respective interests.

Liberal democratic governments had originally attempted to distinguish the economic order from the political system. That distinction laid the groundwork for the maintenance of the distinction between the public and the private sphere. Implicit in the distinction between economics and politics, between wealth and power (political authority), is the autonomy of the public and private sphere. The American constitutional order has buttressed this distinction in several ways. It has guaranteed the protection of private property, as well as protection of individual liberties. Moreover, by not specifying how economic power was to be distributed, the Constitution created a bias in favor of the free market and the utmost liberty of private contracting.

The Constitution had created a limited government, but the leaders of the Progressive movement desired an active government that would be without limitation in its power to pursue social and economic justice. The discrediting of the Constitution, with its emphasis on limited government and the protection of individual rights, was a precondition of the growth of a centralized administrative state. However, before administration could be centralized, politics had to be nationalized. FDR's Democratic Party succeeded in doing this during his New Deal. The Party also achieved centralization of administration in the wake of the "Great Society." In the decade between 1964 and 1974, centralized administrative control resulted in the creation of a large public sector for the alleged purpose of securing social justice through a more equitable economic system.

The growth of the administrative state has blurred the distinction between the public and private sphere, between the state and society. It has altered the relations between the political and economic realm. Indeed, it has transformed the definition of liberalism itself. A liberal was once distinguished by being a lover of the private. New Deal liberals, however, not only tolerated state intrusion into areas long deemed private, they welcomed it. This change in opinion concerning the use of power—or public authority—was necessary but not the sufficient condition for the growth of a centralized administrative state. The sufficient condition was the incorporation into government of a "new class," knowledgeable in the use of "general ideas," with a new function, that of solving the political, economic, and social problems of society by means of the uniform methods of science. The centralization of American politics in the 1960s and 1970s, which depended upon the influence and authority of this new class, resulted in the attempt to replace market processes with administrative ones. As a result, the self-interest of business, industry, labor, and governments at the state and local level were permanently altered by the necessity of functioning within a centralized administration. Washington became the organizational focal point of both economic and political activity. And the existence of the bureaucracy—or the Washington establishment—transformed American politics.

Of the many problems associated with administrative centralization, not the least troublesome has been the regulation of the economic market. The intrusion of government into the economic sphere posed numerous problems for liberal government. At one time, as Assar Lindbeck observed, it was widely believed that "the free market with free individual enterprises" offered the best means of a "complete decentralization of production decisions." Without a reasonably well-functioning market system," Assar Lindbeck suggested, "a far-reaching centralization of economic decision-making and responsibility would be necessary."[21] Indeed, Walter Lippman could still insist in 1937 that "the first principle of liberalism . . . is that the market must be preserved and perfected as the prime regulator of the division of labor. When the collectivist abolishes the market place, all he really does is to locate it in the brains of his planning board."[22]

It was not surprising that opponents of the growing public sector viewed the line between public and private control as the dividing line between coercive governmental authority and individual freedom. They attempted to prevent the expansion of the public sector at the expense of the free market and the private sphere. As one economist noted in 1936, "the public realm is distinguished by the fact that it rests on authority and if necessary even on compulsion, while

---

[21]Quoted in Committee for Economic Development. *Redefining Government's Role in the Market System* (Washington, D.C., 1979).
[22]*The Good Society* (Boston: Little, Brown & Co., 1937), pp. 124–125.

private relations rest on contract."[23] If private relations are characterized by the freedom to engage in contracts, the public realm is not merely distinguished by its coercive capabilities; it rests not only on authority, but on the legitimacy of that authority. The New Deal succeeded in undermining the opinion that private solutions to economic problems were intrinsically preferable to public ones. Hence, it legitimized the use of that authority in the public realm. The growth of the public sector provided the conditions for the creation of a centralized bureaucracy.

The introduction of policy specialists into government in the 1960s provided the catalyst for the solution of the problems of society through the use of a scientific, or uniform, methodology. The "new class" was committed to a complete centralization of governmental and administrative power. It was animated by the expectation that the social, economic, and political problems of society could be solved by what John Stuart Mill once referred to as "general ideas." The importance of "general ideas" was made apparent to Tocqueville in a conversation with Mill in 1835.

> Up to now centralization has been the thing most foreign to the English temperament. Our habits or the nature of our temperament do not in the least draw us toward general ideas; but centralization is based on general ideas; that is, the desire for power to attend, in a uniform and general way, to the present and future needs of society. We have never considered government from such a lofty point of view.[24]

One cannot but be struck by the lofty, even utopian, view of those who assumed power in the 1960s. There appeared to be no limit to what could be done in the social realm if power and knowledge could be united. That unity was achieved by bringing large numbers of "policy professionals" and intellectuals into government. The utilization of such professionalism "means the formulation of an occupational skill by general concepts." Such knowledge is "theoretical," it "can be applied generally to similar problems wherever and whenever they exist." Consequently, the professional brings to government "not just an interest in a specific problem, but rather a preparation to deal with all such problems."[25]

In their desire "for power to attend in a uniform and general way" to the needs of society, a new class interest in the growth and success of the public sector was created. Unlike the political forces that dominated New Deal politics, "the influence of parties and pressure groups had declined, while that of the expert and professional had risen. . . . The new social programs . . . depended on government spending to provide specific services delivered by pro-

[23]Gerhard Colm, "Theory of Public Expenditures," *The Annals of the American Academy of Political and Social Science* (January, 1936), p. 183.

[24]*Journeys to England and Ireland* (Garden City: Anchor Books, 1968), pp. 66–67.

[25]Samuel Beer, "In Search of a New Public Philosophy," in Anthony King, ed., *The New American Political System* (Washington: American Enterprise Institute, 1978), p. 20.

fessionally trained persons, to certain categories of consumers for the sake of designated outcomes."[26]

The new professionalism cut across traditional federal lines. Policies were not to be carried out directly by the federal government; rather, standards and policy would be set at the national level to be implemented by professionals at state and local levels, as well as by quasi-public and private contractors. The policy technocracy was united by a common outlook and a common purpose, and its incorporation into government could not but consolidate centralized administrative control. The growing power of the bureaucracy was not dependent upon an increase in the size of the federal bureaucracy, but in its increased ability to set the standards for all levels of government. Consequently, administrative centralization has resulted in an increase in the size of state and local bureaucracies in response to federal directives reinforced by federal grants.

Bureaucratic centralization increasingly required that participants in the political realm be ensured adequate representation in the administrative realm. Consequently, the organizing core of American government revolved around the bureaucracy. The substance of national politics, therefore, involved attempts by the president and Congress, and by interests and constituencies associated with those institutions, to influence and control the administrative and regulatory bureaucracy. Moreover, each elected branch sought to prevent the other from exercising control in areas deemed vital to representation of its interests or constituencies. As a result, bureaucracy in general has become more autonomous and less responsive to the political order as a whole. At the same time, private autonomy—or those elements that have buttressed individual liberty—has been circumscribed. Increasingly, administrative law and agency rulemaking has supplanted statutory law, which is reflective of the importance of specific interest regulation as opposed to laws that govern generally. Accordingly, the functions of the legislature and the courts have undergone significant change.

Richard Stewart has commented upon the changing perceptions of law brought about by increased administrative centralization. He noted that prior to the 1960s, "the underlying premise of administrative law [had] been the limitation of government power in order to preserve private autonomy." Until that time, "the imposition of administratively determined sanctions on private individuals" would only be "authorized by the legislature through rules which control agency action." The enormous growth of government activity "not only in the regulation of private activity but also in the provision of goods, services, and advantageous opportunities" has transformed American politics and law. These developments, "have necessitated the delegation to agencies of considerable discretion to determine government policy and to distribute the resulted benefits and burdens." The "distinct spheres of private and government activity

[26]Ibid., p. 20.

have melded."[27] Moreover, "our received models of choice—the elected legislature and the market—seem entirely incapable of effectively controlling the expanded machinery of government." Legislatures and courts have consequently added to the responsibility and discretion of administrative bodies. The intention, says Stewart, is to expand "formal participation rights in a fashion that points toward the development of an interest representation theory of administrative law."[28]

The consequence of the extension of the administrative sphere has been to parcel out areas of public concern to "interested publics." It has tended to promote a kind of pluralism, not merely at the expense of community or consensus, but at the expense of genuine—or comprehensive—representation as well. What has become increasingly difficult in the absence of a free market economy and the legal preservation of private autonomy is the ability to provide adequate representation of individual, unorganized interests. As a consequence of bureaucratization, the general interest, reflected in laws made by the legislature, has been undermined by an undue concern with particular interests, given expression in the form of specific rules promulgated by administrative agencies for specialized purposes. At the point at which private activities become increasingly subject to "administrative rules" rather than general laws, or when the individual is most governed in minor details, he has least access to the real center of decision-making authority. The administrative apparatus isolates the legislature from the people by limiting the extent to which specific policy is promulgated in the general interest.

In practice, the bureaucracy and the regulatory agencies are largely responsive to particular committees and individual congressmen. Increasingly, the bureaucracy allows Congress as a body to escape its responsibility as policymaker. Nor is control vested in the president, from whom the independent agencies have purposely been isolated. Moreover, the executive branch agencies, "as a practical matter . . . are no more subject to presidential directives on specific policy issues than the independent agencies."[29] The result of such insulation has not been representation in the public interest; indeed, it may have resulted in the destruction of a public interest.

The difficulty of reconciling the general and particular interests becomes especially apparent as a result of administrative centralization. When the distinction between the public and private remained viable, citizens were made to distinguish between self-interest and the public interest. It was possible, per-

---

[27]Stewart suggested that the "ideal of private autonomy," which had been limited "only through government constraints authorized by a popularly elected legislature—is impoverished and incomplete in an urban, technological society." "The Reformation of American, Administrative Law," *Harvard Law Review* (June, 1975), p. 1811.

[28]Ibid., p. 1813.

[29]Lloyd N. Cutler and David R. Johnson, "Regulation and the Political Process," *Yale Law Journal* (June, 1975), p. 1404.

haps necessary, to think of "self" and the "whole" at the same time. It was possible, therefore, to reconcile the competing claims of the individual and society through rational representation. In an important way, both representation and a concept of the public interest require a kind of abstraction from the particular or individual case; the relative advantage or disadvantage of the parts depends upon the ability to consider the effect upon the whole. The growth and centralization of the administrative process has led to the enthronement of particular, concrete, and material interests. As a result, it has become increasingly difficult to reconcile the particular and the general interest. Rather, the primary necessity of the administrative state is the provision of adequate representation for every particular interest. Without it one is disenfranchised, regardless of the right to vote. Consequently the idea of a common good is replaced by the agglomeration of every organized private interest.

Political administration in the United States has reached the point at which organized politics, especially through the parties, is in the process of dissolving; at the same time, individuals are forced to organize. The "dissolving of organized politics" and the "politicizing of organization life" has not led to increased representation of the interests of individuals or a national majority, much less a public interest. As Hugh Heclo has observed, "society may have politicized itself" at the very time it has "depoliticized government leadership."[30] In practice, administrative politics has replaced partisan politics. The organized groups, created to represent specialized interests before specialized tribunals, carve out distinct areas of policy that have become the nearly exclusive domain of persons knowledgeable of and groups interested in particular issues. A policy technocracy has replaced political parties in dominating the issues and agenda of political life. Not having legally or politically enforced private autonomy, the individual is alienated from the political order even wile he is increasingly controlled by it; even the courts increasingly protect group rights.

The nationalization of politics and the centralization of administration has resulted in profound changes in the national government. Increasingly, politics has centered upon the "importance attached to managerial control of the bureaucracy in general and of government regulatory agencies in particular."[31] The administrative and regulatory battles have occurred within the framework of the executive–legislative struggle for control of those elements of the administration that enable each of the respective branches to fulfill its task of ensuring adequate representation for its constituency. "The politics of regulation rarely is the partisan politics of Democrats versus Republicans. Rather it is the politics

---

[30]"Issue Networks and the Executive Establishment," in Anthony King, ed., *The New American Political System*, p. 124.

[31]Robert S. Gilmour, "Congressional Oversight and Administrative Leadership," *The Bureaucrat*, Fall (1981), p. 32.

of patronage and privilege."[32] The contention between the branches concerning the use of the bureaucracy for patronage purposes is complicated by the fact that the alleged superiority of administration is due to its rationality and neutrality.

The period of the 1960s and 1970s was one of great growth in the administrative and regulatory powers of government. Both the executive and legislative branch, dominated by a single party throughout most of the 1960s and animated by an apparent consensus forged in the election of 1964, cooperated in the growth of the administrative state. But the increased centralization itself transformed the interests of the parties and the political institutions of the national government. The bureaucracy, itself a creation of a partisan majority, offered a means by its continuation and growth to ensure representation of interests quite apart from the political parties. From the point of view of individual members of Congress, the maintenance of the bureaucracy has been considerably more important than the necessity of maintaining a visible partisan profile. Indeed, congressmen quickly learned to take advantage of the ombudsman function, that capacity to intervene with the bureaucracy on behalf of constituents.

The more fully bureaucratized a regime becomes, the greater the possibility that congressmen are able to function as ombudsmen. However, in order to do so, Congress needed powerful instruments of individual control over the bureaucracy. In addition, "the effectiveness of the [control] instrument is made all the more real by the establishment and maintenance of the elaborate committee–reciprocity system. . . . Each congressmen is given the opportunity to exercise disproportionate influence over the segments of the federal bureaucracy that are of special concern to him." As a result, the congressman does not have to mobilize a majority of members to deal with a department or agency; "he need get only four or five subcommittee colleagues to go along." Congress does not want unified control of the bureaucracy; in fact, "part of the agency's activities are typically out of control, but Congress wants it that way. It is a necessary cost of maintaining a bureaucracy sufficiently unconstrained [in law and by its nominal leader] that it is susceptible to congressional influence." Less than total control of the agencies works to the advantage of congressmen satisfying constituents. "Why take political chances by setting detailed regulations [that are] sure to antagonize?" when it is more expedient to "require the agency to do the dirty work and then step in to redress the grievances that result from its activity. Let the agency take the blame and congressmen the credit."[33]

In the 1970s, Congress reformed itself to consolidate the political structure necessary for centralized administration. It was able to do so by decentralizing power and fragmenting unified or central leadership capability within Con-

---

[32]Louis Kohlmeir, Jr., *The Regulators* (New York: Harper & Row, 1969), pp. 34–35.

[33]Morris P. Fiorina, "Congressional Control of the Bureaucracy: A Mismatch of Incentives and Capabilities," in Dodd and Oppenheimer, eds., *Congress Reconsidered* (Washington: Congressional Quarterly Press, 1981), p. 343.

gress. Committee government gave way to subcommittee government. Party influence was diminished. At the very time politics and administration had been centralized at the national level, Congress reorganized itself in such a way as to make it increasingly difficult to pursue or alter national public policy. It was able to do so precisely because a centralized mechanism to administer national policy was in place. Congress has come to see its primary function as one of managing the centralized bureaucracy.

In this same period, there was an attempt to "work a direct transfer of managerial power from president to Congress." The mechanism for such a transfer was the new congressional budget system with a provision for control of the use of executive impoundment, "development of vastly improved management and research capabilities; the application of a wide array of impact statement requirements as a precondition to agency action; the institution of legislative veto and similar pre-audit sanctions to administrative rulemaking, and much increased administrative specificity in lawmaking." Congress also increased the size of its staff for casework and investigation, reverted more frequently to the use of short-term project authorizations, commenced direct oversight hearings, and increased agency reporting requirements. All of these reforms were intended to strengthen congressional control of administration. Congressmen "force agency level officials into regular, nearly continuous consultation with committee overseers and their staffs to justify agency budgets, personnel practices, and even the most detailed aspects of program operations."[34]

Further, Congress pursued policies toward the executive branch that made unified or centralized control of the executive branch by the president more difficult to achieve. As a result, much of the growth of the national government occurred outside of the executive branch. This was accomplished by the wholesale private contracting for government services, and the creation of numerous government, quasi-governmental, and private corporations often called "twilight zone" corporations. By utilizing a variety of specific organizational structures, "private ownership and profit incentives have largely been avoided." Most of these organizations are distinguished by being exempted from "the Government Corporation Control Act and laws applicable to federal personnel, funds, and contracts." Moreover, the number of federally financed enterprises excluded from the budget process by law (off-budget items) increased as well. The intention was clear: the growth of the government sector was ensured while at the same time unified political control was made nearly impossible. In this leadership struggle for control of the administrative sector, Gilmour suggests, "the agencies, clientele groups, and uncoordinated committees and individual congressmen have benefited most."[35]

---

[34]Gilmour, *"Congressional Oversight,"* p. 33.
[35]Ibid., p. 38.

The consequence of the expanded use of the bureaucracy—given the congressional habit of intervening in bureaucratic decision-making on behalf of constituents—has been to undermine the congressional role as formulator of national policies. At the same time, members have become increasingly concerned with satisfying the organized interests on the one hand, and perfecting their role as ombudsman with the general public on the other. The practical effect of this is "that parts of Congress control parts of the bureaucracy, but there is little coordination in such control. Committees control agencies they want to control—but there is no coordinated or centralized control—the bureaucracy cannot be made to work in harness to achieve major policy goals."[36] Nor, it may be added, can the influence of the bureaucracy be lessened without encroaching upon the domain of individual congressmen and the committee structure.

The interests of the president and Congress have diverged, regardless of party, as a result of the new centralization. Although Congress can better represent organized interests because of its access to the bureaucracy, the president is less able to pursue a national interest in the attempt to satisfy his constituency, which is the national majority. It is almost impossible to represent a national constituency without the necessity of abstracting from private interests, which requires the elaboration of a "public interest." This entails mobilization of a coalition explicitly aimed at creating a consensus through a national majority. In doing so, a president creates expectations concerning his ability to carry out his publicly stated mandate. But a national presidential electoral victory based on such an appeal only provides the appearance of an opportunity to govern; it does not give the president the capacity to govern. Increasingly, because control and care of the details of administration constitute the core of governing, an electoral victory merely gives the President somewhat less than equal access— with Congress—to the bureaucracy. But any attempt to govern or rule the bureaucracy in a coordinated or unified way in response to the necessity to attend to the national interest, is strongly resisted by Congress, as has been made evident in turbulent executive–legislative relations in the decades since bureaucratization. The goals and constituencies of the president and Congress differ. The president "as the representative of all the people desires centralized control of the bureaucracy, whether to construct the national coalition he needs to win reelection or to make the major policy initiatives that will insure his place in history." But Congress prefers to attend to the details of administration in support of the local, often parochial, interests of a far different constituency. "Congress has the power but not the incentive for coordinated control of the

[36]Morris Fiorina, quoted in William Livingston, Lawrence Dood, and Richard Schott, eds., *The Presidency and the Congress* (Austin: LBJ School of Public Affairs, 1979), p. 126.

bureaucracy, while the president has the incentive but not the power."[37] Increasingly, competition between the president and Congress revolves around managerial control of the bureaucracy.

Congress has denied the president the ability to control the bureaucracy effectively. This does not mean that the bureaucracy is simply accountable to the legislative body. Rather, parts of the bureaucracy are controlled by individual committee members. It has been argued that Congress has, through the use of the legislative veto, sought to gain a greater measure of institutional control over the bureaucracy in the interest of greater accountability to the legislature as a whole. The evidence appears not to sustain this view. Rather, "the veto power [over administrative agencies] gave rise to negotiation and compromise over the substance of rules between the agencies and the congressional oversight committees." Indeed, "experience under existing vetoes reveals that political accountability is likely to be attenuated in practice . . . floor votes, of an entire house on the merits of a veto resolution were rather infrequent."[38] It appears in fact that the use of this device offers individual members better access to control of the details of administration. Robert Dixon, Jr., noted the extent to which the congressional veto "subjects program administrators to a continuous process of consultation with some members of Congress. Because the latter are in a position to have the last word . . . certain key committeemen in Congress and their staff aides, thus acquire power without responsibility."[39] The legislative use of the veto appears to have as a primary purpose the ongoing control of the details of administration. It appears so alien to the notion of administrative accountability to the legislative body, that "Congress surrenders its role as independent agency overseer in exchange for direct subcommittee and staff participation in the administrative process, in effect, for immediate and particularized control of agency decision-making."[40]

It was widely believed that the *I.N.S. v. Chadha* (1983) decision would alter the way Congress conducted its business. The Court majority held that "legislation by the national Congress [must] be a step-by-step, deliberate and deliberative process." Furthermore, in *Bowsher v. Synar* (1986), the Court insisted that the "structure of the Constitution does not permit Congress to execute the laws; it follows that Congress cannot grant to an officer under its control what is does not possess." Using the *Chadha* decision as precedent, the Court insisted in *Bowsher* that "once Congress makes its choice in enacting

---

[37]Fiorina, "Congressional Control of the Bureaucracy," p. 335.

[38]Harold Bruff and Walter Gellhorn, "Congressional Control of Administrative Regulation: A Study of Legislative Vetoes," *Harvard Law Review*, May (1977), pp. 1417–1418.

[39]"The Congressional Veto and Separation of Powers: The Executive on a Leash?" *North Carolina Law Review*, 65 (1978), p. 463.

[40]Gilmour, "Congressional Oversight," p. 38.

legislation, its participation ends. Congress can thereafter control the execution of its enactment only indirectly—by passing new legislation."

If implemented, the Court's opinion in these two cases would have undermined much of the real power of individual members, and would have required a change in the actual practices of Congress, particularly its role in the administrative process, which is the source of its dominance in recent years. As Louis Fisher of the Congressional Research Service recently noted in regard to these decisions: "This is a caricature of Congress, heretofore found only in the most sophomoric treatment of American government. The Court contradicts everything we know about the ability of Congress to control the execution of laws through hearings, committee investigations, GAO studies, informal contacts between Members of Congress and agency officials, committee subpoenas, the contempt power, and nonstatutory controls."[41]

Despite early claims that the *Chadha* decision would result in the transformation of congressional–bureaucratic relations, very little changed in the way Congress conducted its business in regard to the executive branch. In fact, it appeared that Congress virtually ignored the decision. "In the two years immediately following the Supreme Court ruling [*Chadha*] Congress enacted fifty additional legislative veto provisions." Several scholars have concluded that "the president's position in relation to Congress may actually be weaker than it was before the Supreme Court decision."[42]

CONCLUSION

There is little doubt that the bureaucracy has presented a problem for American government from the beginning. Because many powers are shared, it is not clear where administration fits within the framework of government. Hamilton had argued in the *Federalist Papers* that "the administration . . . comprehends all the operations of the body politic, whether legislative, executive or judiciary." But, he added, "in its most precise signification, it is limited to executive details, and falls peculiarly within the province of the executive."[43] After Madison became a member of the first Congress, he seemed to believe that the administrative sphere provided only an opportunity for both branches to compete for control of the bureaucracy. Nonetheless, both Madison and Hamilton agreed that administration must be subject to the political control of the elected branches of government.

This view is compatible with a decentralized and nonprofessionalized ad-

---

[41]"The Administrative State: What's Next After *Chadha* and *Bowsher*?" Paper presented at the annual meeting of the American Political Science Association, Washington, D.C., 1986, p. 3.

[42]Randall Ripley and Grace Franklin, *Congress, the Bureaucracy, and Public Policy* (Chicago: The Dorsey Press, 1987), pp. 78–79.

[43]*The Federalist* No. 72.

ministration. In 1930 Leonard White could still point to the distinctive characteristic of American administration observed a century before by Tocqueville:

> The centralized type of administration is related to the bureaucratic (i.e., the pro-
> fessional), the decentralized type to the self-governmental (i.e., the amateur) . . .
> the United States, in spite of the technical nature of many aspects of administration,
> is still powerfully influenced by preference for amateur self-governmental forms.[44]

The change in the character of administration, viewed in light of the Progressive critique of the constitutional basis of American government, was revealed
quite clearly in James Landis' seminal work, *The Administrative Process*. In
1938 Landis wrote, "the administrative is not, as some suppose, simply an
extension of executive power. In the grant to it of that full ambit of authority
necessary for it in order to plan, to promote, and to police, it presents an
assemblage of rights normally exercisable by government as a whole." Because
of the necessity "to plan, to promote, and to police," Landis assumed that
government existed to achieve positive purposes and this required the centralization of authority in an administrative class. If the Constitution had attempted
to limit power by separating it, it was united in the administrative realm. In this
view, administration rested outside the traditional or formal powers of government, precisely because it was not political. As Landis observed, "the rise of
the administrative process represented the hope that policies . . . could be developed by men bred to the facts."[45] The superiority of the administrative state
rests upon the specialized knowledge and the uniform methods of the social and
policy sciences. It presupposes the possibility and desirability of separating
politics from administration.

In light of our growing experience with the problems of the administrative
state, few would suggest that attempts to separate politics and administration
have succeeded. It is not clear that administrators "bred to the facts" are any
less political than those who must compete in the partisan arena. It is clear,
however, that those who inhabit administrative offices are harder to hold accountable to the voter than those who are elected to office. In addition, through
widespread delegation of authority to administrative bodies, Congress has obscured its own role in the policy-making process. As a result, the electorate too
is often unable to hold the legislative body accountable for failed policy because
it is not clear where responsibility lies.

The complexity of the American constitutional system, with its separation
of powers, has obscured the relationship between the bureaucracy and the political branches. Even now, many Americans are unaware of the fact that Congress has become, in Morris Fiorina's words, "the keystone of the Washington
establishment." Nonetheless, regardless of the impact of bureaucracy upon

---

[44]"Administration, Public," *Encyclopedia of the Social Sciences,* 1930.
[45]*The Administrative Process* (New Haven: Yale University Press, 1938), p. 15.

American government, it is not accurate to suggest that the fundamental problem in contemporary government is a result of an uncontrolled, or all-powerful, bureaucracy. As Fiorina has observed, "the bureaucracy is not out of control. The Congress controls the bureaucracy, and . . . gives us the kind of bureaucracy it wants."[46] What appears to be lacking is unified control of bureaucracy in the public interest. This condition has led to the "decline of the national government with regard to its special function in the American federal system," one observer laments, "that of promoting the public good."[47] The centralization of administration has undermined the capacity of American institutions to conduct the government in a manner consistent with the form as well as the spirit of constitutional government. At its inception, the Constitution was animated by "principles . . . of justice and the general good."[48] The administrative state has undermined the incentives within the institutions of government that would enable each of the branches to participate in defining and pursuing a national interest. In short, it prevents consideration of a conception of the public good. In doing so, it subverts the aspiration for the fundamental ideal of government and community, the desire for justice. As James Madison noted, "justice is the end of government. It is the end of civil society. It ever has been, and ever will be pursued, until it be obtained, or until liberty be lost in the pursuit."[49]

[46]Fiorina, "Congressional Control of the Bureaucracy," p. 335.
[47]Robert J. Pranger, in King, ed., *The New American Political System*, p. 118.
[48]Madison, *Federalist* No. 51.
[49]Ibid.

Index

About the Author

John Marini is Associate Professor of Political Science at the University of Nevada, Reno. He has worked for the federal government in Washington, D.C., and has written extensively in the areas of American politics and public administration, focusing on the separation of powers and bureaucratic politics. He is coeditor of *The Imperial Congress: Crisis in the Separation of Powers,* published in 1989, and a work in progress, *Bureaucracy and American Constitutionalism* (New York: Taylor & Francis, forthcoming).